MILITARY MEN

Ward Just

MILITARY
MEN

Alfred A. Knopf New York 1970

To
F. W. J.
and
D. H. H.

CONTENTS

MILITARY MEN

PROLOGUE

Stramm

Begin with the view from the inside out: in the fall of 1969, the Washington chapter of the Society of the First Division gathered at the base of the division's war monument, a concrete monolith which occupies a plot of ground catercorner from the White House. It was Veterans' Day and there were two hundred folding chairs set up for the members of the Society, officers and men who had served in the division and felt strongly enough about it to form a permanent association. The ceremonies began at eleven o'clock, with only half the chairs occupied. General Clarence Huebner, who was with the division when it was formed in 1916, spoke very briefly on Army traditions. Huebner is eighty, but he wore a neat black beret and looked fit and lean at the microphone and his voice was steady. He recalled that the first division had lost six thousand men in World War One and when the war ended in 1919 "the thing that motivated men was that the killing had stopped. For those who yesterday had been in combat the killing was over." He said that the rejoicing had been very great in the United States, but it was greatest where the killing was.

"There is a great difference between those two wars and the war where the killing is still going on," he said. "Those men are not being supported as we were supported in World War One." There was to be a demonstration against the war in Washington the next day— The Moratorium—but Huebner did not mention it. Then he said: "We who know must tell our young people what it means to be a soldier." In 1970, the rest of the country had apparently forgotten; or didn't care.

The sense of isolation was palpable. The colonels and majors who had interrupted their holiday to listen to Huebner and honor the division were grim and angry men, or seemed so that morning in November. They sat solemnly and faced the base of the monument, which was inscribed with the names of all the great battles fought by the division known as the Big Red One: Meuse-Argonne, St. Mihiel, and Saizerais in the first war and North Africa, Sicily, and Normandy in the second. There were no Vietnam placenames, although the division had fought in Vietnam since 1966. When the lapidaries got around to it, there would be Tay Ninh Province, the Michelin plantation, and War Zone C. The best known of the division's Vietnam commanders also spoke that morning, but he did not mention the war. He spoke instead of the Society's scholarship fund for the sons of the dead, and there have been almost fifteen thousand of those in the three wars.

It was a hard twenty minutes, and when it ended most of the soldiers went quickly to their cars. Those who hung back stood together among the empty folding chairs in small groups talking to each other, listening to the traffic, standing straight and stiff, their trousers sharp as knives. An occasional passer-by, eyes caught by the uniforms and medals, glanced over at them, then hurried on. A newspaperman's questions were answered

quickly and bluntly. Thirty minutes after Clarence Huebner left the microphone and the color guard had put the
flag away, men were still standing at the monument, talking confidentially. They were old soldiers, one of them
said later, talking among friends.

It is difficult for an outsider to break through it, to relate
to the environment. Society's distrust of soldiers is
equalled only by the distrust of soldiers for society, or
that part of it—a part they still describe as "the liberals"
—which they feel have brought them under attack. Sus-
picious, resentful, angry beyond measure at what they
consider to be indulgent and unfair criticism, the professionals have drawn together at the barricades of the
institution. The thing that binds military men together in
1970 is the belief that the country is falling to pieces and
the military is the only place where duty, honor, and country are put above self. Among themselves, among friends,
they tick off the problems onetwothree: Where are the
American virtues of discipline and sacrifice and patriotism? In an atmosphere so slack and disorderly, the
Army is the only institution in America a man can really
count on. It is not simply a matter of traditions, either;
it is as much, or more, a matter of the military psychology.

There are not very many military memoirs worth reading, and very few that deliver serious insights. Probably
the most appealing are the meditations of the Roman
emperor Marcus Aurelius, perhaps because he declines
to discuss soldiers as such, or even battles, but concen-
trates instead on the qualities of mind and spirit that
produce great men and civilizations. Thus, the ideal mas-
culine temperament: straight, strong, just, forgiving.
Stoic virtues these, and the standard against which men
ought to be measured; they could be taken, as a matter
of fact, from the West Point code. Facing the enemy, any

enemy, the good soldier perceives a demanding and vengeful world. He must accommodate himself to what fate brings, but in the extremity act alone, on an inner motion. Marcus approvingly quotes Plato:

> *The truth of the matter is this, gentlemen. When a man has once taken up his stand, either because it seems best to him or in obedience to orders, there I believe he is bound to remain and face the dangers, taking no account of death or anything else before dishonor.*

That is the Roman standard, and the romantic conception of the hero in America as well: a man disciplined and obedient, brave and fatalistic, Gary Cooper on a street without joy. The Prussians called it *stramm*, military qualities, or more precisely military bearing, without which no soldier could succeed. The American Army, a citizen Army, has traditionally been denied the glamor and prestige of a military caste on the Prussian model, so the American soldier's *stramm* relates less to the uniform or the senior men who wear it than to the society itself. Duty, honor, country, as the West Point motto says; minimum pomp, maximum circumstance. To a professional soldier (the more senior the rank, the more rigid the belief), the army is seen as the agent of the state and the loyalty is therefore indivisible. The one is the other, and has been for some time—with few exceptions, Robert E. Lee among them, southern graduates of West Point fought with the Union in the Civil War. Lacking the caste hocus-pocus of the Prussian junkers, or the social respectability of the British officer corps, the American Army commenced to identify itself with whatever national destiny was current. For an American, the distinction between uniform and country was not great, considerably less than a difference, and it is easy to see where the psychology can lead, or has led. Identifying the army with the society can, with brisk logic, become the

converse. In a nuclear age, a military man naturally con-
fuses one with the other; in an atmosphere of more or
less permanent menace, military strength is the one
thing that makes all of the other things possible. For a
society to succeed, it must first be secure. To be secure,
it must be strong. From the perspective of the soldier,
then, the very life of the society depends on the quality
of its military forces, both men and machines but mostly
men.

In their advertisements for themselves, professional
soldiers like to assemble a picture of fatalism tinged with
a kind of innocent nobility, the brave young men march-
ing off to do their duty, taking their chances with the
dice (I have heard it described just so), some lucky
enough to live, others unlucky enough to die. Since
American wars are never undertaken for imperialistic
gain (myth one), American soldiers always fight in a virtuous cause (myth two) for a just and goalless peace
(myth three). Wars are never fought for the prestige of
the Army—what the hell, they used to say, every time the
Army won the war the politicians demobilized the troops
—they are fought for the vital interests of the United
States, when not for humanity itself. The slogans reflect
the attitude: *Don't tread on me!* the flag said, and Dwight
Eisenhower called his memoirs *Crusade in Europe.*
American wars are defensive wars, undertaken slowly
and reluctantly, the country a righteous gentle giant
finally goaded beyond endurance by foreign adventurers.
Thus armed with moral superiority, the professional
soldier sees himself in a soft, virtuous light: not, with
Nathan Hale, "my country, right or wrong," or even with
George Orwell, "my country, right or left," but with—
who? Colonel Robert R. McCormick?—"my country, always right." Because of the civilian nature of the society,
the soldier would add, drolly and accurately, "and always
unprepared." With a certain justice, a military man
could see himself as both hero and victim: "they don't

give a damn about us until they need us," an echo from the years between the wars. Call it Kiplingism or a savior complex or a martyr complex or incipient paranoia or simply the fatal American fascination with innocence. Given the traditional place of the military in American society, it is essential that sacrifice be appreciated. It is equally essential, or has been, that the burdens of war be distributed equally, either by using volunteers as cannon fodder or by universal conscription. Society, after all, has defined the mission—and no man ever puts another man out there on point and then abandons him. Or on his return gives him the back of his hand. No civilian sitting safely at home has the right to do that; my God, men have been *killed*.

The idea is that there is something virtuous in dying for a just cause; that, and whatever exhilaration may come from close-order combat. If you were ten before 1945 you could not escape the heroes: Washington and Lee and Custer and Alvin York, Barney O'Hare (a pilot), Douglas MacArthur (a general), *Thirty Seconds over Tokyo, Wake Island*, the Marine Corps, Wayne. World War Two itself was a metaphor, real heroes fighting real villains and the propaganda such that only those who were there and understood the objective reality felt the texture of war as Goya felt it and as every foot soldier has felt it before the slow, certain erosion of memory. It was not until D-Day 1944 that American newspapers published a picture of American dead in World War Two; it was a photograph made on the beach at Normandy, the soldier's face buried in the sand. Ernest Hemingway's delicate perception of Greek refugees on the quay at Smyrna deserted him utterly in the second war, when he wrote grandly of strategy in the manner of Basil Liddell Hart. Looking at it twenty-five years later, it is as if the mere introduction of American troops into war made war itself a different, more innocent and ingenuous affair —as the addition of SO_4 changes H_2O. Twenty-five years later, the perspective has swung as surely as a sloop's compass on a tack, and now it is the other way around.

In 1970, there are no heroes and no crusades. There have been no popular heroes in the Vietnam war, a crusade that became a depredation. A man could believe in Captain William S. Carpenter for a while, until S. L. A. Marshall reconstructed the battle in the highlands and found it a mess, and someone else disclosed that Carpenter did not know it was napalm he was calling in on his own position—"Put it right in on top of me," he'd said, and Colonel Henry Emerson, on the other end of the radiotelephone, told Bill he wanted him to know he was putting him in for the medal of honor. No one thought Carpenter would survive and little wonder that the subsequent publicity embarrassed and angered the captain (a genuinely modest soldier). A man is obliged to reach into history for his sense of "what it means to be a soldier." It is less a trick for the older men, who have an old-fashioned understanding of the mission of America (it was re-validated as recently as John F. Kennedy's inaugural address, "We will pay any price ...") and a romantic sense of themselves—attitudes which often produce a conception of war—killing—totally without irony, fundamentally remorseless, and staggering in its sentimentality. Perhaps that is the only way the soldiers of this world can survive. What emerges is this, a colonel of infantry, forty years old, one of the most decorated officers in the Army and a complete professional.

"I'm a soldier and I'm good at it. Nothing unusual in that. It only takes a year to take the average man out of civilian life and really make a storm trooper out of him. We can take the average civilian and really mold him into a very effective soldier. The Army becomes your life and your home, and the mission becomes your job. Nothing else but that. They know they have got to relate to that to stay alive, and in times past there was something all right about it—those who fought forgot the pain and the blood and remembered only the glory, or what they recalled as glory. That's the fantasy world. In the average person, brains are built to remember only the good things, otherwise we'd all be nutty. This war of course is the American outrage. The graduates of Vietnam just don't think that war is fun. The older men are wearying of the burden, and the younger men never understood the reason for it in the first place.

"I remember all the movies, *Dawn Patrol* and stuff like that. It was something inculcated in me at a very young age. I became a super patriot, a hero worshipper, and perhaps I wanted to be a hero myself. As a sergeant, I quit counting at one hundred and twenty-seven dead. I don't worry about it and never have. I was trained to do that. To kill a person is murder, but to kill a man in battle is honorable. It's the mystique of war. There have only been a couple of good war books, Remarque, Crane, and only one good book on the Army, that other book, *Once an Eagle*. The supreme risk, see. A seven or a crap. I wouldn't buy a house without reading the fine print, but I'll say to a man in combat, 'You cover me while I pop a grenade in the hole.' The only thing that's at stake there is our lives. I'll do that, have that trust, because I've seen the man perform in adversity. It's a secret bond that no one else can share. It's highly emotional, very inarticulate. I think that when a man's back is against the wall, that's when he really produces.

"In every great American battle, the United States has had its ass in a crack. Bataan, Corregidor, the Marne. It isn't the splendid victory we remember, but the difficult periods, the near-disasters. You know, people need adventure. The sterner the challenge, the finer the response. Toynbee says that, I think. You've got to test yourself. In Korea, I used to say, 'Oh God, please help me be competent.' I worried about it all the time. I'd up the ante. In combat, you know, you aren't accepted right away. You've got to prove yourself time and time and again. To join the clique. You'd get so you'd lie, cheat and steal for one another. I wanted to prove myself so I had my life on the line a few times, and you get beyond the point of being scared."

What the colonel called "that other book," *Once an Eagle,* tells much about how a certain type of soldier sees himself and the Army. *Once an Eagle* is an 815-page narrative written by Anton Myrer in 1968. Myrer's hero is an up-from-the-ranks Kansan named Sam Damon. He enlists in World War One as a private, ends World War Two a major general, and is killed in Indo-China on an intelligence mission for the Army. Army insiders insist that the book is a *roman à clef,* accurate as history, excellent as journalism, and devastating as sociology. Indeed, all of it is there: the Army command structure, medals and ribbons, post life, blood and guts, pride and prejudice, staff men and field commanders, West Pointers and mustangs, gallantry and heroism, cowardice and stupidity, hook and crook. The characters are pat, and it is astonishing that central casting has not grasped the opportunity: George C. Scott as the brilliantly suave and ambitious general's aide who has troubles with his sex life (a curvy preference, in later years, for fellatio), Deborah Kerr as the embittered (and finally redeemed) Army brat of a wife, Martin Balsam the cowardly general, Burt Lancaster the sturdy colonel, Pat O'Brien the faithful sergeant. There is no role for Dustin Hoffman. Black Jack Pershing puts in an appearance and so does MacArthur, "Dugout Doug." But most of all there is Greg Peck/Damon, a man so pure of heart and instinct that he could only have been drawn from life. Damon wins the medal of honor, marries the general's daughter, thrashes the camp bully, frees the innocent Indian from the stockade, snatches victory from defeat on a dozen bloody occasions, all the time true to himself and loyal to the Army. It is the system, the Army apparatus and its offspring who hold Damon back (Peck/Damon goes to two stars, but Scott/Massengale goes to four), who try to humiliate him, *who are ungrateful*—and who prevail in the end. Damon dies and the Army survives and the appeal is clear: life is a struggle to maintain personal honor and individual courage against the stupidities and caprice of the organization. He who struggles attains a luster that nothing can dim—and what is war anyway but a hideous business in which the fight is to maintain life amid death, to place duty and honor ahead of everything else; duty, honor, country. Or so Army officers have expressed it to me. That is, some of them have. A few have said that *Once an Eagle* is bullshit.

Senior commanders in the Army today have been formed by the experience of World War Two, and are thus rooted in what seems now ancient history, "irrelevant." Lieutenant General William DePuy, the assistant vice chief of staff of the Army, believes it to be central to the conduct, call it the perception, of the Vietnam war. "Many of our senior commanders were battalion commanders in World War Two. They came from an entirely different background than Bradley or Ike. Now we got into Normandy with the battalions and it looked goddam near impossible. We went in there and we said we would do it regardless of cost. You go up the hill five, six times and then you go up the seventh time. You took the hill regardless of cost. Cost was no object. Men trained out of their personalities the ability to dwell on . . . *problems.*" The difficult we do today, the impossible takes a little longer. World War Two, by this view, was one big engineering project. It was clear, *is* clear, to these men that nothing is impossible for the United States if the country has the will and is prepared to pay the price in money and men. The experience of combat in World War Two was indelible, and the approach to Vietnam proceeded from it.

Vietnam. To an outsider, the Army isn't much of a place to be right now unless, like the colonel, a man enjoys adversity. "Oh my God, we hit a little girl," the author John Sack quotes an infantryman in his book, *M*, an account of a company of Americans fighting the Vietnam war; the quotation stands as epitaph. Early in *The Naked and the Dead*, Norman Mailer causes his Gallagher to say: "Of course they died in vain. Any GI knows the score. The war is just t.s. to them who had to fight it." Fifty years before Mailer, in 1895, Oliver Wendell Holmes, then fifty-seven, advanced a different view: "I do not know what is true. I do not know the meaning of the universe. But in the midst of doubt, in the collapse of creed, there is one thing I do not doubt, and that is that the faith is true and adorable which leads a soldier to throw away his life in obedience to a blindly accepted duty, in a cause which he little understands, in a plan of campaign of which he has no notion, under tactics of which he does not see the use."

Holmes does not read so well in 1970, and one wonders what Stephen Crane would have replied in 1895. But his remark is only a slightly more florid version of what officers tell their troops today or (to sharpen the point a bit) what Presidents sometimes tell their citizens. What else can an officer say but, Win One for the Gipper? In the midst of doubt, in the collapse of creed, the professional soldier—as the rest of us—retreats to personal definitions; success or failure, personal endurance, balls.

The soldier sees his life spent in the service of the state, and that in what Harold Lasswell called "the management of violence." It is one thing to take responsibility for your own life, quite another to take responsibility for the lives of 150 or 600 or 5,000 others. The thing goes back to the President, who is the commander in chief, and the population that elected him. The American Army exists to carry out the orders of the government, and if you get into the wrong war that's not the fault of the Army. Or it shouldn't be, given the American system. The Army is responsible for its men and to its commander in chief, the principal representative of the state. So to a soldier the Army is fundamentally innocent, and that is the dilemma.

ONE

The Academy

*"The Army's the only goddam thing holding
this country together."*

In midwinter West Point is bleak and gray, uninviting to
the eye. The hills with their leafless trees come rolling
down to the Hudson River, deep green, swollen now and
shifting with ice. In dead winter the wind rockets up the
valley, and the men march along the road, their chins
buried in heavy coat collars. They walk with economy,
arms swinging to cadence, eyes up and watchful. It is a
gray place all of it, buildings gray, men in gray, the sky
itself reflecting gray and bouncing it back.

The view across the river is marvelous: standing on
the heights of the east bank are the great houses of the
Hudson River squirearchy, heavy places of brick and
stone, built into the woods facing the river. They are far
away, too far for a cadet to see the inhabitants. A prime
situation, the surroundings originally owned by the
banking Morgans and the firearm Colts. Farther south is
Tarrytown, on the edge of ripvanwinkle country, quaint.
But that is not part of the Academy, which is self-
contained as the Army is self-contained, a reservation

with its military switchboards, police, chapel, taxi cabs, taps, and hotel run by the United States Government, Department of the Army.

This is the place where the professional Army begins. The other important places, the infantry school at Benning, the Command and General Staff College at Leavenworth, the Army War College at Carlisle Barracks, the E-Ring of the Pentagon, come later. What Lee and Grant, Custer and Pershing, MacArthur and Eisenhower, Bradley, Taylor, Lemnitzer, Wheeler, Johnson, and Westmoreland have in common is West Point, the Army alma mater.

But in winter, the winter of 1970, it is gray. From the wide gates, the road runs along the river past the brick houses of the colonels and the white frame houses of the lieutenant colonels and majors, the still smaller dwellings of captains, and finally the dormitories, where lights switch off each night at eleven. The houses are neat, symmetrical, and austere; each has a nameplate with the name and the rank of the occupant. At West Point, Army officers are educators, teaching engineering and mechanics, physics, history of the military art, French, American history, English literature, the social sciences. The sounds of progress echo and clatter across the post . . .

"What's the new building?"

"Science building, Sir. New large science building . . ."

. . . but otherwise it is still, so still, so little noise. Traffic halts on Thayer road when the classes change each hour. The traffic halts for about five minutes and the cadets, rigid in their uniforms, pass by. If there is an officer in the car, they salute, looking to a point at the right of the nose, saying very clearly and definitely *good morning, Sir.* No roughhouse, nor horseplay; no dishabille nor signs of disrespect. The uniforms are old-fashioned, tight tunics with enormous stripes on the upper arm. Cadet caps are pulled down low over the eyes, the bills like hoods, and the scalps shaved so close you can see the contours of the bone. In midafternoon during semester examinations, the parade ground, "the plain," is filled with men wearing parkas and carrying skis, bound for the slopes. Back of the plain around a curve are other faculty houses, large well-tended houses with porches and wide lawns where the children play soldier and the enemy is VC. They hide behind oak trees, taking the car in defilade as it drives by, tatatattattattat.

For a school so old and laden with tradition, its aspect is surprisingly modern. The stone of the new dormitory looks clean—new stone, the sort of stone that goes into expensive bungalows in the suburbs to the south. But the landmarks remain. The names of celebrated battles are carved in concrete above the entryways, and in front of the library stands an heroic statue of George Patton, blank-faced, pistols at the ready, his silver general's stars, the real ones, buried deep in the bronze fist. There are other statues, of Kosciuszko, of Washington, and the newest, of General of the Army Douglas MacArthur, superintendent of the Academy in 1919, winner of the Congressional Medal of Honor in World War Two, Army Chief of Staff in the nineteen-thirties, the man who returned to the Philippines, who devised Inchon, the embodiment of the West Point motto, Duty Honor Country. "Your's is the profession of arms," he told the cadets in 1962, "the will to win ... the sure knowledge that in war there is no substitute for victory, that if you lose the nation will be destroyed, that the very obsession of your public service must be duty, honor, country."

No substitute for victory . . . if you lose, the nation will be destroyed. At West Point it comes down to that, words, deeds and men; those are the tangible spirits, but difficult to recapture at this point in time. There are the statues and the words beneath them, legends living and dead, jumbled together with the sense of things as they are now. What came to mind was an anonymous quota-

tion in a wire service dispatch from South Vietnam,
which sought to gather reaction from the troops after
Senator Edward Kennedy's criticism of the assault up
Hamburger Hill. "Victories, heroes," a lieutenant colonel
of infantry said, "they must mean something different to
Americans now."

But on the sidewalk, moving swiftly to the Officer's
Club for lunch, those matters were part of some other
time and place. Army men, immaculate in their uniforms, clicked down the paths, saluting, murmuring
greetings to the cadets, short nods, the right hand to the
visor and down again; nod, up, down, and walking a few
more feet, good morning, good morning; the shoes
polished, the trousers creased, hair trimmed, eyes clear,
eyes as gray as the day.

The cadets advanced on the dining hall, an immense
room in the shape of a star, constructed in the baronial
style of an Elsinore. On one far wall of this building,
Washington Hall, is an immense mural depicting great
battles. The colors are light, almost pastel, and in the
confusion of it one battle spills over into another, Wel-
lington and Napoleon at Waterloo with William The
Conquerer at Hastings, Miltiades at Marathon, Joffre at
the Marne, Gates at Saratoga, Arminius at the Teoto-
burder Forest, Cyrus at Babylon, Jeanne d'Arc at Or-
léans, Marlborough, Mohammed II, Alexander the Great.
The commanders stare down at the refectory tables with
fixed, iron stares. Morning light angles through the win-
dows of Washington Hall, catching a corner of the mural
and turning it yellow-bright. Odd mural. There is heroism and martyrdom, but no blood nor suffering. There is
gallantry and heroism, victory and defeat, but no blood
and no tears.

The old buildings of the quad are stone, gothic fortifications, some of them dating from the establishment of the

Academy, March 16, 1802, mid-point in the first administration of President Jefferson. It is nearly as old as the
Army itself, and something of an ivory tower. The Academy is a presence, evidence of continuity, and in the
winter of 1970, seven years after the assassination of
Kennedy, six after Berkeley, five after the Marines landed
at Danang, officials at West Point were proud that the
place was still solid, hard. There was a revolution of
sorts in America, but no challenge to the status quo at
West Point; some students and some faculty at the Academy were concerned, but expressed their concern with
restraint: the Academy was very old, the revolution very
new. The war in Vietnam was discussed, but with detachment. Many of the younger faculty had served their tours
in the war zone, but reported that the cadets were not
anxious to hear war stories. Brigadier General Sam
Walker, the commandant, admitted with a smile that he
felt like he was sitting on a powder keg, but there was
not much evidence of sparks. It was possible to hear one
or two snide remarks about the Navy and the Pueblo
disgrace . . .

"Don't give up the ship unless, uh, absolutely necessary."

. . . and a few of the younger officers were blunt in their
criticism of American leadership. One of them called Vietnam a chickenshit war, shaking his head in distaste and
grimacing, as if he were watching a beautiful woman
making love to a troll. At West Point they were training
men for serious business, not the interminable Vietnam
war, which the civilians had bungled from the outset and
Westmoreland had finished with his witless policy of
attrition. Forget about it and move on to other, more important, things; things that mattered, and would endure.

Time and again, the senior colonels at the Point would
reach beyond Vietnam and urge me to do the same. They
were thinking about the curriculum and the role of the
Army in the nineteen-seventies, and the really serious

threats: the Soviet Union and China, and the international conspiracy. They seemed to be trying to blot Vietnam from their minds, a bad dream that recurred and kept recurring. As often as not, a conversation about the war would switch to the domestic upheavals in the United States, "the other insurgency." This was examined with puzzled interest, as an English professor might discuss a best-selling contemporary novel by an author he knew only slightly; sometimes it seemed a subject best passed over in silence. A few colonels declared that the Point was a bit remote to thoroughly understand student radicals and radical blacks; there was the library with its 285,000 volumes and everyone knew that ninety-five per cent of the faculty had master's degrees and nine per cent held PhDs. So it was not a matter of intellect or scholarship. The *brains* were there, but it was an Army post and the atmosphere was one of discipline. The chaplain called West Point "the beautiful ghetto." The rage was elsewhere, and it was difficult to make the connection—to the blacks or to Woodstock Nation, one of the colonels said, and added: "Well, as in any academic environment."

These impressions were assembled in January, 1970, two months before the Army commission headed by Lieutenant General William R. Peers recommended that two generals and twelve lesser officers be charged in connection with the massacre at My Lai; two generals, and one of them was Major General Samuel Koster, the Academy's superintendent.* West Point's reaction to My Lai and to Koster was more complicated than the general Army reaction, due to West Point's tradition as something of a conscience for the Army. The general reaction was paradoxical: anyone who had spent any time in Vietnam knew that there had been "incidents," usually "isolated."

*The commanding officer of West Point. The commandant of West Point, a one-star billet, has charge of a cadet's military training and the disciplinary apparatus.

The policy of heavy tactical air strikes and the indis-
criminate lobbing of artillery shells into the countryside
had made a wasteland of certain parts of the country.
But this was destruction by remote control, and anyway
not very different from the rules of engagement in Germany or Korea. When Seymour Hersh broke the My Lai
story, most soldiers didn't believe it; then they thought
about it a bit, and commenced to search their memories
for any incidents in which *they* may have been involved
(or so I was told by a thoughtful major who had spent
five years in the war zone, and was there when the
My Lai disclosures came). The disposition was to accept
a massacre ("if you insist on calling it that") of a dozen
or two dozen people—you could never tell those gooks
apart anyway, and it was *war*—but not 119 or 156 or 306
or 600 or whatever the figure was. Not shot in the back.
Not by American troops led by American officers from a
division whose commander was now the superintendent
at West Point. That was the average reaction, as best I
could read it. But there was one other view, a minority
view, which held that of course it could happen and
given the way the war was conducted was bound to happen. A colonel: "You go through those hamlets in company and battalion strength and you get a sniper round
and hell, yes, you level the place." But unarmed women
and children? What if there was no sniper round? "The
distinction's pretty slight," said the colonel. "Pretty
damn slight."

Most military men with whom I spoke were torn between a desire to cover it up on the theory that it would
indelibly tarnish the Army's already soiled image and a
pride that the service had moved to clean its own house
(no one mentioned the assist from Hersh). At West
Point, attention was focused on what My Lai meant to
the Army's traditions, to its officer code, and not least
the melancholy fact that the superintendent was among
those charged. The accusation against Samuel Koster

was violations of Article 92, Uniform Code of Military
Justice, failure to obey lawful regulations, and derelic-
tion in the performance of duty. A man is presumed
innocent, at the Point as elsewhere in America, but in
the cadet honor code (Koster is West Point '42) there is
a strong strain of innocent appearance. More specifically,
"quibbling, cheating, evasive statements or recourse to
technicalities will not be tolerated." There is something
of the cadet code in military justice as well, a notion that
what matters is the spirit and not the letter of the law. A
charge against a major general by a commission headed
by a lieutenant general (you could be sure there would
be no charge unless the commission had all the evidence
it needed to convict) was regarded in the Army as solid
proof of guilt *of some kind.** So however the inquiry
would come out, Koster had been tainted, and when he
left the Point for Fort Meade to await trial, the Academy
was shaken. Nothing remotely like it had ever happened
at West Point before.

A few officers at the Point had been told privately of
the charges, and were prepared to resign from the Army
publicly and with drama if Koster were not among those
charged. Copies of the Peers report were circulated and
made a heavy impression. One of these officers, referring
to the statement that Koster read to the cadets the day
he left, was appalled: "Why did he have to use that line,
Duty Honor Country? It will haunt him, that one will."
The information that Edward Bennett Williams would

*A note on the Peers commission. Its members were very
carefully selected, and it was no accident that Peers himself was not an Academy graduate. One senior colonel (a
West Pointer) attended the opening session, and then was
replaced. The reason was his outspoken, by Army standards, opposition to the American conduct of the war. Westmoreland wanted, by this account, a "pristine" commission
of moderate men, Army regulars, who "knew the score."
Peers, a gruff professional, has a reputation for both
toughness and fairness.*

plead the defense was greeted with restraint. (There is a darkly amusing aspect to all this. The Academy has a number of ways it traditionally honors its outgoing superintendents. These range from a full-dress parade to a quiet leave-taking. It is said that the senior colonels at the Academy worried the Koster problem for two days, calculating the precise azimuth of his dishonor, and then decided it would be appropriate to have a mill-in in front of his house. This the cadets dutifully did, parading by for forty-five minutes, with little visible emotion either way. Tradition was satisfied, and a day later the new superintendent arrived. He was Major General William Knowlton, West Point '43, whose record is clean as a hound's tooth. Knowlton, a onetime aide to William Westmoreland, is regarded as one of the smoothest men in the Army.)

I returned to West Point in March, ten days after the charges had been made, and found surprisingly little discussion of Koster as a man. He was said to be a good officer, a fine officer, who was either being (1) railroaded or (2) made a casualty of war. The fact was that the general had made very little impression on the Point, despite his almost two years as superintendent. He was widely regarded as a "comer" in the Army, proof of which being that he got the job at all. At the time of my January visit I had interviewed him, a tall, iron-gray-haired, cautious officer, fifty years old, a product of West Liberty, Iowa, whose son is West Point '72. In Korea, he had directed the Eighth Army's guerrilla warfare operations against the North; in Vietnam, his reputation is best described as mixed. Commanding an undistinguished division (the Americal, which was stuffed with draftees), he produced undistinguished results. He was steady, conservative, and unspectacular. His area of operations was rough, so his own divisional tactics were rough.

When I saw the General in January, we sat in the superintendent's handsome office in the headquarters building, Building 600, and drank coffee and chatted. It was an obligatory interview, and Koster was subdued. We talked of discipline, the permissive society, the role of the Army now. "I'm not sure all youth wants to be completely free," he said. "Some respect discipline and control. Here, there is so much to be accomplished—not much time to be nonconformist. One of the main goals is to teach self-discipline. We get a certain number who do not conform, and they leave during the first two months . . ."

I later found out that this was not precisely the case, but no matter. I was then preoccupied with the education of Army officers, and inquired why the Academy had produced so few military philosophers. America had never sired a Clausewitz (unless you counted Alfred Thayer Mahan, the naval strategist) and I wondered why. "We're more interested in the 'doer' than the thinker," the general said. So I turned to Vietnam. "I think it has had no great effect on the cadets," said the general. "A tarnished image? The Army is carrying out the wishes of the political leaders of this country. You shouldn't criticize the Army for being there . . . anyway, it is not lasting and will have no significant effect."

That was that.

When My Lai became known, a year and a half after the event, there was little reaction among the cadets. To the extent that true attitudes can be known, it appeared that the older officers, the colonels who chaired the departments, tended to disbelieve what they had read. And when the superintendent was charged, many did not believe that either; or believed that when all the facts were known, the general would be exonerated. "The supe" would ride it out, true to what he had told the cadets: *Don't let the bastards grind you down.* There were only two reactions, really: disbelief or disgust. The disgust was centered in the younger instructors, captains, majors, and lieutenant colonels, who reckoned that the massacre probably did happen (most of them were veterans of Vietnam, and knew the madness) and that it represented a stain upon *their* honor. There was a platoon leader and a company commander and a battalion commander and a brigade commander and a division commander and all of those men were responsible; and the senior man was the division commander, and that was Koster. These men did not like what appeared to them to be low-ranking scapegoats, small fry like the enlisted men and Lieutenant Calley and Captain Medina. The fact that the Army had proceeded against its own, that a major general could be named in what civilian law would call an indictment, seemed to many of the younger men a vindication of the system. Thank God for the Army and its traditional ways. The old ways. Would Congress ever move against its own?

But the crucial point was the stain upon professional honor that resulted from My Lai. One of the young men who felt strongly about it was Lieutenant Colonel John H. Johns, associate professor of military psychology and leadership.

"My Lai," he said. "I wanted an uproar around here. But there wasn't any. I even tried to provoke one, and got nowhere. We rationalize too much. We have a . . . different problem in Vietnam because of the frustrations, and anyone who has been there understands those. I can understand it. But look, once you begin to break down, break down discipline and break down in general, it tears into a man's self-concept. I wanted the people here to grasp that, to look at it and understand it, to renew our own integrity. I wanted more of a reaction. I wanted us to clean it up in-house."

But West Point stayed cool; not indifferent or callous, just cool. A colonel, a chairman of a department, said of Johns: "He was more upset about My Lai than the damned chief of staff of the Army." And after Koster was charged, I returned to West Point to talk with Johns again. We had a long and detailed discussion of ethics and the breakdown of visible symbols of stability in a society. We spoke of the cadet honor code, and what was crucial to a man's honor and what was not. "Look," Johns said, "I don't want to say that morality is collapsing in the Army. It's not. It's just that . . . I think that the Army is slipping as the rest of society is slipping." He mentioned the curriculum, and shrugged. There were two hours of ethics, *only two hours*, in the entire MP&L course; the staff of the department had met for two hours assembling their reaction to My Lai, and the gamut ran from blame of the media to blame of the American system. Johns handed me a paper he had written on the subject. At the end of it was a notation that any member of the department could go to Professor X of the English department for a briefing. Professor X was a recognized authority on ethics and morality, and he would give a briefing to anyone who wanted it, a briefing on ethics and morality.

Anyway, Johns said, he intended now to leave the Army for a career in law. He'd leave next year, with twenty years in, get a pension, his law degree. Johns looked an unlikely attorney, and I could not picture him in mufti. When he put on a business suit, he would dress like James Gavin. The suit would be wonderfully cut, but he would wear brown socks and a blue tie and his shirt wouldn't fit.

The cadets were preoccupied with the superintendent for about two days, and then the matter was dropped. According to John Johns and others, the examination never plunged very deep. The cadet corps is not a monolith, and there are distinctions within distinctions as in any subculture, which West Point certainly is. Yet Colonel Harry Buckley, the chairman of the department of military psychology and leadership, is probably accurate when he says, "the response to My Lai, General Turner, Sergeant Major Wooldridge, and the others— well, it was the response of Middle America." The deputy chairman of the English department said that the cadets have "made a truce with the world as they found it, or they wouldn't be here."

Quite possibly so, but I doubt that a survey would support it; or, rather, it would in some particulars and it wouldn't in others. What is given here is not a survey, but the result of conversations with Cadets Barbour, Knight, Postell, Bishop, Weddle, Sullivan, and Folk, among others. These men, all of them selected by Academy authorities, appeared to be a reasonable cross-section of cadets, from Weddle, who admires Eldridge Cleaver and Congressman Allard Lowenstein, to Knight, who admires the late General George Patton. These cadets were well turned out, carefully groomed, and unfailingly polite.

To one degree or another, all of them were conscious that the uniform set them apart, and not always in agreeable ways. Knight, son of an Army colonel from Alexandria, Virginia, described an evening at the discotheques in Georgetown: "I try not to get caught up in it. I avoid letting them know that I am from West Point. In Georgetown, I tell them I'm from an upstate New York college or the U. Va., some place like that. Once I said I was from West Point and it stifled conversation for the rest of the evening. I feel, you are really branded."

Vietnam: "We get into some pretty deep discussions. You remember the October and November moratoriums. The Vassar girls came up here and they had a total ignorance of our problem. Total ignorance. My God, if there is one group of people who have a vested interest in peace, it's us. I mean, *we are the ones who have to fight the wars.* When guys go home, they get a lot of questions about it. We are the ones who get the questions, who are quote unquote the defenders of the faith."

Patton: "I saw the movie. I admire him as a tactician. You know, he's a simplistic, uncomplicated guy—straightforward, no curves, just fastballs. I like that. I'm not so sure about the remarks that his son [Brigadier General George Patton III] makes, though. He said about the war in Vietnam, 'I do like to see the arms and legs fly.' Huh uh."

And Koster: "He got the shaft. He was a Congressional scapegoat really. Of course he had the responsibility but did he have the *guilt*? That's the real question. We all understand command responsibility. But what about guilt? He may not have known about My Lai. The railroad job on Koster could be attributed to a cry for blood. If you want it bad enough, you are going to get it."

But what about Peers? If it was a railroad job, then Peers, a respected Army lieutenant general, was in on it, an accomplice.

Knight thought a moment, and then shook his head. "Well, that connection wasn't made," he said. "It just wasn't associated with it."

All of the cadets thought that the Army's mission into the nineteen-seventies would be some variation of counterinsurgency. Conventional war was finished and if there was a nuclear exchange—well, that was that. So the spot for the talented officer in, say, ten years' time was in something to do with the underdeveloped world. The lesson of Vietnam? That was difficult because the U.S. was only now learning how to fight that war, and it certainly wasn't a war of attrition. At least a war of attrition like World War Two was a war of attrition. "What works in one country doesn't always work in another," Cadet Bishop said. "In small countries, you won't be able to apply all your force."

The problems lie in the small countries, the ones Bishop described as "not satisfied . . . and there is no other organization that can do it (satisfy them) except the Army." The cadets were fuzzy on these points, which seemed ill-defined; one of them said that while Vietnam was not a war of attrition, the Americans had fought the war in the only way they could. Most of the cadets thought of the world as one of menace to the peace and security of the United States. One of them saw a possible tactical role for nuclear weapons, "small tac nukes," in places like Latin America:

"Well, you have got to hold the spread of Communism down, and keep whoever is in government *there*. That's what's important." I remarked to the cadet that it was the first mention of Communism that I had heard from a student; most of them used the word "enemy." The cadet shrugged and replied that he didn't mean, necessarily, ideological Communism but "sedition and so forth."

Fairly conventional military world-views, I thought. But Knight gave it a new twist. When I asked him what he thought the role of the Army in the nineteen-seventies should be, he spoke first of counterinsurgency, then this: "In between wars, what does the Army do? Why should we be passive when we could be doing something which might prevent a war? Why can't the Army have civic action? A peacetime mission is at least as important as a wartime mission. There's so much wasted time in the Army. Guys could be learning a trade, going to school, building a dam—anything. Hell, that's the trouble with places like Fort Hood. Guys get into trouble because there's nothing to do."*

The discussions became more revealing when they turned to the nature of West Point itself. Cadet Postell: "A good friend of mine left in his sophomore year. He was very methodical about it, talked to officers around here for six months. We tried to dissuade him because he was a really good man, number one in aptitude. But it

---

*The Department of the Army has a committee studying this question, what to do with all the men and money, post-Vietnam.

didn't work. He said, finally, that he had talked to the officers and decided that when he grew up he didn't want to be like them."

What this cadet meant can only be imagined, but in the others there seemed a distrust of what is conventionally described as the military mind, and the environment surrounding it. Weddle: "Look, we are part of the same world as the rest of our generation. We react to the same things. The world goes on. Now is not when MacArthur was here."

Cadets Weddle, Sullivan, and Folk were leaning forward in their chairs. We were back in a dark corner of Grant Hall and the Mothers of Invention were pounding from a stereo. The three of them confirmed that some of the best men were leaving (some of the worst, too). The First Class, the class of 1970, was down to 1,050 from 1,400; the sophomore class was just over 1,000 men, down from 1,244 admitted. There were a number of reasons for it, as many reasons as cadets, but the principal theme seemed to be disappointment. The Army wasn't what they thought it would be. One of the other cadets had said that he was appalled on his first visit to a military post, "the enlisted men very sloppy and undisciplined, and the same with the officers. I can't figure it out. We have three times as much discipline around here [West Point]. Really, it was very sloppy." And a remark made by Cadet Bishop: "There are a lot of people at the Point who really don't take to discipline. They don't look at West Point as a training vehicle. I don't know why they suffer here for four years without benefit. But they stay. I don't know why."

Weddle, Sullivan, and Folk—the last demurring part of the time—were discussing the education, which Weddle described as appealing to the lowest, the worst, common denominator. "If we could go into one, just one, subject really thoroughly. There is no depth at all," Weddle said, "just survey courses. A man can't pursue his field in depth." One of the others added that the entire system was at fault, the daily grading, the rigid classroom atmosphere, the Mickey Mouse. The damned Mickey Mouse all the time. Shined shoes. Haircuts. Bracing. Niggling rules that tied you down like the Lilliputians did Gulliver. Weddle: "We are supposed to be the cream of the crop. Very well, if that is so, why is the whole system designed for a man who has ab-so-lute-ly no responsibility? They give us none. None. There is no sense for a cadet of any sort of responsibility, personal or otherwise."

They had all spoken of that, the Army's obsession with appearance, with cleanliness and tidiness and care. Did it make a better general to have his shoes shined and his hair cut short? What difference did it make to anyone? To the real world? Grant had a beard and drank. Eisenhower's disciplinary record was so uneven that he very nearly didn't graduate, and when he did they wanted to post him to the Coast Artillery. *Now is not when Mac-Arthur was here.* The details overwhelmed, they had said; the details became so great that it was impossible to concentrate on substance. One did not deal with ideas at West Point, one dealt with facts. The instructors did not encourage reflection or imagination or wonder. There was no time to *think*. "No time at all to sit and wonder," said a sympathetic major in one of the humanities departments.

"Well," I said, turning to the three of them who were sitting almost primly in the heavy Grant Hall chairs. "What do you think the Army is going to be doing in ten years? Or let me put it another way: What do you think you will be doing in the Army in ten years?"

They exchanged smiles and didn't say anything for a moment. I didn't catch the look, so I rephrased the question and still they didn't say anything. The three of them looked like they were sharing a joke together.

"That's a very important question," Weddle said.

Then I understood. "Oh."

"Look. There isn't a single member of the junior class who is going to stick with this Army after the five-year commitment. None of us is going to be here in ten years."

"Are you serious?"

"No one that I know," Weddle said with finality. "The guys will do their five years, and then out. Who needs it?"

"Oh, I don't think that's right," Folk said. "It's not that way with the people I see. My friends."

Weddle smiled and nodded, turning to Sullivan. Okay, the smile said. You have your crowd and I have mine. Your bunch does one thing and mine does another. "Call us the underground," Weddle said.

We talked about that a bit, and then I asked them the question I had asked all the others. Sitting around a table with the younger faculty of the MP&L department, I had asked who the heroes of the 'fifties were at West Point. The answer came quickly: James Gavin, and before that Eisenhower and Patton, possibly MacArthur. So I put that question to Weddle, Sullivan, and Folk. Who are the heroes of these students? They grinned at me as a majority of the other cadets had done. These were men —boys—who had been born during the Korean War and were eight or nine when John Kennedy was elected President. They were eleven or twelve when he was murdered, fourteen or fifteen when the Marines first waded ashore at Danang. The entire period of their public consciousness had been dominated by Vietnam and murder, and for much of their generation the two words were very nearly synonymous.

"There aren't any heroes any more," Folk said.

"I guess not," I said.

In light of these attitudes (if they are representative, and I believe they are), it is worthwhile to examine the curriculum at West Point in some detail. The math, science and engineering requirements are these: at least three semesters of math, two of engineering, two of mechanics, two of chemistry, two of physics, two of electricity, two of engineering fundamentals, one of astronomy/astronautics, and one of world regional geography. West Point requires four semesters of one foreign language (French, Spanish, German, Portuguese, Russian, or Chinese), two of military art, three of English, six of social science, and two of law. That is the core academic program, and beyond that all cadets must successfully work their way through the department of tactics and the department of physical education. Those two departments will supply the crucial comments on "aptitude."

It is a staggeringly heavy load, even granting that cadets attend classes six days a week, nine months a year. (Two summer months are devoted to military training, and a third is vacation time.) Reveille is 6:15 each day, and each day carries its full complement of tactics and physical education as well as academic subjects. Seventeen per cent of the courses are elective, and the core breaks down to forty-four per cent humanities and thirty-nine per cent mathematics, science, and engineering. Despite the apparent disparity (it is the exact reverse of the percentage a decade ago, when the Academy first introduced electives), it is in the hard sciences and math that the more sophisticated courses are given. West Point's degree is a bachelor of science, and that is where the concentration is: there are no courses in history or social science, which are the equivalent of nuclear reactor theory, heat mass and momentum transfer, or numerical analysis with digital computation. The chairman of the department of history, Colonel Thomas E. Griess, defends the emphasis on the hard sciences this way: "We have to give the cadets the sciences because the Army is highly technological."

Just so, but a run through the catalog confirms the impression that the Academy is relentlessly stuffing ten pounds of sugar into a five-pound bag. Repeatedly, de-

partment heads would concede that there was a danger
(as one of them put it) "of squeezing the cadet between
the ceiling and the floor, covering him with mediocrity."
But the case was made that it was a complicated world,
and a complicated institution, and the objective was not,
after all, to develop a scholar—a political scientist or an
engineer or even a platoon leader—but an Army officer.
A generalist, a man at home in both cultures but oriented
to science. West Point was there to give a man a platform
from which to pursue advanced studies. No course, or
series of courses, was meant as an end in itself; each led
to something else, and when one asked why, given the
world-wide responsibilities of the American Army, the
language requirement was only two years (and completed
in the freshman and sophomore years, at that), the chairman of the language department could only smile and
repeat the theory of the generalist officer. The generalist
officer, one might add, firmly rooted in an earlier American tradition.

West Point began, and through much of the nineteenth
century remained, as a school of engineering, a natural
reflection of one prevailing theory that successful armies
were the product of a superior technology. It is part of
the lore of the Academy that in the years before the
Civil War, West Point produced more railroad presidents
(the most notorious was George B. McClellan) than generals. Its pedagogical influence on other colleges was
very great, on the technology of the time enormous, and
on the Army (until the Civil War) slight. It was not until
1858 that a department of tactics was established, and
not for 110 years after that that the department of military art and engineering was split into two separate dis-
ciplines. The intellectual father of the Point was Thomas
Jefferson, the man of the Enlightenment, and he built
himself an *école polytechnique*—not a Sandhurst and
certainly not a *Kriegsakademie*, whose director in 1810
was Gerhard Scharnhorst and in 1818 was Carl von

Clausewitz. West Point was organized in 1802, and its
first superintendent was a grandnephew of Benjamin
Franklin, a scientist named Jonathan Williams, an Army
major with some knowledge of fortifications but no real
military background at all. Sylvanus Thayer came in
1817 and stayed nearly sixteen years; rigid, narrow-
minded, autocratic, and brilliant, Thayer, as Jefferson,
conceived of the military art as a technical specialty and
of France as the primary source of military wisdom. So
there were French textbooks and French professors, and
West Point graduates were sent to Paris, not Berlin, for
advanced study. The resident genius was the former
Swiss bank clerk, Baron Antoine Henri de Jomini, not
Clausewitz—and the informing vision was the drive to
expand the American frontier. Neither Grant nor Lee
took to it very well. On his return to civilian life after the
war, Robert E. Lee remarked that "the greatest mistake
of my life was taking a military education."

Thayer's ideal was the Enlightenment ideal, and as
West Point officials today point out, he sought to build
men, with the Academy not an end to an officer's education but a beginning. More important, the Army officer
was not to be trained as a professional and set aside from
what one of the early documents describes as the "other
orders" of society. A soldier's responsibilities were
different, it was true, but he would deal with them
through force of character, not special privilege. Thayer
established small classes, no more than fifteen men to
each, a principle that endures at West Point today. Then
as now cadets were subject to frequent tests, and even
more frequent oral examinations in class; there were to
be no major subjects, or specializations. One course of
study would suffice for all, the objective to produce an
officer corps of interchangeable parts: a colonel who
could command a brigade, build a bridge, calculate supplies, assemble intelligence, be truly capable of serving
wherever and whenever the Army directed him to serve.

A West Point education is not an education in war or the techniques of war or the nature of violence or its causes. Still less is it a restrictive education, and the lengths to which the Academy goes to produce the well-rounded man have to be seen to be believed. In his senior year (they call it the First Class at West Point, the freshman year being the Fourth Class), the cadet scales the summit of English 402, Advanced Exposition-Readings in Philosophy. There are forty-three meetings of this class, and students are expected to read, and digest, selected works of Socrates, Descartes, Bertrand Russell, Thucydides, Nietzsche, Machiavelli, W. H. Auden, Jeremy Bentham, Epicurus, Epictetus, Robert Lynd, Aristotle, James Thurber, Emmanuel Kant, Martin Luther King, John Dewey, William James, David Hume, Francis Bacon, Henri Bergson, Benedette Croce, Plato, Henry David Thoreau, Jacob Bronowski, Lucretius, John Dalton, Spinoza, John Henry Newman, La Rochefoucauld . . . but that only takes us to Lesson Fourteen. There are twenty-nine more lessons, and Camus, Buddha, Hemingway, and the Old Testament (among many, many others) yet to go. It is the survey course to end all survey courses, matched only by H.M. 401-402, History of the Military Art, which deals with wars and warriors from Herodotus to Mrs. Meir in ninety-five eighty-minute classes. An Army officer dealt with facts, a colonel said, and from facts he could proceed to judgment; but first he had to know all the facts, every fact that there was.

The department heads are permanent staff, men who have chosen to end their careers at the Point; upon retirement, a man is promoted from colonel to brigadier general. There are no civilians at all, except in the language department, and they are required to wear army uniforms sans badges of rank. All of the department heads and three-quarters of the rest of the faculty are West Point graduates themselves. The instructors and most associate professors are temporary. They stay two or three years, and then move on to another assignment, the Pentagon or Iran or Vietnam or Fort Hood. The faculty like it that way, because the new men bring the new Army with them; they are not at West Point primarily as teachers, but as Army officers. Colonel Edwin B. Sutherland, the chairman of the English department, sports handlebar moustaches and wears leather arm-patched tweed coats over his regulation Army greens. Put him in gray flannels and he would be a fixture at Deerfield. Sutherland did not appear convinced that the Army atmosphere was appropriate for the teaching of English, but he had made his own peace with it. Henry James? "I tell them that Henry James is like a major general standing in the middle of the road. You must salute him whether you want to or not."

It was tempting to put down the colonel of infantry who had done his master's thesis on Emily Dickinson. But the men of the English department were so demonstrably defensive about the course of study that after a time I felt sympathetic; clearly, these men were the outcasts of the Academy. (Much later, a friend told me that the Tac department regarded them as effete, as they did many who taught the soft sciences.) Colonel Jack Capps, Sutherland's deputy, was anxious that it be understood that the cadets were good scholars; the department had devised a survey which showed that incoming cadets read poetry, *outside of assigned work,* from four to five per cent more than men entering Ivy League schools. Four to five per cent more, Capps said. It was true of course that there was no literary magazine at West Point—"there are so many which are disasters, and we'd have to be looking over their shoulders all the time"— but the idea, after all, was to educate Army officers. No, it was not a disadvantage that the instructors were Army officers first and teachers of English second, and that *Heart of Darkness* (wonderful choice) was the only novel the cadets were required to read in its entirety.

Far from being a disadvantage, it was a positive plus: "The instructor tells them, 'Byron was important to me. Byron will be important to you.' And the man who is saying that has a D.S.C. and a silver star and was in the Special Forces." They were soldier-scholars, Capps was saying; "when this major or lieutenant colonel is talking about Camus he has that row of ribbons that shows he knows something more . . ."*

Lieutenant Colonel Charles R. Kemble, B.S. USMA, M.A. University of Pennsylvania, PhD George Washington University, agreed with Capps. He appeared a tough hombre, and he said that when the cadets listened to the man with the ribbons they said to themselves: "I want to be like that man." The ribbons meant Korea perhaps, Vietnam almost certainly—the young platoon leader or company commander who took the hill and protected the wounded, who had been there and knew what it was like, had commanded other men, required them to move into the killing zone; he had met his responsibilities, and the tickets on his blouse showed that he was not a spectator. This man had read Camus and Thucydides, perhaps Proust, and liked what he had read. He was not some dumb son of a bitch who thought that a stanza was an Italian general.

*Many faculty members of the English department have written their master's thesis (or "major research paper") on fairly conventional literary subjects: "The critical reputation of Robinson Jeffers," "Technique of narration in Conrad's Marlow stories," "The structure of the Jacobean family in Shakespearean tragedy," "Swift, Pope, and Satire." Others have chosen military themes: Major Benjamin W. Covington III, "A short history of key terminology pertaining to mounted combat"; Lieutenant Colonel Robert L. Merrick, "Stephen Crane as a war correspondent"; Major William B. Gard, "An Edymological history of the military terminology in Tristam Shandy"; Major Walter R. Good, "Contributions of army language habits to civilian usage," and Major Harrell G. Hall, "Artillery terminology before 1600."

Byron is important to me, Byron will be important to you. These students, Colonel Sutherland said gently, "most of them are incurable romantics."

Military history is taught in the department of history, one of the smallest departments at West Point. There are only five courses, including the survey course, History of the Military Art. The other four are Revolutionary Warfare, Evolution of Modern Warfare, Twentieth-Century Warfare, and an individual history project, a long essay on a military subject. Next year, Colonel Griess is thinking of adding a course on the military philosophers, Sun Tsu, Machiavelli, Clausewitz, Jomini, Mahan. These men are now treated only superficially in the other courses. Warfare is handled largely as a function of technology, and the heroes are Alexander, Hannibal, Frederick the Great, and U. S. Grant ("better than Lee, when you look at him from all aspects . . ."). Griess said that there were no villains, as one commonly thinks of villains. "When we talk about generals, we look at the whole man—we teach cadets that everyone is human and can make mistakes. The more you read the documents, the more gray areas there are." Under interrogation, Griess admitted that McClellan was "a little less satisfactory" than he might have been and Marshal Pétain, "due to age," a little less able to cope. Why is there not more on the history of warfare? Griess, a tall, careful man, smiled. "Then we'd be vocational."

Most of the action at the Point is now in the social sciences department, whose chairman, Colonel Amos A. Jordan, and one associate professor, Colonel Rogert W. Nye, are extremely well known and admired throughout the Army. Social science undertakes to instruct cadets in comparative political systems, anthropology, economics, the problems of "the developing nations" and simple history. The spin appears evident from the description of SS 381, History of Russia, "a study of the historical development of the Russian nation and its relations with the western world, with particular emphasis on the nature of the Russian revolution, the regime which it produced, and the Communist bloc as it presents a challenge to the West." In other words, a history of the cold war—and it is safe to assume that no major college or university in America approaches Russian history from quite that angle.

Safe to assume, but perhaps wrong. A number of otherwise critical officers indicated that whatever the catalog says, the department itself is straight. No inflammatory histories of the cold war, and certainly no descriptions of monolithic Communism. But it is an uphill battle for Jordan and Nye. Tac officers who occasionally listen to the lectures are prone to complain, in writing, that this course or that is excessively "liberal" or, occasionally, "peacenik-oriented." Two officers did that not long ago after hearing a professor discuss the roots of the First World War, which he described as more or less rotten, resulting in appalling loss of life for no reason other than—what?—stupidity? avarice? To the credit of the department, the complaint was slapped down. But it is the sort of thing that happens. One former teacher laughed and clucked wryly: "Sure did keep us on our toes."

At West Point the Soviet Union is not a problem. Khrushchev's remarks, though made a decade ago, are fresh in everyone's mind. But some of the senior officers and many of the junior ones, especially those in the humanities, know that the course of instruction must change to meet the peculiar complexities of 1970. As Jordan put it: "The institution is now beginning to question its own character. We know how to fight the conventional war. We are equipped to handle it. We are very certain in the second mission also, the thermonuclear deterrent. We feel relatively comfortable with these, conventional and nuclear. But we must develop a doctrine to cope with the other, the counterinsurgency. We are divided on that.

The professional soldier finds himself with a mission, and in typical can-do fashion, he sets up the schools and writes the manuals to deal with it. Well, counterinsurgency isn't all that simple. Look. In the other, you employ combat formations, you seize terrain, you destroy the enemy's will to fight. But these might stand in the way of achieving certain other objectives in a . . . a quasi-political war. The destruction of enemy forces may get in the way of certain political objectives. Often . . . well, often you cannot find and fix the enemy. Vietnam is the worst possible mixture of circumstances from the point of view of the United States. The nationalist and the Communist are all mixed up together in Vietnam."

Vietnam. What Nye and Jordan were saying was that it did not fit neatly into any doctrine that the Army had, or right now was willing to stand by. The evidence was contradictory, and all the returns not in. Evaluation would have to wait on events. The general of the future, Nye said, "has to understand combined arms, artillery, armor, infantry, signals, and so forth, but these are skills that you don't need if your are pursuing a war of counterinsurgency." He corrected himself then to say that it wasn't that you didn't need them. You did. But you needed other skills as well.

The professional soldier, Nye went on, had to understand political science, economics, and history, "the social framework in which he practices his profession." Martin Luther King and Che Guevara become as crucial as, perhaps more crucial than, Clausewitz (whose principles do not adapt easily to guerrilla war); and viewed from this angle, where did technology stand? Was war now a soft science? Nye didn't go into that, but said instead: "If a military man wants to have his advice taken, he must be an all-purpose man. He must understand the context of the thing. The core of his advice must be military. But he must be sensitized. He must understand the sense of his advice in the total situation."

But what happened when political judgments contra-dicted military ones or vice versa? In "the total situa-tion," where was the military man's specific gravity? What do you do when the President asks your advice on whether or not to invade Cuba? Do you confine your advice to strictly military matters—it will require X boats and Y troops and Z aircraft to secure the beach-head—or lace it with political verdicts? Or both?*

Nye and Jordan insisted that the military officer must now have a political component. But what that com-ponent should be, and how it should be exercised, re-mained a mystery. As much a mystery, one supposes, as the manner in which impartial historians will view American foreign policy of the nineteen-sixties from the perspective of 1990. The question of the "political com-ponent" is now bedeviling the entire Army (see Chapter Seven), not just the social science department at West Point. And no one seems able to supply a satisfactory answer, or analysis.

When I had asked the professors about heroes, their heroes and the heroes of the cadets, the replies had been

*The disaster at the Bay of Pigs illustrates the problem. A member of the Joint Chiefs of Staff at the time told me that "the military"—meaning the JCS—approved the origi-nal landing site, provided there was air cover. This general insisted that the JCS role was purely advisory, and there was no question of the military having operational control. When CIA switched the beachhead to the Bahia de Cochinos the JCS reaction was negative. But Arthur Schlesinger in A Thousand Days declares that JCS papers contained a sharp political spin, to the effect that any effort against Castro was on its face a worthy one. The general with whom I spoke denied it, saying that "it was a CIA thing and we didn't have anything to do with it. We were asked our advice and we gave it. No military man would ever approve the sort of plan that finally emerged. For crissakes we have more experience in amphibious landings than any nation in the world!"

James Gavin, and from the older men, wistful references to Patton and Eisenhower and MacArthur. (Dwight Eisenhower, a tough-minded man, had no trouble with distinctions: "Such people as Hannibal, Caesar, Pericles, Socrates, Themistocles, Miltiades, and Leonidas were my white hats, my heroes," he once wrote. "Xerxes, Darius, Alcibiades, Brutus, and Nero wore black ones.") They thought that the cadets probably admired Peter Dawkins, the Rhodes Scholar and football hero, West Point's First Captain in 1959 who had gone on to do everything and do it well and with modesty. He had gone from the Point to Oxford, where he took up rugby and starred in that as he had starred in everything else. But none of the cadets had mentioned Dawkins. The cadets hadn't mentioned anyone, except young Knight who liked Patton the elder. Or maybe it was just George C. Scott.

I had been advised to look up the West Point chaplain, James Ford, whose connections with the cadets were very close. Ford is not a career Army chaplain (the Army has career chaplains as it has career infantry officers), and, even rarer at West Point, is not an Episcopalian. He is a Lutheran and a Hubert Humphrey Democrat from Minnesota. He doesn't know what got him the job at the Academy (Westmoreland was superintendent then), only that he applied for it and somewhat to his surprise was accepted. West Point, Ford explained, was always a citadel for the Episcopalians, "who paid their own man to come down here." Once in the mid-nineteenth century a Methodist had breached the walls, but converted to the high church once installed. The strong Episcopal tie was broken in the nineteen-fifties, and now seems ended for good with Ford, who likes the Point and intends to stay. He is arch about it: "There are two boats which are sinking today, the military and the church, and I have got a foot in both."

The chapel is important to the Academy. There are 184 cadets who teach Sunday school, and the choir is one of the really important extra-military activities. Eisenhower was a choir boy, and so were Ridgway, Westmoreland, and Dawkins. Cadets are required to attend chapel on Sundays, and many of them attend every day. Ford is not light about his spiritual responsibilities. "Sometimes during the fourth week of the second summer (each summer, the cadets take basic training), men come to me and say, 'I cannot kill.' This is usually after the first bayonet practice, which is pretty tough. I say to them, 'the commandment Thou Shalt Not Kill is best defined, Thou Shalt Not *Murder.*' More pertinent," he said, "is the commandment, Thou Shalt Love Thy Neighbor As Thyself."

"Well, then you get into the personal equation. We are all involved. How many M-16s have I purchased with my taxes? In killing, there are rules, religious rules—no more violence than necessary, legitimate authority, a just and goalless peace, the defense of the nation . . . and you go through that and you make your decision. You are involved. Everyone is involved. We are all involved. Jesus said to the centurion, 'Never have I seen such faith, no not in all Israel.' That was an accolade given to very few. So in that way, Jesus honored the profession of soldiering."

We had been sitting in his study, drinking whiskey sours. Ford looks like an Irishman, black hair and unlined face, but speaks in flat Minnesota tones. He rose from his chair and walked over to the wall and motioned for me to follow. He pointed to a class picture. They were a group of cadets, standing in rank. "I have buried ten that I have married," he said. He thumbed the picture, placing his nail on the face of one, then another—this one killed near Dak To, that one killed in the Delta of South Vietnam. This one at Tet 1968, that other one, the one there, killed a little later, just before he was to go home. Then he brightened and pointed to a Negro. "That's Joe Anderson, you remember the Anderson Platoon—that French documentary?" I remembered. He talked about Robert Lucky, the head acolyte, killed at Tet 1968. Just after they received word that the boy was dead, Ford was talking to his younger brother, also a cadet, and down the hall—"well, down the hall we were having a seminar, 'What did Jesus mean when he said we should love our enemies?' You have the natural feeling of despair, but the soldier ought not to lose sight of the fact that there is an overriding concern, the nation, and that may sound pious or pompous but it is *right*." He paused to answer the telephone, spoke into the receiver for a few moments, then put it down.

"That was the young wife of a soldier . . . I mean a young widow," he said slowly. He repeated that he had buried ten that he had married. The widow was lonely, and wanted to come and see him. Ford shook his head. "That has been the most difficult part, really. It has been the part that has taken the most out of me." He went on to say that the chapel was an extension of Duty Honor Country.

The same things concern cadets that concern college students everywhere: haircuts, pot, women . . . the general liberalization, "if that is the word," of society. "West Point? Well, West Point is the beautiful ghetto. Everyone is healthy here, and if they are not healthy they are discharged. We do not see these social problems, because they are not a part of our lives here. We're a world apart. We don't see the problems." Ford said that the difficulty of loosening reins is that the Army has never lost a war, "so you are reluctant to change, because you don't know what part of the system gave you a winning team. Parades? Compulsory chapel? The system? Military instructors? We have got an Eisenhower Barracks and a MacArthur Barracks, and Patton, Thayer, and Washington statues . . ."

"Will there be a Westmoreland statue?"

"No, probably not," Ford said sadly. "And you know, these guys are all of the same cut. All of them."

The chaplain sighed. The sentiment of West Point lays over the land like a blanket. There is a plaque on a rock near the football stadium, a quotation attributed to George Catlett Marshall, *I have a secret and dangerous mission. Send me a West Point football player.* In the gymnasium, MacArthur's charge is chiseled: *Upon the fields of friendly strife are sown the seeds that on other days in other fields will bear the fruits of victory.* They are trying to preserve the old ideals, Jim Ford had said, and they are going to do it, believe me they are going to do it. Thank God West Point does not change, or at least does not change much. But in the barracks, the cadets worry about haircuts and Mickey Mouse—trivial, very trivial, until one learns *why.* It is because the Army haircut, the old white sidewall, instantly identifies a student as an Army man. *I tell them I am from an upstate New York college, the U. Va., some place like that,* Cadet Knight said. In Washington or New York or Boston or Los Angeles or San Francisco, Army is no longer what a man wants to be, at least not all the time, everywhere.

Major Ramon A. Nadal II, the assistant director of the department of military psychology and leadership, and an uncommonly introspective officer, observed: "It is much tougher to be a cadet now than it was ten years ago. Hell, I went home and I got a pat on the back. These kids go home and the first thing they do is take off the uniform and say they go to Yale." That was hyperbole and Nadal knew it, so he looked up and smiled. "One boy I knew broke up with his girl because they were always arguing about the damned war and the Army. Another cadet lives near Berkeley and he told me, 'I'm home for thirty days and I'm dueling for thirty days.' Guys don't like to go to Wellesley for dates, for example, because it's nothing but a big hassle all the time about the war, My Lai . . . But look. It's not the biggest deal in the world. Last year, at the November moratorium, some Vassar girls came up here to demonstrate and they handed out flowers to the cadets. One of them gave a lily to a football player and he took it and ate it."

There are paradoxes. A man has come to West Point, not to Yale, and is proud in a perverse way of the restrictions placed upon him. A soldier suit is still glamorous, and discipline still appealing as a way of life. It is an attitude which leaks down from some of the senior officers, inside the Academy and out, men who see the Army as savior. "The Army's the only goddam thing holding this country together," one of them said, believing it, believing that the Army was the only solid foothold in a country gone soft. To the cadet, something of the same psychology applies to the Academy. Nadal, Colonel Johns, and others say there are frequent complaints that the Point is not tough enough, not strict enough, and not sure enough of its own values. "They are very conscious of the purity of the corps," Nadal said.

Some of them. And no less conscious than the officers in charge. "Our whole tradition is that the cadet should be immersed in the military atmosphere..." It is the reason why civilian instructors are addressed as *Sir!*, and why the corps itself is broken down into regiments and companies, with regimental commanders, company commanders, platoon and squad leaders. From the moment a man enters he is understood to be within the military system. This has been described elsewhere as a process which point by point transfers a man's primary reference group from family to Army. Army is home, mother, dad, wife. The first summer there is beast barracks, less tough now than it used to be, but still tough enough. Twenty-eight per cent of those admitted wash out at one time or another, and something under ten per cent of those during the first summer. That first day, the cadet is acquainted with the peer-rating system: everyone rates everyone else, on intelligence, on competence, and crucially, on attitude. Attitude: toward discipline, the military way, sports, studies, comrades, the Academy, the Army itself. Command and obedience, instant obedience to orders. Before a man can lead, Commandant Sam Walker had said, he must be able to follow; follow absolutely. After seven months at the Academy, a cadet's file is an inch thick. It is filled with documents, reports from professors, physical education instructors, tac instructors, fellow cadets. In January of 1970, the most damning indictment in the file of the cadet who was rated number 1,273 in a class of 1,273 was: "He fails to respond to orders."

The orders are everywhere to see. Some are unwritten, reflected only in the conscience of the cadet. The honor code, simplicity itself: the cadet will not lie, cheat, or steal, or tolerate anyone who does. There are books and pamphlets written about it, but there is nowhere a definition of it within quotation marks, like the Ten Commandments or the Articles of the Constitution. It is finally an appeal to honor, not to law, and is expressed this way.

> *Honor, as it is understood by cadets and those responsible for training them, is a fundamental attribute of character. Its underlying principle is truth; the cadet is truthful both by act and by implication. The cadet honor code has, as its objective, fearless honesty in setting forth the truth regardless of consequences. Quibbling, cheating, evasive statements or recourse to technicalities to conceal guilt or defeat the ends of justice are not tolerated. The Corps of Cadets is responsible that all cadets meet the standards of the code. Cadets are expected to adhere to the spirit of this code at all times and without reservation.*

. . . *recourse to technicalities to conceal guilt or defeat the ends of justice are not tolerated.* The assumption is clear: it is that each man knows when he is guilty, knows when he quibbles and evades, knows what justice is. Law is not a matter of procedure, evidence, extenuating circumstance, shades of gray. It is Duty Honor Country, and those are plain enough. A man knows when he has sinned. He knows right from wrong. American society may change its rules, the Supreme Court may make sociological law, but not West Point. For an Army officer, morals and ethics do not change. Cadet Barbour, a first classman from the Chicago suburbs, a fine-looking, chain-smoking, poised, and confident young man, put it this way:

"When a new classman comes in, he comes in from a pretty permissive environment. He is used to getting away with things, and perhaps he is not completely honest. You are always going to have one or two who are not, and they are eliminated. On the Honor Committee there are thirty-six representatives of the companies, plus the officers. The very first night you are here you get a lecture, not to lie, cheat, or steal and not to tolerate anyone who does, and right from the first day you are culpable. There is no statute of limitations. Just because you make an honest mistake is no excuse, and if you say you have six pairs of white trousers and you only have five, and you discover that mistake, you'd better own up to it.

"This is the way it works. The other day I told a cadet that the shower water was cold, but then I stayed in it awhile and it got warmer. When I got out of the shower, I went by this cadet's room and I corrected myself. I had made an untruthful statement. You . . . ah, you make a real effort to be honest."

When a man comes up before the Honor Committee, the proceedings are open and it is customary for some cadets to attend. But is is not customary for plebes to attend the hearings of yearlings (third classmen), nor is it customary for yearlings to attend the hearings of cows (second classmen). That would be the equivalent of a GI observing the court martial of an officer, and would tend to breed disrespect for rank.

Barbour: "We are not interested in whether it is a big lie or a little one. One dollar or a thousand dollars. The only way we can administer the code is to be completely honest and fair, *completely*. A man is requested to resign, and if he refuses he can go before a board of officers. At the initial hearing he can bring witnesses in his behalf. But if all else fails, the corps takes action and a man is silenced."

"Silenced?"

"Frozen," Barbour said. "No one talks to him."

"There are about thirty hearings a year," Barbour said. "It becomes very foggy sometimes which ones are real violations and which are not. Some of the men who are caught have simply lost confidence in the system. There is no one I know who at some point or other has not been close to resignation. You see, a man may come to you and say, 'I have committed a violation and my violation is saying I have committed a violation because I haven't.' It is a way of getting out of West Point with a minimum of fuss. When we think this is what is happening, then the cadet goes through an elaborate counseling process. Sometimes he stays, sometimes not."

There are a number of written rules, and many more which are unwritten. One of these is the ban on P.D.A., public display of affection. The unwritten rules center around propriety, seemliness, what is proper for an officer and gentleman and what is not. At West Point, drugs apparently aren't—in a college of 4,400 men, only two were dismissed for smoking marijuana in 1969. Barbour: "The firsties [seniors] are the most reactionary people I have ever met. But you value the refinement that the Point gives you. It's nice to have a certain amount of restraint . . . Maybe I am Victorian or something. I value the idea, the propriety, of maintaining certain standards and ninety-nine per cent of my contemporaries value the same things. You are searching for certain values, and one value of this system is that you are forced to maintain them. At twenty-two you don't all of a sudden decide that 'this is not right' or 'that is wrong.' I came to West Point because of the discipline. I wanted a career in some kind of service. If you maintain yourself in a rigid hierarchy, you often have to do things you sometimes don't understand. Isn't that right?"

Of course there is pressure for reform, Barbour said, but the pressure decreases the longer a man stays; it is like the Army itself, greatest in the beginning, less toward the end. In the beginning, a cadet does not see the need for stiff discipline, but he learns. To Barbour it was clear when he took instruction in tactics, when the Tac drilled into him the demonstrable truth that when a man has said he has covered your flank, that no enemy is there, that *he means what he has said*. No quibbling, no evasion by means of technicality. He said he has swept the flank, and he has. So your unit can safely move out and you take less risk because a man has given his word that the field is clear. You can trust a West Point man.

It is a bad time for the Army, and West Point feels the strain no less than the other parts of the institution. Admissions applications remain high, higher than ever in fact, but quality is said to be lower. Many of the younger instructors are disappointed in that, and point to the college board scores on English aptitude of entering cadets. They average 550 of a possible 800. With considerable energy, West Point has sought black cadets, and in 1969 there were thirty-eight fourth classmen admitted. In the past, blacks have numbered less than one per cent of the total; the facts of discrimination are obvious, in the admissions machinery as well as in the atmosphere of the Academy itself.

Younger instructors, less satisfied than their older colleagues, wonder where the George C. Marshalls of the future will come from (to which an outsider might add,

Virginia Military Institute, Marshall's alma mater). The cadets seemed to me in flux, no more certain of the future than their contemporaries elsewhere. What was the future of an infantry officer? The shape of the next ten years was not clear, and, lacking new signposts, the Academy was sticking with the old. Until someone else came along, MacArthur would have to do. But he was clearly not very satisfactory, not in 1970 and surely not in 1975. Everything was changing, the society and the Army, and one could not see where either one was headed. But there wouldn't be any heroes now for some time to come.

In Thayer Hall, the two new wooden plaques with the names in black continued to fill. *In proud memory of these graduates of the United States Military Academy who died in defense of freedom,* the legend said. It was the war roster, row upon row of names, more than two hundred dead now since 1961. Name. Rank. Branch. Class. Date of death. And the single word: Vietnam.

TWO

Hood and Lewis

Fort Hood curls around Killeen like a claw, a 341-square-mile government preserve. The land in west central Texas is hard, stark and bitter rather than austere. Compare it to Castile, except there is nothing picturesque. It is 100 miles south of Dallas, 50 north of Austin, Lyndon Johnson Country.

British generals retire to Ireland, the Americans go to Texas. In Killeen and Temple there are eighteen retired generals. The environment is congenial, and directorships in banks or insurance companies or defense industries are available. Money for right-wing political causes is plentiful, and a retired general can take up politics the way a retired doctor takes up golf. Paul Harkins, Westmoreland's predecessor in Vietnam, is a political dabbler now (The American Security Council and other vigilantes). Killeen is a military town: the Chamber of Commerce has a military affairs committee over which the leading banker, Roy J. Smith, presides. The economy depends on Hood, with its 50,000-man payroll (military and civilian), and $22,000,000 in monthly disbursements. Killeen has grown from 1,200 people in 1940 to more than 35,000 today, and the reason for that is the base. The American government built the town's sewer system, and the schools receive large government grants. "Hood is a very positive influence for good," said the editor of the local paper, J. C. Gresham.

The base has made rich men. Killeen yielded up more members of Lyndon Johnson's President's Club than any other town in America. (The President's Club was one of John F. Kennedy's nifty fund-raising ideas, a man paid $1,000 for membership and once a year got to shake the President's hand at a reception; presumably there were other, more practical advantages as well.) The base has not brought any industrial spin-off, but Killeen is filled with automobile agencies, pizza parlors, insurance offices, real estate agencies, and banks. Lieutenant General Beverley Powell, the base commander, has instructed his command to have friendly relations with Killeen because he knows that whatever happens on the base has a dramatic effect on the region around it, principally an economic effect but also a social one. Powell's G-4 (supply) has been designated director of industrial relations. Powell says that seventy-five per cent of his time is spent on management problems, and much of that with the civilian community outside the base. "Relations are excellent," editor Gresham said. "We like the Army and the Army likes us."

Fort Hood lies to the west of Highway 190, a sprawling collection of sandy buildings and rolling land. Two armored divisions, the ones called "Old Ironsides" and "Hell On Wheels," call Hood home. A top-secret Army project called MASSTER is down the road. The terrain is said to be excellent for tank maneuvers, which are conducted almost daily. The only two fully equipped armored divisions in the United States are at Hood, and they are targeted for "the plains of Europe" in the event of a war with the Soviet Union; the time from here to there for one division is said to be twenty-four hours, because a full complement of gear—uniforms, weapons, tanks—are cached somewhere in West Germany. A man puts the best face on it, but Hood—well, about the best that can be said is that it is neither Huachuca nor Bliss. Huh! scant comfort, the officer's wife says; thank God there is air service to Dallas. At Hood, even the water is hard as a rock. Generals live in the sort of houses they gave light colonels before World War Two. No, there are very many better places to live than Hood. In recognition of the maximum leader of armored divisions, generals' row at Hood is called Patton Drive.

In the barracks, men live forty to a room in double-decker bunks. During the day, the rooms are silent and spotless, the troops falling silent when a visitor enters. During the day, the doors are kept locked: barracks thieves. The base is known as Fort Head for the quantity of marijuana available and used. It is less social protest than an expression of unspeakable, stupefying boredom. The trooper lies on his back in bed, drinking a Pepsi-Cola and reading *Hot Rod* magazine, hearing the vroom-vroom of powerful engines, seeing the long ribbon of vacant highway, thinking of Fonda and Hopper, moving on. The pages crinkle in the silence. It is hot inside with the smell of sweat and disinfectant. The objects on the bureau, combs, brushes, packages of cigarettes, are impersonal objects. The long row of buildings spins off into the desert; in March it is cool, but in high summer they say that Hood is a sweatbox, the worst place in America.

There is not enough to keep the men occupied, so they are sullen. The Army does what it can. There are two golf courses and a swimming pool, and an officers' club and an NCO Club and an enlisted men's club (beer only), bowling alleys and gymnasiums and movie houses and a large PX and an education center plus a rod and gun club, a lake to sail on and a stadium for ball games. The wives band together, work in the hospital, produce a play, sit four to a table at canasta. The guidebooks had spoken of history living in the sun-drenched hills, the remains of an earlier, more romantic Texas to observe from your car window. A man wanted a good car at Hood, an LTD or Camaro or big Pontiac, soft, air-conditioned, fast. South to Houston or north to Dallas, but slow as a big cat on the base itself; Powell is a son of a bitch on traffic accidents and had the big sign erected, CAUTION YOU ARE ABOUT TO ENTER THE MOST DANGEROUS PLACE IN THE WORLD THE PUBLIC HIGHWAY. The sergeant said that for real excitement you had to go see the under-water ballet or the Spanish Hanging Gardens at uh San Marcos. A real carnival atmosphere, the sergeant said.

The troop train doesn't stop at Killeen any more. Troop trains have disappeared along with gold star mothers, and now the recruits arrive by bus or by air-craft to do their time in the Army, to train at Fort Hood for the plains of Europe and then fight in Vietnam. The cars carry signs, E.T.S. and the date. Estimated Time Of Separation: 1 June, 1970. The best thing about Killeen is leaving it, they say, sitting on the edge of a bunk nodding with grim understanding. In the afternoon you can see them waiting at the bus station, preparing to leave on pass. Trailways buses in and out, and the GIs sitting on the benches, their packs in front of them, staring across the street. The dark green soldier's hat with its long bill is curved down over their eyes, and they sit and watch a girl in a miniskirt move up the street. Look but don't touch, she's young, their age. They coldly watch the girl's ass, the skirt moving over it like liquid, watching it tremble up the street and into the camera shop, the Kodak. She's somebody's wife, no quiff in Killeen would look like that. One of the GIs has a pint of Schenley's in a brown paper bag, and he takes a swig from it and replaces it in the rucksack where it won't be noticed. Killeen is dry, no beer and no liquor except for the strip outside town limits, and the Cowhouse Motel, where travelers can get a card for a bottle club; visitors and officers. The soldier's fingers are thick from the whiskey and his face is flushed. He is not smiling but staring grimly into the street. The soldier with the whiskey takes a final drag on his cigarette, drawing the smoke down into his gut then releasing it with a rush into the airless street. Then he puts it out on the sidewalk. He does not flip it away, but gently eases the burning coal into a crack. The girl is gone now, and the street is empty. Sitting on the bench, he can hear the whirr and click of the apparatus that runs the traffic lights. The soldier field-strips the butt, doing this very slowly and carefully, tearing down the seam. He sits looking at the brown tobacco rolling off his fingers onto the pavement, then meticulously rolls the thin paper into a wad. He places that between thumb and second finger, tucking the paper into his fingernail and flipping that into the street. It dribbles off the end of the nail and bounces twice and comes to rest. With his boot, the soldier mashes the fallen tobacco into the sidewalk. He pushes the boot back and forth over the tobacco, pushing hard, scraping, and then sighs and leans forward, his head wilting between his knees. Drops of sweat rise on his forehead. The bus is late. Swaying slightly, the soldier will presently reach into his pack and take another sharp swallow of the Schenley's. But now he sits on the bench, his head between his knees, feeling the thickness in his head, waiting for the Trailways bus that will take him out of Killeen.

II

At Fort Hood, the putative martyr is Robert Bowers, and the coffee house in Killeen is called The Oleo Strut. At Fort Lewis he is Bruce McLean, and the coffee house in Tacoma is called The Shelter Half. At Hood, the under-

ground newspaper is *The Fatigue Press;* at Lewis it is
Fed Up. The protest moves ahead: "My military history
includes a stockade sentence at the Presidio of San Francisco stockade. During my confinement I met the Presidio 27, the GIs the army was trying to make an
example of by sentencing them to sixteen years each in
Leavenworth for their crime. What the GIs did was sit
down on the grass of the Presidio stockade and submit
a list of grievances to the IG [inspector general]. A
prisoner at the Presidio stockade was shot in the back of
the head by a stockade guard . . ." So runs the lead edi-
torial in *Fed Up.*

The dissent is everywhere now, Fort Lee, Fort Dix, Fort
Carson, Fort Bliss; West Point graduates sign stiff letters
to *The New York Times,* retired colonels write commen-
tary for *The New Republic.* The war is no longer remote.
Anyone who hasn't been to Vietnam himself knows
someone who has, and has kept the letters. They are
letters like this one, from a trooper named Sammy Washburn, who in the winter of 1970 was stationed near
Di An, South Vietnam:

> . . . *in a way I've learned to love and hate war and
> fighting. But the people in them are my concern for
> someday I'll publish a picture book of people and war.
> Not the kind you see every day, but real people. Not one
> side but both. The tears, smiles, loves, hates, happiness
> and sadness for people to see and feel the pain of
> people fighting, dying, and living in a thing most people
> talk about and never see for themselves.
> . . . most of what happens, people wouldn't read in a
> newspaper. A book about here and the people fighting
> it, it seems to me more people would read than the
> crap in the papers. . . . I've grown up right before my
> eyes and have saved and killed people many times. I
> have been to many services for the lost in combat and
> received and seen received the medals (rewards the
> army gives) for killing and hating the enemy.*

I've cried many times and laughed less each time I returned. I cried as I picked up my friends who were killed in a fire fight. Funny thing is, I've cried for perfect strangers I didn't know and I either carried or tagged and put the body on a chopper. In turn, I learn to hate and be cold as I never could believe I could be like.

The terrible thing is that the fearless leaders fight this war like a game. Human life doesn't mean anything to them at all, except it decides whether they get relieved or get a few medals. That is all the freaks really care about, whether men eighteen to thirty-five are dying in the jungles, swamps, paddies, mountains somewhere people don't really know where it's at except on a map and newscast and papers.

. . . too bad most of the news about Nam in the world isn't completed the way it should be. Most of the facts and the truth about this war like the rest won't come out until much later, after it slowly becomes another Korea. Then and only then will people know what really happened here in the war on the other side of the earth we all live on.

You know, a couple of us sat down a little over a year ago and figured what a dead GI is worth to the army and the government in material things. A metal coffin draped with an American flag. A two and a half page telegram from DA [Department of the Army], saying how sorry they are your son etc etc was killed on 12 March 19??. A bronze star, purple heart or whatever they think your death is worth in medals and ribbons. A military escort from Oakland and six soldiers to be pall bearers. And a uniform to be buried in and a lot in a military graveyard. To be sure, the family is given some kind of compensation to help them live. They are given six months base pay and $10,000/00 which cost the soldier who's dead $2.00 a month ever since he came into the army.

This is the price tag we came up with roughly that the army puts on each GI who comes to fight a war that he cannot comprehend or see what it's being fought for

*by the Americans. So they [we] go Blindly Into Battle
into the hands of death with our price tag.*

*Sometimes it doesn't seem worth it. Then you look at
the kids and say "I could be Vietnamese and these kids
could be mine." For the first time since I've been here
I've seen more old people smile more than they did
before. Then it happens and you get a feeling that it's
worth all the hate and killing and even the loss of
a friend (brothers-at-arms) that you've known only a
few months who lives 1,000 miles from you in the
world.*

*But after losing so many friends you begin to hate it
all over again. For another man you have lived with in
war, slept with, eaten with, shared jokes together and
the times he or you help get rid of the feeling that the
world has ended when your chick writes you a Dear
John . . . You start hating the gooks not just the enemy
and the brass that sent you to die and he is a man who
says My Men and I did a good job in killing The enemy.
Funny how the brass appear afterwards and if ever
and I do mean if ever they are on the ground with [the]
men fighting. He is usually in his command chopper
four thousand feet above you giving orders for you to
follow.*

*Then he gets the glory, the family gets the body, and
you get another operation. If you by chance are a
platoon sergeant you get to write a letter to say how
sorry you are that their son etc. etc. was killed. Also
saying he was a brave and a great person. Saying all
kinds of crap just to say that you really are sorry that
he died and all the crap that goes into these letters.
Even if he was really brave or a coward who got some
people killed before he finally got killed, it's a good
thing that I've only had to write three of these my last
tour and don't want ever to do it again. For it is
harder than anything I've done in my life.*

Thus Sammy Washburn, far from the atmosphere of The
Oleo Strut or The Shelter Half, coffee houses in Killeen
and Tacoma. The Shelter Half is vaguely reminiscent of

Peter Verkovensky's apartment in *The Possessed:* dark talk, violent dreams, and the smell of theater. It is not necessary, and probably not even fair, to approach the Army from the perspective of a radical nineteen-year-old. Approach it instead through the eyes of an average middle-class boy, or, more typically, lower-class, the Army reflecting as it does the lower depths of American society. The Army and the war seem so mindless, such creatures of other loyalties. No one else supports the war, why should they?

It is no trick, now or twenty years ago, to find dissent and discontent among military ranks; draftees by definition would rather be someplace else. But there is something new about it now, and the newness goes to the heart of the Army's problem: it is that many young men feel no particular obligation to serve the nation in its armed forces. John Kennedy's fatalistic remark that "life is unfair," a remark made at the time of the Berlin call-up in 1961, has no pertinence for a nineteen-year-old activist in 1970; pessimism and fatalism are traits of the old, not the young. College students, through the deferment apparatus, can escape it—a fact which yields paradoxical emotions in those who can not. Some of the ranks hate the collegians, as poor kids hate the rich; others, alley-wise, nod approvingly at men smart enough to beat the system, or anyway work it to their advantage. Meanwhile, Jane Fonda arrives at Fort Lewis and tells enlisted men to resist; she is arrested, thus proving sincerity of a sort, and what the enlisted man is just beginning to understand is that if he wants to make trouble, and has wits enough to put a political spin on his motivations, there is a significant segment of American society which will be sympathetic to him. It is a revolutionary idea, and while it is penetrating some, it is not penetrating those with IQs of eighty, the ones called Shitkick and Fuckhead, the clumsy ones who arrive at Lewis and are instantly diverted into remedial reading drills, instruction in third-grade grammar. These men proceed through the Army as they proceed through life, walking wounded in the center of a monstrous joke, forced to struggle with basic training as they are forced to struggle with everything else . . .

"Nineteen times, I had it *nineteen times*," the kid says, grinning.

"Bull," his buddy says.

"Yeah, Fuckhead, you talk to the fucking medic, he's got my chart. It's all there. Clap, nineteen times . . ."

. . . There is no radicalization of the dull; they arrive at Lewis or Hood or Benning and they serve. The Army keeps them out of trouble by training them and sending them to war. ("Well, what the hell, you have got to have those guys who will go out there when no one else will," a major at Leavenworth told me and when I didn't say anything but just sat looking at him he colored and half-apologized and said that he didn't mean it quite the way it sounded. But he did.)

The Army's troubles grew as the percentages changed, as the casualties among blacks and poor whites outran the manpower pool and the Army was forced to go to the colleges. The Army did not know then how fortunate it was that the cannon fodder was black and lower-class or poor white, either rural southern or big-city northern; either way, not educated in the complexities of draft evasion. Barracks lawyers came later. Still, in 1969, of 283,000 men drafted only 28,500 were college men—ten per cent, in a country where forty per cent of the college-age young do, in fact, go to college. If the war goes on long enough quite possibly there will be no lower-class young in America; the war will nearly have eliminated them.

At any event, the Army does not know how to contain the revolution. Its senior officers, most of them, do not understand it and do not like that part they do understand. The wall posters of Mao and Che Guevara are only the tip of the iceberg. Real alienation, as *Ramparts* once put it, is when your country is at war and you want the other side to win. To the regular Army officer, this indicates a cynicism and a slackness which are literally impossible to comprehend. How to deal with them? A simple appeal to patriotism is obviously the wrong end of the stick, and pure discipline useful only up to a point. A colonel complained that some of his men were "like foreigners," speaking another tongue. None of it fits: not participatory democracy, nor controlling your own destiny, nor personal definition through action; not any part of what those who protest profess to believe.

For the average draftee, there is the war and boredom and not much in between. The Army of 1970, moreover, is not the Army of 1966 and 1967. Now there are negotiated settlements on the battlefield. A tyro company commander orders the troopers of Company C down an open road, and the troopers refuse to go; too many good men get killed that way. They refuse to go and tell the television newsman all about it. So it is negotiated over the CBS Television Network a few nights later. Field Commanders were saying in 1970 that American aggressiveness was way down, genuine daring almost nonexistent. One of the mottos of the 101st Airborne Division was STAY ALERT, STAY ALIVE. The motto survives, with the emphasis very much on the last two words. The draftee negotiates with his officers, alternately furious with the enemy and furious with a society which would put him where he is—out on the line, with no visible means of support. The anger is centered on the Army itself, at the lifers and the straightlegs, the witless military mind, spat on and polished to a high sheen of . . . nothingness. If this is the way an army runs, *My God how did we ever win a war with these people.* In 1970, a young man does not accept an iniquitous condition with fatalism; he tries to do something about it, and the wonder is that there has not been a major revolt on the battlefield before now. An observer can only marvel at the internal discipline of the average GI, and the strength of the military institution. And recall the lament from *The Time of Your Life:* "No foundation—all the way down the line."

When the mayor of New York declares that the real heroes of the war are those who refuse to serve, a hatred fierce and white-hot burns inside the professional soldier. What he has left now is his honor and his uniform, his institution; although Spiro Agnew encourages him to believe that if the country were permitted to speak, it would speak in support, the profession prefers to turn inward. It is paradoxical (don't make too much of it) that some soldiers hate the establishment almost as much as the students do. These are the professionals who believe that the civilians, by their timidity and desire not to disturb, needlessly wasted American lives in Indochina; too much death, to no end. If you are going to do it, *do* it; don't screw around with it. Bomb Hanoi. Bomb Haiphong. Invade Laos. Seal Cambodia. Put a million men in the country and any solution short of that is criminal murder. "Criminally insane," to quote the Nobel Laureate George Wald on another matter. There is no such thing as a *limited* war. "Let us not hear of generals who conquer without bloodshed," Clausewitz wrote. "If a bloody slaughter is a horrible sight, then that is ground for paying more respect to war." So perhaps there is a connection after all.

Nothing about it is very complicated. A soldier's commitments, personal and professional, are stern and unambiguous. One night at Fort Lewis an older officer was talking about one of the legendary American commanders in Vietnam (there have been about four), Colonel Henry Emerson. Emerson, by force of personal example, could lead men and get them to do whatever it was he wanted. He could do that even in Vietnam, take his battalion and make it a world of its own. By force of personal example, the man at Lewis meant personal courage; Emerson could lead men the way they do in films, and no one ought to discount that. But the story had an anachronistic taste to it in 1970; it sounded like a story out of World War Two. Only among the junior officers is there a link with the atmosphere of young America. The "Captains of Algiers" (the name taken from the Jean Larteguy books about disillusioned French officers returning from Vietnam after the fall of Dien Bien Phu), all of them Special Forces veterans, have quit the Army, many to work in the ghetto. To them, the Army is as rotten as the rest of society—that is, its structure is based on privilege and prejudice and is therefore suspect. Its leaders refused to fight the war as it ought to to have been fought, and the fact revealed the collective mentality of the military. These are the men who told the Department of the Army that if the widely admired Colonel Robert Rheault was courtmartialed for his part in the assassination of a Vietnamese double-agent, they would hold a press conference and tell the world everything that went on in the war zone: the random assassinations, the ground raids north, the elimination of villages, the falsifying of statistics, the incursions into neutral territory, the calculated use of terror. They knew, and were prepared to tell; however Colonel Rheault may appear to an outsider, to a Special Forces man he was one of *us*. You stick with your own, and Bob Rheault was one hell of a fine officer. "The trouble was, he came up against the Army establishment."

The Captains of Algiers were and are a small group, maybe two dozen men, most of them out of the Army now. An aberration, one is told; non-typical. Probably so, and ditto the proportion of dedicated protesters in the Army. But taken together, the rise in AWOLs and desertions, the off-base newspapers, the draft "counseling" offices, the prevalence of marijuana and acid on the battlefield and off, the casual life-styles of nineteen-year-olds —that, plus the craziness of the war and the fundamental unfairness of the burden, and it is obvious that the discontent is very real and very deep. And the propaganda engine very powerful. All the Army has to counter it is its traditions and its discipline, command and obedience. It can relax the regulations on haircuts, and it can tell the drill instructors to ease up; it can supply lawyers for protesters, clean up the stockades, assign more public relations men to the bases and more gumshoes to the antiwar movement. But the protest is growing and cosmetics won't stop it. The truth is, the Army doesn't know what to do about it.

One argument runs that the institution must face up to its responsibilities. It isn't a university, never was. War, they say, and the face grows stern; war is a serious business. At Fort Lewis in Tacoma, Major General Willard Pearson, the commander, spoke repeatedly of the black demands for "Afro-Asian haircuts." He slapped one GI in the stockade for distributing *Fed Up*, and declared that dammit he was not going to lie supine while dissidents and misfits tried to undermine his command. Despite the fact that only about 150 GIs (of some 34,000 at Lewis) have joined the American Servicemen's Union (as of March, 1970), the organization which is the center of organized resistance at Lewis, Pearson believes that political agitation is the major threat to his command. He appears to see it as a genuinely subsersive activity, abetted and encouraged by outsiders, and informed by a communications net that refuses to enlist support for the war and the Army that is fighting it. By this analysis, the coffee house The Shelter Half is something of a Finland Station, and Bruce McLean—the most celebrated of the dissidents at Lewis—the exiled Lenin. That is Pearson's analysis, but lower-ranking officers in his command disagree. To them, "the race thing" is far more significant and potentially disruptive (or disastrous, depending on whom you listen to). I think Pearson is wrong and the others right, but it is easy to see why a professional sol-

dier fastens on the political dissidents. The dissidents
and misfits, as General Pearson would have them, attack
precisely those points most dear to military men: duty,
honor, country. They revile the soldier as a hired killer,
and his commanding officer as a butcher. Duty to one's
own conscience. The slogan is F.T.A., which means Fuck
the Army. Honor is personally defined. Apart from that,
with their long hair, the men look like women; *fairies*,
as one senior officer spat out, and the women, "My God
the women, you just don't know the women. Why [lean-
ing forward confidentially], the things they will say to
the MPs, particularly the man in charge of the stockade.
They yelled at him [the officer leans farther across the
desk, so no one could overhear], 'Jackson, I'd like to
f u c k you.' Well now, what kind of women are these?
Are they prostitutes or what?" Whose country?

Others at Lewis worry about "the new rules," the change
in atmosphere. They mean society's rules. Brigadier
General Thomas Tarpley, the assistant base commander,
shook his head: "AWOL. Take AWOL. It used to be
purely a military offense, and now we find that society
doesn't think it's so bad. Men go to Canada and there's
no hue and cry. The press doesn't think it's bad. There
are hundreds of AWOL-deserter types, and this is dis-
turbing. Society doesn't care. They say that a kid doesn't
know enough or know any better. But . . . Well, once
the service was in great demand. Now a kid—or a
pack of them—can go wash dishes and make enough
money to tide them over. It's a distressing thing to me,
though."

Pearson: "You have got to address these problems
head on, like the Afro-Asian haircuts. In a military organization you have got to have teamwork, you have got to
have esprit. You must have uniformity. The Army has
been uniform since the days of Solomon. If you train
people to fight and die, you must have esprit not separatism. Well, the Russians started out with no saluting,

but even they went back to it. Fundamentally, the American people accept discipline. But I want to tell you that the young man coming into the Army today is tremendous. Eager, intelligent, alert, and responsive. And you can quote me on that."

At the end of March there was an anti-war (or anti-Lewis) rally on a baseball diamond in American Lake Park, which is hard by Tacoma and near the bottom of Puget Sound, about a mile from the base. About two hundred people assembled for it, and ninety per cent of those were young. Many of them sported beards and feathers. They were very orderly and met the remarks of the speakers with polite, sincere applause and murmurs of "Right On!," the Panther slogan. Off to one side was a police car, inconspicuous under the trees, and on the fringes of the crowd were the C.I.D. men with their cameras. Lewis has a very active (and by most accounts inept) military intelligence unit, and these men could be instantly identified because of their short hair; also they looked like top sergeants (after you have been around the Army you can spot a top sergeant).

The theme of the rally was the return of Bruce McLean, a nineteen-year-old GI who was dispatched to Vietnam by the Army against his will. The ones in the park said he was kidnapped to Vietnam in punishment for his war views. "We want Bruce McLean back and we want him back right now," the speaker said, and the crowd muttered its agreement. McLean's sister, Sylvia, a long-haired distracted little girl of about sixteen, crossed the infield and took the microphone. She swayed with it, and spoke rapidly.

"In the Army you have no freedom. Zero freedom. GIs have no freedom, it is the most repressive institution . . . I just think it is about time we understood our connection with the GIs. I hold General Pearson personally responsible for sending Bruce to Vietnam." She paused, and rushed out the rest of it, close to tears: ". . . and next time I'm not going to come down here all drunk and stoned and shit like that."

Next speaker was Paul McLean, the kidnapped's brother. He talked along the same lines, but now at the edges of the infield neighborhood kids came with their bikes and were skylarking along the third-base line. They were riding in circles and making sarcastic remarks, wheeling around the infield on their bikes. Someone had put up a huge poster picture of McLean and one of the kids looked at that and said to a friend, "Who's the creep?" Bruce McLean's brother finished off: "Freedom of speech and assembly. That's in the Constitution of the so-called United States."

As the speakers trooped to the microphone, the kids in the infield began to giggle more harshly. It appeared that the march which had been planned would be called off. One organizer said, "What is the point of demonstrating in front of a bunch of MPs?" What indeed? The officials at Lewis had replaced the traditional WELCOME sign with an austere board which listed the conditions under which a civilian could enter; it also listed the penalty for disruption of the installation. But the rhetoric now was mild, and the audience leaned back on the grass, enjoying the spring weather. The speaker stood with the microphone in one hand and the other in his trouser pockets. "Power and peace to the people," Paul McLean concluded, and strode off the field.

The master of ceremonies was keeping it together. Bruce McLean, he said, escaped one kidnapping attempt and went AWOL. Found, he was placed in the stockade and then sent to Vietnam "at four in the morning, February nineteenth . . . He doesn't want to be there and he should have the right to decide whether he goes to fight an imperialist war. The choice now is five years in jail or one year in Vietnam."

Those who had spoken earlier were not GIs. Now an American Indian came to the microphone, and identified himself as a member of the Third Cavalry Regiment. Very appealing, lithe, short-haired, with moccasins on his feet, the Indian was less concerned with the war than with the riot training the troopers were receiving. "They put Bruce McLean on a reactionary force, the riot patrol. You are totally suppressed in the Army, we are going to have fascism in the United States." All of this was said very distinctly, with hard drama. You could see that this Indian, a Sioux, would give the drill instructors fits; so light and polite, and that expression on his face which seemed to be a smile, but at times looked more like a sneer . . .

"But Sarge, I'm *smilin'*."

"Wipe that fucking grin off your face!"

"But *Sarge* . . ."

. . . and he said that all of it was part and parcel of the Army's system of fear and repression; fear part of America now too, and the coming of fascism. More people will start resisting the Army, the Indian said, when they realize that in the Army the GI is a second-class citizen. Zero freedoms. "Power to the people," he concluded, and there was a short burst of applause and cries of "Right On!" The Sioux then had a second thought and returned to the microphone. "I want to tell you about one of those sergeants who teaches riot control," he said, and waited for the crowd to quiet. "Well, he said in class: 'If one of those creeps threw a rock at me I'd shoot the motherfucker before he picked up another . . .' " There was mild laughter from the crowd and the Sioux smiled and nodded his head, as if in admiration. "Well, at least he knows where he's at."

The rally was like a miscellaneous bulletin board, anybody could make a contribution. They talked about good Steve Gilbert, sent to a military post deep in the Arizona badlands, repatriated to Lewis, and finally sentenced there to the stockade. "It's okay with me," Gilbert was reported as saying, "then I will organize the stockade."

It was true too. Gilbert was happy in the stockade, where God knows there was no lack of grievances to satisfy, and no love for the Army either . . .

"The Army doesn't treat you men right."

"You're fuckin-A it doesn't."

. . . Steve Gilbert and Bruce McLean: symbols of fascist repression in America, political prisoners now in order that the country can run its insane militaristic course, slaughtering civilians and freedom fighters in Vietnam, and suppressing the Panthers at home. Undermining Castro, and entreating with dictators in other countries. And doing it on the blood of its youth, who had no understanding of or use for these commercial wars. One of the boys who came to the microphone was pudgy and blond, a boy with a broad western accent, who said that they had to get Bruce McLean back. He said he knew he was jeopardizing himself by appearing at the rally. But he had to speak. He was in the Army, but he didn't want to go to Vietnam. It was not his choice, the Vietnam war; but the alternative was five years in the stockade. No one wanted that. He seemed uncertain how to proceed, now that he was speaking. He mumbled a few words in conclusion, and it was clear that what he wanted was to bear witness; to be *there*, to have spoken in the face of discouragement, of threats from the Army. He said that he would not give his name, and there was applause.

Well, the way to deal with that, the last speaker said, was to topple the government. He was very musical, this last speaker, fast on his toes, red hair billowing out of his head like smoke, which surely would be Willard Pearson's last word in Afro-Asian haircuts, although the boy was white, white as snow. "A little party in Seattle tomorrow night," he said, eyes moving sideways like Mae West's, "and you're all invited." What would the C.I.D. make of that? Pederasty. Dope-taking. Gangbang. Shifting now a little to his left, up onto the pitcher's mound, slyly looking at the kids on the bikes who were silent, listening. Everyone in the audience was grinning at the sheer graceful nerve of the boy on the pitcher's mound, a red-haired leprechaun of menace, who moved with deft rhythm and craftiness of expression. "A little party then, all invited, come and bring a little wine and dope"—he mentioned an address in Seattle—"and we'll sit and grooooove all night, and early into the mor-ning." Dead silence, pause, and very neatly, as neat as a patent leather shoe, he grinned again and his arm went up, and he tucked the microphone into his face and murmured, "Right on, brothers and sisters."

The crowd began to move out of the infield, and onto the road leading to the base. They were going to march after all, MPs or no MPs, go right up to the gate and let the Army know where the youth of America stood. The sun was glinting wonderfully off their hairy heads, the light coming from one side of Mt. Rainier, the heads of the kids back-lit better than Avedon or Karsh could do it. There was that huge wonderful solitary mountain, the afternoon sun over its left shoulder, and the kids were walking into it, hand in hand, chanting, *Brass lives high while GIs die.*

The day before that, Pearson came with his suite to speak at an initiation ceremony of 1,000 recruits. They had arrived forty-eight hours before, newly minted infantrymen. They were in a gymnasium sitting in rows, by company, sitting very quietly with their gear arranged in piles before them. There were packs and a helmet and blankets, and their deep green field jackets. None of them had their name tags yet, the strip of cloth that was sewn over the left blouse pocket. Pearson, who is a slight man, hair going to gray, hawk-nosed and full of *stramm*, came up the aisle to Ruffles and Flourishes. The men bowed their heads as the chaplain read the invocation, part of it

calling down God's blessing on drill sergeants. The ranks
were seated after shouting their unit designation. That
is part of what the Army is about, identification: with
your buddy, your unit, your battalion, brigade, division,
the Army, the country. There were two speeches, one
from the brigade commander, Colonel Louis North, and
the other from Pearson himself.

North: " . . . maximum harmonious relations among
yourselves. You are living close together with little privacy, and what I am saying is that you must be an effective member of the team. Also I want you to bear in
mind the senior-subordinate relationship, and the importance of hygiene. Everyone in a short haircut. Quick
response to orders. Don't shirk duties. The buddy system should be employed in everything you do here . . . "

The young men, almost all of them white boys from
the far northwest, looked blankly ahead. They were
sitting and listening with cocked heads. It seemed odd
to me that they were actually listening to North, and I
thought of the song from *Midnight Cowboy:*

> *Everybody's talkin' at me*
> *I don't hear a word they're sayin'*
> *Only the echoes of my mind.*
> *People stop and starin'*
> *I can't see their faces*
> *Only the shadows of their eyes.*

The gymnasium was dark, and it was difficult to see the
men on the platform. The voices came from a loud-
speaker, very clear but remote and disconnected. Disconnected the way bayonet practice was disconnected,
if you watched it from a hundred yards away: pull,
push, *thrust*; a wavy line of men in new fatigues, some
of them scared, all of them uncertain—and the drill
instructors in the wide-brim hats, allrightyoumen, *thrust*.
The sound volume was up, and I looked at the men sit-

ting, perfectly respectful, listening. I remembered the
GI who drove me to the airport at Bragg:
"Oh dear," he'd said. "Oh God *damn* the Army." The
words came in a low monotone, trouble with his wife,
who was sixteen years old, now back in her hometown
of Ohio. He was writing to another girl, and when he got
rid of the wife he'd think about marrying the other one.
"She's waiting for me, she's the one who's really waiting
for me." As for the wife, "I don't care what she does.
She can do anything she wants." His wife was with him
at Bragg while she was pregnant, but it didn't work out
well and she left and went back home. What tore it was
the morning he'd come back from driving in the motor
pool, and his wife, pregnant, kept waking him up asking
for money to buy a . . . doughnut. A doughnut!
  "Well, she wanted doughnuts," the boy said in a deep-
south accent. "I told her, you eat so many doughnuts
that kid is going to be born with a hole in his head."
  Of course the wife began to cry, and he turned over
and went to sleep. She left home shortly after that. The
boy poured all this out in thirty minutes, and ended by
saying he's re-upped for Vietnam. The last time he'd
been in a construction battalion and had built a swimming pool at Pleiku. What the hay-ell, the pay was good
and he thought the Americans were winning the war
now. One more tour wouldn't hurt and might help, and
would get him out of the United States, which was the
important thing . . .

> *I'm goin' where the sun keeps shinin'*
> *Thru the pouring rain*
> *Goin' where the weather suits my clothes*
> *Bankin' off of the northwest winds,*
> *Sailin' on the summer breeze.*
> *Skippin' over the ocean like a stone.*

  But in the gymnasium at Lewis, there was only the
silence of listening. Colonel North spoke of basic train-

ing, and then he stood back and introduced the commanding general. Pearson. When he had a brigade of the 101st Airborne in Vietnam he was something to see. He had Hackworth and Emerson as battalion commanders and there isn't any doubt that the brigade was the best that there was as a fighting unit. Pearson allowed his commanders wide latitude, and the result was a certain amount of innovation, something as rare in Vietnam as victory. Bill Carpenter was in Pearson's command when he called napalm on his position at Dak To, and today Pearson has a picture of Carpenter in his office, and it is not usual for generals to display photographs of captains. Pearson then as now is a man fond of slogans: *Find, Fix, Fight; Stay Alert, Stay Alive.* At Lewis he passed out buttons at the reception center: *Every soldier a V.I.P.* When he launched a haircut campaign it was called, *Look Sharp, Feel Sharp, Be Sharp.* He called the non-coms into his office for little twenty-minute lectures, and he made certain they understood that there would be no dissent at Lewis, no undermining of the command. Because that was what it was all about, the command and its effectiveness. The Department of the Army had not sent Willard Pearson to Fort Lewis to preside over another Woodstock or Fayerweather Hall. *I will not lie supine,* he'd said. Now he was standing at a microphone in the gloom in front of the recruits and telling them something of what they could expect at Lewis. He did not speak of the war.

"You are going to get along well together," Pearson said, and it sounded like an order. "You are going to succeed! It is teamwork, not the degrees that you have but the degree to which you are accepted by others, that's the key to success in life. By your presence here you are demonstrating a love of country, and this will loom larger in your life." But there were also a few practical things to be said: Drive vehicles cautiously. Never aim a weapon at another man unless you intend

to use it. No senseless horseplay on the Confidence
Course. What could be more tragic than for a parent
to hear of a broken arm or worse. *We have all learned
from experience.* (What the recruits would find at Lewis
was classic basic training, plus the mine and booby-trap
obstacle "confidence" course. It is a course containing
two dozen—or three—different mine and booby-trap ar-
rangements, including cyanide in Coke bottles and a
flying mace strung from a tree. The punji stakes are
realistic, and the men are warned they are smeared
with feces; in Vietnam, one sergeant got a stake *right
through the balls,* and when he went on a five-day R&R
with his wife in Honolulu he ripped out every damn
stitch. That anecdote was supplied by the instructor, a
young lieutenant who had never been west of Tacoma.)

But Pearson was not talking details, he was talking
of the Army and the country, and what the two meant to
each other. It was a period of life when a man must
accept discipline, and accept it without question. There
were senior officers and junior ones, non-coms and enlisted men, and in a war a soldier must obey his superiors to stay alive. Stay alert, stay alive. Command and
obedience. The recruits were not civilians any more,
not college fraternity men or farmhands or checkers in
a supermarket. They were soldiers, and that made them
different. It made their responsibilities different. "We
have all learned from experience," Pearson said. "And
one final point: The time will go by quickly, and you
want to look back on it with pride. Some of you will
go AWOL. Now if you go AWOL, you won't solve the
problem. I get letters every day from soldiers in the
stockade who tell me their wife is pregnant. So resolve
to keep your service honor. So that you will be proud of
what you have done."

He sat down to scattered coughs (there was not meant
to be applause) and still there was the listening silence.
Heads descended as the chaplain delivered the final

prayer. The men sang the National Anthem, and then Willard Pearson marched from the shadows to the sound of the old Army song:

> *Over hill,*
> *Over dale,*
> *We will hit the dusty trail*
> *As the caissons*
> *Go rol-*
> *ling*
> *Aaaaaaaaaaaaaaa*
> *long.*

THREE

Three Sergeants

Fort Hood. Fort Bragg. Fort Leavenworth. Fort Benning. Fort Lewis. The big Army bases in the United States are tight societies, forts in more ways than one. A man and his family need never leave the post, not for birth, marriage, or death, nor for shelter, food, fuel, or clothing, nor for golf, drinks, dinner, dancing, and movies. A man is encouraged to spend his salary on the base—as who would not, considering the bargains? One hundred and fifty dollars for an AKAI tape recorder worth two hundred, fifty cents for a VO and soda at the NCO Club. A man can worship a nondenominational God ("Army God," a senior soldier described Him) and putt on an Army green and listen to Army radio while having a tooth pulled by an Army dentist, and all the time call it home. There is only one thing that the Army doesn't have. It doesn't have schools for the children, at least in the continental United States it doesn't.

The regulars call it a decent life, and insist that a few years ago it was better. A man trains for sixteen weeks at Benning and then is assigned to a division at Hood, say, or Lewis. He stays there for a year or perhaps two years and then is assigned to some other base as a squad leader. Now he is a sergeant and from that base, Riley in Kansas, say, he does a tour with the 7th Army in Bavaria or the garrison forces in Korea. If there is a war he will go to it. But in twenty or thirty years in the Army a man will see duty at five or six Army bases. There will be at least one tour in Europe and one in the Far East: Korea, Japan, Taiwan, Thailand, Vietnam. The professional soldier will return to the stateside bases, however, his life a series of rotations. We are talking now of the single relentlessly stable element in the Army, the senior non-commissioned officer, the top sergeant or sergeant major. The senior non-coms are likely to stay in one place for three or four years; they watch the officers come and go. The wise officer knows that the sergeants run the Army, so the first thing an officer does on assuming command is have a friendly chat with his top. Master Sergeant John Gillis, a career man now at Bragg, explained the stability element: when he was at Lewis he put in two years with a tank detachment and in those two years he saw four company commanders, two squadron commanders, two regimental commanders, and three post commanders.

The names may change but the environment does not. At Fort Lewis, company grade officers live at Clarkdale, a collection of wooden bungalows; the field grade officers (major and above) live at Broadmoor, conservative brick dwellings; the NCOs live in semi-detached wooden houses, in areas called Greenwood, Parkway, and Davis Hill. Call these Wilmette, Winnetka, and Evanston, if my sociology is straight. Life revolves around the clubs, the post exchange, the neighborhood— the Army itself. If there is a certain regimentation, it is because the senior people like it that way. When Willard Pearson assumed command at Lewis he built a flagpole in front of his house and flew an American flag from it. It didn't take much more than a month for flags to be flying from every brick house in Broadmoor.

Senior sergeants would be above that sort of thing, not that they are any less patriotic but simply that they would reckon flag flying unnecessary. The wise sergeant waits it out, knowing that sooner or later the commanding officer will leave and he will stay. The old ones, the lifers, know everyone in the Army, from four star generals on down, and an extraordinary bond grows between them. We are the backbone, they say to each other; we run the Army. Standing atop the NCO corps is the sergeant major. It is in all senses of the word a privileged rank, every bit as much as a general officer. He is addressed respectfully, by full title,

"Well, Sergeant Major Hickey, how is it going today?"

"Fine, sir. Just fine."

"Good work, Sergeant Major."

The most impressive looking NCO I ever saw was the former Sergeant Major of the Army, William O. Wooldridge. Tall, tough, knowledgeable, he had fought in three wars and understood the Army about as well as a man can. One of Wooldridge's patrons was the assistant vice chief of staff of the Army, Lieutenant General William DePuy. (DePuy, in turn, was something of a protégé of William Westmoreland.) Wooldridge was DePuy's sergeant major when DePuy commanded the 1st Infantry Division in South Vietnam. Around the base camp of the Big Red One, it was well known that whatever you wanted, Wooldridge could get it for you. He was said to be an excellent soldier, with a fine military bearing and all the ribbons a man could want, and no one has satisfactorily explained why a man like Wooldridge would become accused of involvement in bilking NCO clubs (through a complicated apparatus where he and other senior sergeants bought companies which furnished liquor and equipment to the clubs). The Army didn't have enough evidence to prosecute, or so it said; Wooldridge was permitted to resign.

The presumption is that Wooldridge's ambition outran his pride in the Army and perhaps that is so. At any event, it was subsequently disclosed that Wooldridge used General Creighton Abrams's personal airplane for the import and export of whiskey from Vietnam. It is an index of the authority of a senior sergeant major that he could commandeer COMUSMACV's airplane. It is arguable that Wooldridge is typical of the NCO as Ponzi was typical of Wall Street or Eddie Cicotte of professional baseball; not a type but an archetype. One sergeant major, displaying a most unmilitary tolerance, explained that Wooldridge's activities were nothing more than an extension of what was always expected of sergeants; something extra, a little something for nothing. In the old days, if there was a crap game in the barracks, the sergeants supplied the dice and the drinks and took a fat cut of the pot; no one questioned it, a natural perquisite, like an automobile for a company director. There are a hundred ways for a smart sergeant to skim a buck here and a buck there, this source said, and Wooldridge and his friends just expanded the opportunity a little. They looked about them and figured it would be simple enough to make a couple of hundred thousand bucks, which by most accounts is what they did. A sergeant traditionally has had certain privileges in the Army.

To an extent greater than the officer corps, the NCO lives and breathes the Army. The officer is obliged to mix with the civilian community, and to a degree derives his prestige from it. The NCO does not. The public does not distinguish between senior sergeants and junior ones; to the average civilian, "if they were any good they'd be officers." The largest clubs on any base are the NCO clubs, and they are filled to bursting most evenings; the NCO tends to stick with his own. Senior sergeants affect a cool disdain both upwards and downwards, toward the unprofessional enlisted man on the one hand, and toward the better-paid officer on the other. An officer is respected precisely to the degree that he allows the NCO to do his job with a minimum of interference. Gillis: "I can always tell a good officer because he walks through that door and he *asks* rather than *tells*. My job? My main job is to make that troop commander look like the best troop commander in the Army." Beyond that, it is to see that orders are carried out. The officer commands, the subordinates obey, and the job of the sergeant is to enforce, to see to it that subordinates obey. Because he understands the process, the adroit NCO can make it work for him precisely as a mechanic can tune an engine. If you are the only one who understands the machine, you are very close to being the indispensable man.

The senior NCO acts as a buffer as well: he looks after "the welfare of the men" (the phrase recurred a dozen times in interviews), and expects that when the commander wants to know what the men think, the commander will come to him to find out. The role is somewhat Miltonic: explaining the ways of God to man, and man to God. The NCO is successful to the degree he protects his men and serves his commanding officer. It is a job which calls for enormous objectivity, a total dedication to the rules of the institution, and a thorough knowledge of the Book, both that which is written and that which is not. Regulations govern, and the looser the organization is, the less the sergeants like it. NCOs are unhappy now because of the rapid promotion of buck sergeants: "We don't have the authority we used to," one of them said, "because there are too many punk sergeants who don't know the score." Not that an NCO would trade his job for any other. All of the good ones are encouraged to go to Officer's Candidate School, but few of them take the offer. Gillis: "I don't have the desire. I like to get really involved with the men. I want to do it myself, or see that it is done. You can achieve that, *see it*, more than an officer can." Others worry about the social rounds, white gloves for their wives, which fork to use at dinner in the general's quarters. An NCO does not have to be a social lion (none of them are), and his origins do not matter. What he must do is his job. Nothing more. All that is required is that he understand the system; he has that, and the knowledge that the Army is run on the wits of sergeants.

There is a personal element as well. If a base commander wants something extra done for him—his house painted, a stereo system installed—he does not speak to his chief of staff or his aide-de-camp. He speaks to his sergeant major, and the sergeant major sees that it is done. He has it done promptly with no fuss or complaint. Sergeants run the officers' club, and the CG and his wife have been known to arrive late for dinner. Cocktails will precede steak, and the evening will end with cognac all around. No bill will ever be presented.

The NCO grades run from E-4 to E-9, three stripe sergeants through command sergeant majors. The E-4 with six years service will earn around $4,000 a year and the E-9 with, say, twenty years' service, will make around $9,500. That is exclusive of combat pay or jump pay or quarters allowance, if the man is obliged to live off post (senior sergeants almost never are). The senior men have their pick of NCO quarters on the post, and there are ways and means to supplement income. A number of senior generals acquire a sergeant when they are colonels, and keep them as they rise through the ranks. More often than not, he is a sergeant who was with the officer in combat somewhere, in World War Two or Korea, and distinguished himself. "These guys may turn out to be drunks or thieves or anything else," observed a lieutenant colonel now in the Pentagon, "but it doesn't matter. What matters is the combat bond, and nothing can break it." When the general leaves the Army, his faithful sergeant will often leave along with him and continue to serve. It is not exactly the relation of a batman to a British brigadier, but there is something of that in it. The most common phrase you hear on both sides, general to sergeant and sergeant to general, is that the other is "a hell of an Army man, a hell of a man."

The lives of sergeants are different, and the way a man proceeds is different. A man can become stymied for one reason or another, including the accident of birth. Here are three sergeants, one white, one black, and one young.

Command Sergeant Major Lawrence J. Hickey works out of a small office down the hall from the commanding general of Fort Lewis. Hickey is big and leathery, an Irishman who enjoys talk. He is an uncommonly modest man, troubled now by the Army's difficulties but confident that they will be weathered. He won a silver star in World War Two and added an oak leaf cluster to that in Vietnam. He has three bronze stars and a legion of merit, all of them won in the Korean War when they were tough to win. He has been an Army man for twenty-six years.

Hickey said he came out of World War Two as a technical sergeant, thought about quitting, but re-enlisted. After a tour in Europe, he was assigned to Fort Lewis. "They didn't have thirty-five hundred sets of quarters like they do now and the only housing was in wooden barracks. So my wife lived at home in Vancouver, one hundred and twenty-five miles away and I'd commute by car. My wife's father had made some money in Saskatchewan, but the goddam socialists came to power so he left in 1943. He said the hell with it, and moved to B.C.

"There was one funny thing then at Lewis. While I was there, we had one training exercise. It was Operation Miki. Hah! It was an amphibious training mission, and really what it was was a political deal to pump some money into Hawaii. We did the mission in Hawaii, see. Hell, they could have held the thing in Puget Sound.

"Well, Korea came along. When we got to Japan, the regiment only had two battalions. They cannibalized the units in the States to get us up to full strength. I was then a first sergeant. Sooooo we got on the ship and instead of having two hundred forty-six men in my company, I had twenty-seven. We went to Japan and they gave me a hundred seventy-five Korean civilians. I was to train them and make soldiers out of them. Well, you know how they found these men; they swept them up from the Pusan waterfront. They didn't even want to be in their own army, much less our army. So we gave them a month of training and then we went into combat.

"We had forty-six American GIs and six officers and a warrant officer and we went to Korea and met the North Koreans. Well, you know what happened. Arrrrgh. We didn't do very well. It wasn't so hot."

Hickey paused there and shook his head.

"Can you describe that?"

"I guess so," he said. "It was south of Ham Hung, near Wonsan. That was the X Corps area. The Eighth Army under General Walker had the west portion of the peninsula. The X Corps under General Almond had the east. The two commands had nothing to do with each other at that stage of the war.

"In November, 1950, the Chinese came into 8th Army sector. They engaged the 8th Regiment, 1st Cavalry Division. Then they withdrew from the 8th Army Area to the X Corps area. That's where I was. In November, 1950, we were trying to hold them. We had two battalions, maybe a thousand men, and we could contain them all right because they had no really heavy firepower, and they were limited on supplies.

"In December they broke through with fresh troops. The main body came in with weather that was twenty-

five to thirty degrees below zero. We were given an order
one day to hold a hill and an American division ahead of
us was to withdraw through us. We were supposed to
cover them. On the second of December, the division commander came back through the area.

"Well, from the hill we could see these bastards, about
five thousand of them, coming down the road. They were
Chinese. There was a creek beside the road, and it was
frozen. Huh! We knew we were in for it, but we had
mortars and fifty-calibers. We had those, so we were firing
mortars and machine guns and, hell, they just walked off
the road. During the night they moved in around us.
At daybreak, they rushed us and just walked through us.
We were all wounded. The company commander and I
were wounded and we slid down the icy slope on our
asses. There were a few other guys with us and we got to
the road and ran into the Chinese. We opened fire and
they ran away. And we went down into the creek, trying
to get into the rear portion of our own battalion."

Hickey was leaning across the desk, moving his
hands to show where the hill was and where the creek
was, and the distance between the Chinese and the
American battalion.

"The Americans thought we were Chinese and the
Chinese *knew* we were Americans, so it was pretty
tough. We were caught between two fires, and we were
all wounded. We were being shot at all the time. We were
trying to . . . well, they call it now, exfiltrate. Hah! We
were trying to *exfiltrate* the area.

"We weren't doing any fighting. All we were doing was
evading the enemy. Hell, we couldn't do anything else.
We were pinned down. So we made our way back and I
was taken to the 121st Evacuation Hospital. It was like a
big brick schoolhouse . . ."

"Wait a minute," I said. "How did you make your
way back?"

"We exfiltrated."

"But how?"

Hickey grimaced, anxious to get on with the story. ". . . so the hospital was like a schoolhouse. By this time, the evacuation had begun at Ham Hung so they put me in a ward with a bunch of goddam Koreans. They sent me to Japan, then to Seattle. I stayed there a year, wounded in the legs, shrapnel, and my left foot had gotten frozen and they had to amputate right at the metatarsal joint. All the toes went. I stayed in the hospital for awhile, and they damned near forced me out of the Army."

"So you were pretty badly wounded on the hill?"

Hickey nodded impatiently.

"How did the Americans perform?"

"Not too good," he said. "The original twenty-seven were all right, but look: I had a master sergeant. He was old, forty-seven. His name was _____, and he had a big family. He also had a problem with booze. When he was sent over, his wife came and saw me, and asked why her husband had to go." Hickey shook his head sadly. "There was a lot of crap like that."

"And the Koreans?"

"The only way I controlled those guys was with my fists. They didn't have names, they had numbers. I had a pretty good interpreter; he was from the North. I had some PFCs acting as squad leaders. But, you know, when the Oriental tells you something it's about four layers below; the meaning, I mean. Well, I would catch them eating out of garbage cans and I would beat the shit out of them. Rough, you think. But what did they do in the *Korean* army? They would take them out in front of the company and slap their faces. For a worse offense, they'd stand them in front of the company and beat them with two-by-fours. I asked one of these guys, 'What do you do for something really serious?' He looked me in the eye and said, 'We shoot 'em.'

"Anyway, they sent me east to Murphy Hospital in

Waltham, Mass., and this was Christmas of 1951. God damn, they put me back to bed and started operating again. Osteomyelitis. My foot got black. There was a pretty good doctor there, a Harvard man, Doctor Fisher. 'Body By Fisher,' I'd say and he'd laugh like hell.

"From December, 1950, to June, 1952, I was in the hospital. I was sent to Devens to the Admin school there, and did one tour at West Point. From 1952 to 1963 I was in the twilight zone again as an Admin man. Oh hell, I was in Heidelberg, one place and another. See, I had no choice. It was either do what they wanted me to do, or get the hell out of the Army. They had me brainwashed, and said I couldn't go back to the infantry. In 1963 I made E-8 and thought, 'Hell, I'm not getting anywhere.' I wanted back into the infantry."

I asked Hickey why. "Why was the infantry so important?"

"Why? Oh, maybe I wanted my masculinity back. I don't know. Something. But I also wanted to get promoted. At Fort Harrison in Indiana I went to see the doctor (he was a Swiss, very militaristic). I started a program of training, and even now I run two miles a day at lunch to keep in shape.

"See, the amputations had left me not very confident at all. So I went out there one day at Fort Harrison and I was really scared. But I ran for the first time since I'd been wounded. The first time in thirteen years. I ran a quarter of a mile that day, and I couldn't believe it. A major told me: 'Run a lap and walk a lap' and that is what I did. Every day. Then I saw another doctor and asked him to certify me for the infantry, and by God he did. I got back into the infantry and they sent me to the 7th Division in Korea. I was first sergeant for Bravo Company, 1st Battalion, 31st Infantry. I walked in there as if I'd never been away from the infantry. The weapons had changed, but the problems hadn't changed. The people hadn't changed. In 1965 I came back to the 4th Division at Fort Lewis because my wife wanted to come to the West Coast. So I found myself training guys, just like I had in 1949. It doesn't change, you know. There they are. They get off the bus in civilian clothes, and I was standing there, saying you go into that barracks, you go into this one . . .

"In January of 1966 I made E-9, and then I was lucky enough to get to Vietnam. I served under Lieutenant Colonel Vollmer, a West Point graduate, and a tremendous guy. I knew every man in that battalion, every NCO I mean, his strengths and his weaknesses."

Hickey smiled. "We sat out there on the Cambodian border as bait for forty-two days."

Sergeant Major Fletcher Cummings has eyes like black onyx, hard and dark as a stone, and a fringe of white hair that coils around his head like steel wool. He speaks very slowly and deeply, chain smoking cigarettes, occasionally tapping the table for emphasis. He has strong, thick fingers and heavy arms. Sergeant Major Cummings, though occasionally droll, does not laugh much.

"When I first got into the Army, I'd lived in a segregated community," he said. "Tupelo, Mississippi, and so I didn't give segregation in the Army much serious thought. I did begin to think seriously about it, I guess, about four or five months after I got in. Think about this seriously and there is some indication that this being separate has something to do with your advancement. We were kept out of artillery, infantry, armor, anything that you got combat glory from. We weren't permitted in it. By the time the Army was integrated, I was one hundred per cent for it. One hundred per cent.

"I daresay during the basic training there were separate units but integrated barracks. There was no favoritism. You did the same basic training, training as an infantryman, a rifleman. But when you got out of basic you were put into a . . . working capacity. Ware-houseman, quartermaster, labor service company, fire-fighting, things like that. Now I am talking about 1941 and 1942.

"Of course at this time, most Negro units . . . well, I was in horse cavalry basic training. Then they would put us into something entirely different after basic (of course we knew it would be different since the Army wouldn't send us to Europe on the backs of horses). This was more evident in nineteen and forty. That was when I went overseas. On arrival, in North Africa, we received trucks. There was a convoy going to the front lines on a Friday, and we had received no training at all in truck convoying. None at all, and it is more compli-cated than perhaps it might sound. I thought it was a stupid thing, 'cause we were hauling ammunition. They put us in a position where we could blow it. I felt then and I feel now that they did that on purpose. All we had was that little carbine. We were an all-Negro outfit, with white officers."

Cummings was speaking very quietly, in an off-hand tone of voice. He was talking without prodding, except a short question here and there to clear up a point. Then his voice took on an edge.

"I was all the time with the truck," he said, "first in North Africa and later in Italy, through the war. In North Africa once, they put us to putting up an airplane hangar. There were more than two hundred of us and we worked at it for six weeks. Then a ninety-eight-man engineer battalion came by and put it up in three days. Two and a half days it was. We had more than two hun-dred men and we couldn't do it in six weeks. But we didn't know how to erect an airplane hangar. *They . . . hadn't . . . trained . . . us.*

"In Italy—well, in North Africa, rather, we expected to play some sort of combat role. But they didn't have any Negro troops in a combat role. Then later they brought two or three Negro regiments into Italy, and all of us tried to join up, but we were not successful. I'll tell you something: When I found out how those Negro units were organized, I stopped all my efforts." The eyes were very black and hard now, and looking right across the table. "I saw that those regiments contained all the rejects from Fort Riley—the sick, the lame, and the lazy. I didn't want to join up with an outfit like that. It's sure death.

"At one point we had fifty-caliber machine guns on the trucks and we were told to give them to this infantry unit. But they were on ring mounts, do you know what I mean? They were fastened to heavy steel rings, back of the cab of the truck. Well, we took those off and gave them to the troopers. But there were no tripods to use. The men had to put bags over their arms and shoot the guns that way, like a rifle. They shot them against aircraft, and you know those guns weighed more than twenty-five pounds."

I nodded, because I had seen John Wayne or Bogart or somebody do it in a movie. It looked simple the way they had done it. I asked Cummings if the rations were the same, if in most respects the Negroes were at least *eating* as well as the whites. Cummings smiled a wintry smile.

"It was pretty tough to know, because I saw no white units. But we were pretty well off, you know, we were *hauling* it—and one way or another we got our share. The point of it is this: we were denied the right to fight as a combat soldier in a combat unit for our country. That was the only thing. The rest was equal.

"After the war I left the infantry as a first sergeant. I had made that grade four months after I was in—10th Cavalry, Troop E. I had twenty-two people who had more than two years of service, and of those twenty-two, twenty could not read or write. My supply sergeant had a third-grade education. Anyway, after the war I went to work for the Frisco Railway Company and I had the distinct impression that I was about to be fired. So I went back in. I was an E-7, a first sergeant, so I went back in. I enlisted and was sent to Germany and at that time the units were being broken up and abandoned. This was already in the making before I realized it . . ."

"What was that?"

"The desegregation order. President Truman's desegregation order. I don't remember exactly when it was, but I do remember that the Korean conflict set it in motion. It had no effect on me, not really. I was pleased with it, but I knew that there would be bugs in it. The American people are so accustomed to living apart— there can't be a quiet and easy turnover. I didn't think that that order would be the ultimate, uh, word."

I asked Cummings how he had been treated by white Southern officers.

"I think that so far as me personally was concerned I got more cooperation from Southerners than from others sometimes. I can't pinpoint it, really. I got better cooperation from Southern officers, though. Well, of course I was a first sergeant and perhaps they bent over backwards. But I have sat in the orderly room and listened and seen it happen with the troops.

"In that first integration go-around, my truck company was not integrated. We had a perfect record, no accidents or AWOLs in a year, which is *some* record, and they decided to leave the well-knit organization together. Well, after that I was sent to the First Battalion of the Eleventh Infantry Regiment in Pennsylvania. The regular commander—well, he refused me the job of troop sergeant major, and I went to supply again. I was not quick to jump to conclusions. But look: why did he send me two letters before I got there, telling me what my job would be—that is, troop sergeant major—and then change his mind? He didn't know the color of my skin when he sent the letters. But the regiment was breaking up so I got both regimental sergeant major and regimental supply.

"At Fort Knox, Kentucky, there was an almost similar situation. It may not have been racial, but there was a lieutenant colonel there, his unit needed a supply officer, and so I looked at it, and said that if I had a choice, my answer would be, No. That's what I told him. He said to me, 'I KNOW you will be better off here in the supply.' Well, I had no choice. Of twenty-two companies, only three passed inspection. So they put me out ahead of the officers on the inspection tours to get these companies straightened out. So that was the end of that.

"I left Knox in July of 1959 for Korea. I was the only E-8 there, there were no E-9s. I was the only E-8 in the 55th Quartermaster Depot in Korea. It would appear that they would assign me the job of sergeant major for the Depot. But then at the last minute they jumped an E-7 over me for the job. But I don't know. Look: for the Army, they made the right decision. They were much better off because the company they finally sent me to was the worst I have ever seen in my life. And I fixed it up. The base commander later said that I was one of the best NCOs he had ever served with. Well, why didn't they put me where I would get promoted? I knew then and there that you had to fight for what you wanted. The quartermaster job only called for an E-8, and I was an E-8. If they would give me a command job, that calls for an E-9 and they would have to make me an E-9.

"Well, there was an investigation of treatment of Negro troops at that Depot. They called me in and asked me if there was maltreatment. They asked me, 'Do you feel maltreated?' Well, you don't have to ask me down here to get an answer to that question, I said.

"It is not always true that if you do a good job, people will recognize it and will reward you accordingly. I thought it was true, but it isn't."

Cummings had said that as he had said the other things, coolly and unemotionally. He lit a cigarette and continued: "At Fort Riley, Kansas, I was with the 1st

Infantry Quartermaster Section. There was nothing to fight there. My MOS [military occupational specialty] was supply. I was there two years and one month.

"In Germany, I was with the 56th Quartermaster Battalion. In 1962 this was, and the battalion was run down. But the sergeant major of the battalion retired, and I went in and talked to the battalion commander and led him to believe I would talk to someone if I didn't get the job. That is, I would talk to someone *else*." Cummings smiled, and explained that he was talking in code; someone *else* meant a Congressman. "But I was fortunate to come out a winner. In 1964 they promoted me to E-9."

Cummings speaks about racial problems now with enormous detachment, qualifying everything he says, putting the most generous interpretation on his own experience. He is personally so self-possessed that it is difficult to argue with him or fault that interpretation. Sergeant Major Cummings is a man who has definitely got himself together.

"I have had a couple of NCOs come to me and tell me they have not been promoted because of prejudice. Because they married Caucasian wives. But I was promoted to E-8 and E-9 and I am married to a Caucasian."

Cummings shrugged, as if that ended it. I asked him where he was married.

"When I was stationed in Germany."

"She's German?"

"Austrian," Cumming said, those eyes as hard and opaque as eightballs.

"You have got to put the military and the civilian together," Cummings said. "Now my secretary for instance. She told me the other day that they told her she would have to get rid of her Afro haircut. She questioned that authority, and she made her feelings clear to the commander. It makes a big difference when you put the commander on the spot, and this is not good.

We have got the IG [inspector general] channel and the equal opportunity channel, and finally there is a Congressional channel. To do it otherwise is not military: You *must trust* your military commanders. Now she should have discussed the haircut business thoroughly with me, and let me go to bat for her. I've got means and ways to do it. But I don't believe—well, that her complaint was aired the right way. She says, 'I've got a right to talk about it.' Well, no. In the military, you don't.

"I have had very few racial complaints in my job here [at Lewis], very few directly related to race. I have heard statements, but no official complaints. They know you have got to have grounds. Once, it was some time ago, there was a kid who wouldn't take a shower, wouldn't take one at all, and they were having a tough time about it, the CO and the kid's sergeant. I had them bring the boy (he was white) to me and I rose up from the table and swung at the kid and said, 'Goddam it get your ass into that shower and WASH!' Well, he sure as hell did. If a man is stupid, you deal with him on a stupid level. So we were walking by the shower and I heard him telling a buddy that I was a black bastard. The CO got all upset and said to me, 'Don't worry, Top, we'll court martial him.' And I said to him, 'Now you stay out of it. If that man gets his ass clean and I'm his black bastard, it's all right with me.' "

Cummings's voice got lower and colder as he told the story, and then he turned to me and said that just the other day a trooper, a black trooper, had made a pass at his secretary. He explained that the soldier was unmilitary, that he had a goatee and was a bad soldier. Cummings said that he called the trooper into his office and told him to produce his ID card. The soldier denied that he had one, and Cummings ordered him to put his wallet on the table. Cummings wouldn't handle the wallet, and instead he gently fingered the ID card out of it. All the time he was fingering the card out of the wallet, he was looking at the trooper. "I did it so damn slow, looking at him all the time," Cummings said. The dialogue went like this:

"So you got an ID?"

"But . . ."

"You said you didn't have one."

"But."

"No explanations. You got the ID. Yes or no?"

"Yes."

"Yes goddammit *Sergeant Major.*"

"Yes, Sergeant Major."

"Now I am going to ride your ass right into jail if you don't shave the goatee, and don't start behaving like a soldier. You'll do what I say and you'll like it *because you know I mean business.* Is that right?"

"Yes, Sergeant Major."

The trouble, Cummings said, was that the white officers were scared to go to the mat with the blacks. There was too much potential for trouble. But you've got to be damned firm, Cummings said. "People ought to mean business. That's what it's all about."

Sergeant Major Cummings doesn't think he would have done any better out of the Army than in it. He has two brothers who are college graduates, and neither of them make any more money than he does. Beyond that, he has had the experience of working with men, boys really, and nothing could have been better than that. "If I can take a kid and make him see the light, that's okay. I sure do understand human nature better. I've . . . well, I've been in the Army twenty-eight years and I'm fifty-three years old. I'll retire soon, couple of years maybe. I like to tend my rock garden now. I like that more than the parties, and I don't really care for post life much. But it's been a real good life. The Army has been real good to me."

•   •   •

Sergeant Rick Meeks is twenty-four, a business-administration major from Indiana University. He is light-haired, slight, very articulate. Meeks is in the Army for two years only, a draftee. He tends to analyze the institution from the perspective of a businessman.

"It's organized effectively on paper, but putting it into effect is something else. There is so much paper. So damn much paper. There is paper supporting the paper. Why? It's always been done that way. We thought about trying to reduce the paperwork, but then we were told that it takes even more paper to reduce the paper. There are quite literally reports on reports."

I said that one of the senior NCOs—I think it was Hickey—had told me that the reason there was so much paper was a kind of built-in inefficiency because of the low quality of some of the GI clerks. Meeks bridled at that.

"Low quality, hell. Some of the clerks in my outfit are brighter than the NCOs, and brighter than the officers too. My company is two hundred men. At Christmas time we were operating on one-half schedule. We could do that all the time. There are guys who are doing nothing but picking up cigarette butts and counting tent poles and field packs. You see, there is all this equipment that is never used. Guys are treated like children: they don't tell you, 'I think you need a haircut.' They'll say: 'Go get a haircut.' When you go talk to them about it, they'll tell you: 'I am training men for the Third World War and this is part of the process.' Christ. I thought of taking that down and sending it to someone to publish.

"One battalion commander forbade tape recordings and television in the barracks because he said it caused too much noise. The other barracks had them, but not this one. The morale here is nothing to write home about, I can tell you that.

"The trouble is that they try to keep everyone keyed up. You have an inspection on Saturday, and you do the same damned work week after week after week. It is hard to explain. No matter how good you do, they are going to chew you out, and the one thing you are sure of is that you are not going to get a break."

Meeks was saying all this in the calmest possible way. He seemed to regard the Army as a wondrous institution, well worth further study. I asked him where the quality was.

"The quality would be in the people who are not institutionalized. The trouble is with . . . the people who . . . the many who don't question a damned thing. They accept whoever is above them. There are so many people in supervisory positions who just don't deserve to be there. But I'll tell you this: GIs stand up for their rights now. A lot of guys used to accept an Article 15 [a guilty plea, with punishment to be set by the commanding officer] because it was less trouble, and because he was scared of a court martial. But not any longer. They'll try to get you on an Article 15 for things that would never pass a court martial.

"I'll give you an example. I was at Fort Jackson for basic training in November of 1968. That's in South Carolina. Well, after we were in the Army for three weeks we got a seventeen-day leave. Hell, half of us were sick and we didn't want a leave after only three weeks. But we took it, because we didn't know the regulations. We didn't have to if we didn't want to, and that's in the regulations. But I didn't know the regulations then. If I went back to basic again, knowing what I know now, I wouldn't put up with half of it.

"The Army is what you make of it. I knew I wouldn't like it, but I decided to do what I could with it. I have made enough money on the outside, and I've learned a lot about people. I mean, how to deal with people. A lot of guys only saw the officers when they were playing their role, but I see them when they're doing other things." Meeks said that to make a little extra money he tended bar at the officers' club and occasionally the NCO Club. That job turned into something else, because when there were hints of irregularities in the NCO Club accounts, Sergeant Major Hickey suggested to Major General Pearson that Meeks be placed on a committee to look into the matter; Hickey thought that Meeks's business administration education might come in handy. According to Meeks, it did.

I asked Meeks what roles the officers assumed, and he laughed.

"Oh, you know, Mr. Cool, the Know-It-All lieutenant. I see these guys, a couple of years younger than I am, and they are playing a role. They are trying to fit themselves into what they think they ought to be. Their image of themselves as officers gives them a snobbery and superiority toward the enlisted man. Well, maybe they know about their specialty, transportation or whatever, but they don't know anything about life. Most of them couldn't make it in the competition on the outside.

"Morale here really isn't too good. I had a second lieutenant who was getting married. He and the captain, his company commander, were talking at the club. The CO wouldn't let the lieutenant have the morning off— it was Saturday morning—to go to his own wedding, and the wedding was in *Oregon*. He was getting married in Oregon. This was not right at all, in my opinion.

"Then there's the problem of race. It is a problem, even at company level. Look, I have no prejudice at all. I guess I wouldn't marry a Negro woman, but I have no prejudice . . ." Meeks thought about that a moment, then smiled shyly. "I guess that means I *am* prejudiced," he said. Then he cocked his head and smiled again. "Well, you find out things . . .

"Anyway, if some of the NCOs are partial, there is trouble. I had a white friend who was buddies with a Negro. Well, some of the Negro's black friends came to him and said, What are you doing palling around with a white man. It's a problem, like I said, a much more serious problem than the anti-war thing."

I asked Meeks about the system.

"It's an inner contradiction," he said. "You can't worry about your career and your men both. You can't make brownie points with your boss, and support your men. It's impossible. If you argue with the boss, then there is a problem with the hierarchy. If you don't support the men, there is a problem below and it results in low morale. Of course, if *your* boss is good and *his* boss is good, then it's no problem. But that isn't the usual situation.

"I recommended to my brother that he take ROTC because the officer's life is more bearable . . ."

"It is?" I asked.

Meeks took some time before answering: "Well, yes— but again, the one thing I found out, the more you work like a horse, the more they kick you. Everyone gets the same pay, but some men don't work at all—it is a psychological war between you and the guy above you. It is a game people play. You are told to do this, and what you try to do is get out of it, and some of them spend all their waking hours trying to figure out how to get out of it. You are told to do this, and you get out of it if you can. And it affects the morale of those who *stood and did it*. That's what's really challenging in the Army: 'Getting over.' That's an Army expression that means getting out of it.

"The hierarchical thing is obligatory, I guess. I don't think that after having the experience of power, they could stand taking orders from someone younger. Some officers on off-hours treat you like an NCO. They respect you—they know you have a job to do. It's a better relationship. On duty they snap their fingers and want you to jump. Some of them asked me to call them by their first names when I was working at the club. But, you know, I once called an NCO 'Sir' at the NCO Club, and he got mad as hell and told me never to do it again. Well, heck, it was just a courtesy thing, you know, like you'd say 'Sir' to anyone if you were serving him a drink. 'I'm no SIR,' he said to me, and when I got back with the drink he was still complaining.

"I came in the service because, heck, I didn't know what to do. I was eligible for the draft, so I thought I'd go in and get it over with. It's an experience all right, but I'll be glad to get out. You know, a lot of guys get out of basic and volunteer for 'Nam just because they want to get off this base. This base is something else, a little world all its own, let me tell you. This post here, Lewis, just isn't in any system. The treatment of the men is bad. If a guy comes in here with a chip on his shoulder, well, he is done for. *Done for!* They'll never let you forget it."

FOUR

The Generals

Shortly before he [Ludendorff] left Berlin, he was visited by Sir Neill Malcolm, one of the English generals. Ludendorff began indulging in the most violent abuse, both of government and people, who, he claimed, had left him in the lurch, and declared that Germans had proved themselves to be no longer worthy of their warrior ancestors. General Malcolm thereupon asked, "Are you endeavoring to tell me, general, that you were stabbed in the back?" Ludendorff was delighted with the phrase. "That's it!" he shouted. "They gave me a stab in the back—a stab in the back!"
—Walter Goerlitz, *History of the German General Staff*

As a professional soldier climbs in rank, his perceptions change. Put a star on a man's shoulder and he is a different man, his responsibilities different, his outlook altered. The myth of the American Army is that only the most careful and circumspect officers succeed, but the myth is wrong. Grant is an example of one sort of eccentric, Patton of another, and MacArthur of a third. Eisenhower is often cited as the quintessential bland harmonizer, but that is to misread Eisenhower's career as well as underestimate his considerable energy and strong intelligence. In today's Army, three of the most prominent three-star generals—DePuy, Stilwell and Peers—spent part of their early careers with the Central Intelligence Agency (convenient in assembling a conspiracy theory, useless in explaining advancement in the self-centered, not to say narcissistic, U. S. Army).

Generals are now managers, and the Army may have seen its last great combat leader among the senior men. Men of action exist (Creighton Abrams and Major General James Hollingsworth come to mind), but they are becoming obsolete. The Army technocrat, careful and circumspect not so much from personality as from training, is on the rise. "Army technocrat" in this sense does not imply any special skill, other than that of executive and manager; put a general in charge of an ironworks and he would perform just as well. Partly it's the nature of the job. From the time of Napoleon a general officer has acted more or less in isolation. Westmoreland, in his written testimony on the Vietnam war, does not differ markedly from Omar Bradley, who does not differ from Marshal Ferdinand Foch. In the memoirs of Foch and Bradley the face of war is almost never seen. There are no mangled bodies, no stink, no blood, just generalship and logistics, command and control. Foch at the time of Flanders Field:

Even if one of these actions should come to a standstill or one group of these forces be particularly tried, the commander of the whole must unflinchingly stand by his general plan, at the same time stimulating or sustaining the failing action, but never admitting that it can be wholly renounced or that its weakness can cause the relinquishment or even any change of that plan. Losses suffered at any given moment by a group of forces even so great as an army cannot justify any disturbance in the combined operations of the other armies . . .

Or Bradley at D-Day:

. . . The Plan took over.

That is what a general officer deals with, The Plan. To jettison a plan is to admit failure, either in the mechanics of the plan itself or (more devastating) in one's execution of it. "Losses suffered at any given moment by a group of forces even so great as an army cannot justify any disturbance in the combined operations of the other armies," Foch writes. But then it is Foch who described Flanders as "the terrific encounter."

The higher a man goes, the farther he removes himself from the materials of war. A sergeant commands a squad, a lieutenant a platoon, a captain a company, a lieutenant colonel a battalion, a colonel a regiment, a brigadier general a brigade (supposedly the largest unit one man can control within the range of his voice), a major general a division, a lieutenant general a corps or an army group, and a general an army group or a supreme command.* The loftier the position, the more distance he puts between himself and point—the squad scout in closest touch with the enemy. At battalion and lower the threat is immediate and direct, and at brigade and above it becomes increasingly remote and complicated, and the presence of death correspondingly distant. That is one reason why the generation gap in the Army breaks at lieutenant colonel.

The more remote the commander, the greater his

---

*A squad is 12 men, a platoon 40, a company roughly 150, a battalion 800 to 1,000, a regiment 3,000 to 5,000, a brigade 4,000 to 5,000, a division 15,000, a corps two or more divisions, an army two or more corps, an army group two or more armies.

responsibility. Bradley and Foch speak of an army here, a corps there—this thrust and that, wheeling 50,000 troops at a time to meet the enemy. At the highest levels the distance is astronomical: Winston Churchill speaks of an assault against the soft underbelly of Europe, and a rifleman crawls forward on his knees. Add to it the fact of confusion. The charts and the maps are there, the communications net is in, and the four-star general is linked in a command chain down to the lowest squad sergeant; but no one knows truly what is happening. No one knows for certain what the enemy is plotting, nor one's own capacities. Marshal Saxe observed that war "is a science replete with shadows in whose obscurity one cannot move with an assured step. . . . All sciences have principles and rules, war has none."

But that is not the impression gained from the memoirs, nor from the briefings in the field or at headquarters. In Saigon, General Westmoreland would meet with newspaper and television correspondents once every six months, stand before them in beautifully starched fatigues and tell them what was happening in the war. Surely he believed what he was saying, and the correspondents watched the pointer drift across the waist of South Vietnam, indicating a division here, a battalion base at the junction of *these rivers*, COSVN (the Viet Cong GHQ)—well, COSVN probably somewhere in this province, the one next to Cambodia, Tay Ninh. Yes, Tay Ninh. It is the rhetoric of a man trying to make sense of the senseless, trying to bring order and logic to the chaotic. Even with a four-star general, desperation was there because lives were at stake; you caught a whiff of the stink no matter how far back you were.

Occasionally it comes through in the memoirs. The tone of General Bradley's book changes when he undertakes to defend his estimates at the time of the Bulge:

> While G2 at First Army did accumulate a few vital shreds of intelligence for the record, he no more evaluated that information to predict the Bulge than did any of the other clairvoyants who afterward claimed that distinction. Although First Army's observations could have been read so as to suggest the *possibility* [Bradley's italics] of attack in the Ardennes, its warnings were not convincing enough to justify postponement of our winter attack to meet this new threat . . .

Yes, he says, there were reports that Manteuffel's and Dietrich's troops were lying in wait, that von Rundstedt was carefully preparing his assault, but these reports were never seen by him or his staff, nor were those that he did see conclusive. The cool, confident tone of the lieutenant general, the army group commander, wavers and breaks for a paragraph. Bitterly, he recalls that he was obliged to hand over one of his armies to Montgomery, then on the left flank of the Americans. He submits evidence in detail of the poor weather, the difficulty of obtaining satisfactory intelligence. Still, he does not explain how the Germans were able to mass— how many was it?—ten, fifteen divisions in the face of the Americans, to break out across Belgium inflicting appalling casualties. Bradley ends the passage on the melancholy note that it is difficult to know enemy intentions, that if you are a bold commander sooner or later you will be hit. Then, defiantly, he announces he would have done nothing differently. Even in retrospect, he concedes nothing. In a letter to George Marshall, written after the Bulge, he declares: "I do not blame my commanders, my staff or myself for the situation that resulted. We had taken a calculated risk and the German hit us harder than we anticipated he could." Bradley concluded in 1950: "Time has not altered my opinion. I would rather be bold than wary, even though wariness may sometimes be right."

Read that, in another context, *I would rather be wrong than right*. So for Bradley there was no post-mortem critique; he did as he was taught to do at Leavenworth, adhere to the plan. Better be bold than wary, even though wariness may be right. To admit error would be to admit quite a lot. There were 59,000 American casualties at the Bulge, 6,700 killed, 33,400 wounded, 18,900 captured or missing. Read the memoirs and wonder. Ludendorff liked to think that the German armies were victorious and the civilians gave the victory away. The allies unwisely supported the contention when they did not insist on a specific capitulation from the German general staff. That's it, Ludendorff told General Malcolm, *a stab in the back*. The nation did not support the army. Napoleon, who lapsed into irony from time to time, regarded all military history as *une fable convenue*.

There are no iron rules or unbreakable laws by which a soldier proceeds through the ranks of the American Army. The only universal is that there is a system and a man must understand it to succeed. The system does, or is meant to do, two things: (1) establish objective criteria for promotions and (2) make an officer as versatile as possible. Until promotion to general officer, a man will stay within his branch; the infantry, say, or armor. Within the branch he will move from command to staff, from field to headquarters, indiscriminately. An infantry officer may proceed from the command of a company to command of a battalion but he will not do so without intermediate assignments which have nothing to do with a field command. The education of an Army officer is entirely non-exclusive, and no matter that he is the most charismatic battlefield leader since George Patton or the most adroit staff officer since Walter Bedell Smith. The theory is that a man cannot know one job without knowing the other, cannot understand "line"

without knowing "staff" and vice versa. The officer will
proceed as prescribed, skipping when he can but being
careful not to skip too often; the process is known as
"getting your ticket punched," and it means you must
get off at all the stops. There has never been a Clausewitz
in the American Army because the writing of *Vom Kriege*
took time and serious thought.* An Army officer has no

**With the result that the serious strategic analyses are
now done by civilian scholars at the Rand Corporation or
the Hudson Institute or the Institute for Defense Analysis,
private corporations which exist on government contracts.
Economists and political scientists are doing the work that
soldiers ought to be doing, but are not. It is a pathetic (also
laughable) experience to attend a seminar at the Hudson
Institute, up the river from West Point, where Herman
Kahn and his sleek staff undertake to instruct selected
officers on Threats To America. The officers, most of them
colonels, are dazzled by the intellectual pyrotechnics, the
metaphors and scenarios which serve as reality at Hudson. Kahn, who is one of the most articulate men in America, normally appears at the beginning and at the end, to
first set the stage then draw down the curtain. In 1968
one of his major proposals was a television circuit which
would link the major provincial and district capitals of
South Vietnam with Saigon; the idea was that if a prisoner
were taken at Camau, the head of military intelligence in
Saigon could interrogate him via closed-circuit TV right
away without delay. The network would also be used by
the government to propagandize the villages. "If it's a Hoa
Hao village, we'll give them a Hoa Hao kind of program,"
said one of the staff. "A little Orwellian, but a helluva
idea." The cost was many millions, but Kahn observed that
money shouldn't enter into the considerations because the
U.S. government was already spending $30 billion a year in
South Vietnam, and what was a few millions more or less.
The colonels sat raptly through five days of metaphors and
scenarios, each one screwier than the preceding. When Kahn
came to the proposal to flood the Mekong Delta, one
colonel—a veteran of the war—embarrassed his more
respectful colleagues. "Oh bullshit," he said, and closed his
notebook.*

time to think, and imaginative reflection is discouraged. Tours of duty are rapid, and designed to thrust a man into as many different situations as can be managed. The emphasis is on procedure, detail, fact, nut and bolt. It is the theory of the utility infielder, and supporters of it cite the Second World War as proof of the soundness of the doctrine. At a time of rapid full-scale mobilization, the military establishment has no time to sort out abilities; the assumption must be that lieutenant colonel A is fully as competent as lieutenant colonel B, whether the assignment is command of a battalion or division intelligence officer. To make it a bit more complicated, it is worthwhile recalling that in the Second World War, as a matter of fact, Patton *did* have his field command, as Bedell Smith operated exclusively at staff. But the Army, not so dependent on hardware, was less rigid then.

The system begins at West Point, which is an important requirement for the highest commands. When the Civil War ended 16 of the 17 regular generals in the Union army were West Point graduates; in World War Two, 57 per cent of the 155 most senior generals (supreme commander through division commander) were West Pointers. In today's Army, although only 5 per cent of the Army's officers are West Point graduates, 30 per cent of its generals are (154 of 520 general officers). Of 16 four-star generals, only one (William B. Rossen, the deputy commander in Vietnam) is non-West Point. Of 47 lieutenant generals, only 11 are non-West Point, and of those one is Chairman of the Board of Engineers for Rivers and Harbors, another is head of the Combat Developments Command, a third is Deputy Chief of Staff for Logistics, a fourth is Surgeon General, a fifth (Lieutenant General Peers, who headed the My Lai inquiry) is Chief of the Office of Reserve Components, a sixth is Comptroller of the Army, and a seventh was military adviser to the U. S. delegation to the Paris peace talks. These are not field commands. In 67 years there

have been only 2 non-West Point chiefs of staff. George
Marshall (V.M.I.), 1939–1945, perhaps the most successful; and George Decker (Lafayette College), 1961–1963,
perhaps the least. So the first station of the cross, as it
was put by a young lieutenant colonel now in the
Pentagon, is the West Point class ring. It opens doors,
and beyond that establishes a certain seriousness of
intent. West Point is less influential now than it was
between the wars, but there is no doubt that a sort of
Academy protective association persists. It would be
unrealistic to expect otherwise, given the strong streak
of sentimentality in soldiers. A West Point-educated
captain or major is assigned a staff job, and all things
being equal he will receive preferential treatment. More
often than not, the deputy chief of staff for personnel
(DCSPER) will be an Academy graduate. R.O.T.C. and
O.C.S. (officer's candidate school, which takes promising
non-coms and turns them into officers) men tend to drop
out of the Army at major or lieutenant colonel. Occasionally it is their choice ("twenty years and out"),
more often—if my interviews are any indication—it is
because they see their way blocked by the old-boy net.
There is a concomitant to the advantages of an Academy
education: familiarity with the system from age eighteen, and the astonishingly strong ties that old grads
have with West Point and hence with the cadets. The
West Point ring will not indefinitely protect a real
maverick or a definite incompetent, but in the great
middle range of Army officers it does a good deal more
than a Harvard Law School degree does for an ambitious
corporate lawyer.

The point is that a man must be *known*. It was well
put by a very senior general, a West Pointer now retired
and a salesman in Washington: "I was a major at the
beginning of World War Two, and was stationed in
Louisiana. I left the building one night and passed a
tent, and a couple of guys, older colonels, were having a

drink and they invited me in. They were talking about the Army and one of these men said to the other, 'What shall we tell this boy?' The other one said, 'I think if I had a few words to tell a fellow about how to get ahead in the Army I'd say, be known. And take steps to be known. Be known by a large number of senior officers and be known *favorably*. Doesn't matter how. By polo, athletics, football—but get known all over the Army.' This fellow went on to say that he had just returned from a selection board in Washington. It was selection to the War College. He told me, 'The board studied the names and the records and then we started talking about the people, and we picked the people that we knew.' I followed that advice myself. I never forgot it."

For every young officer, the object is to get to the war, if there is one, as promptly as possible. "It doesn't matter which war you were in," the stations-of-the-cross man said, quoting the old line, "as long as it was the last one." The Army is relentlessly anti-specialist, so an ambitious infantry captain would want, first, to command a company in combat and, second, to go to staff as an assistant G-3 (operations). In Vietnam, despite the homage paid to "Vietnamization" no career-oriented officer wants to spend his time as an advisor; he wants to command *American* troops in a highly visible role. Under the policy of the one-year tour for officers in Vietnam, this means as a practical matter that as soon as a captain learned his job as a company commander he was transferred to staff, and as soon as he learned that he was rotated home (unless he chose to re-up). Upon return, the wise careerist would try for a teaching billet at West Point (if he was a West Pointer) or, better still, a master's degree in—almost anything, business administration, history, accounting, political science, physics, sociology. According to Army statistics, more than half of all field-grade officers "go on" to earn advanced degrees. The leadership, fascinated now with the concept of the scientist-soldier and the military manager, believes that only the highly educated are capable of taking the institution through the nineteen-seventies. The most prestigious of all the appointments is emplacement at the Harvard Business School as a colonel (Westmoreland did it in the mid-1950s and proved so adept a student that he collected half a dozen job offers before he was through). The index of the importance the Army attaches to advanced degrees is the fact that only two of the sixteen four-star generals now on active duty have them; more than sixty per cent of brigadiers do (155 master's degrees, 12 PhDs among 250 men). The desirability of an advanced degree is now a matter of policy, and reflects the Army's judgment that warfare is a matter of management and technology. One may define technology to mean political technique as well as nuts and bolts; that is, the soft sciences along with the hard. With its passion for objective thinking, the institution tends to regard an advanced degree as *prima facie* evidence of scholarship, brains, and, therefore, wisdom. The Army has permitted Major Peter Dawkins to spend seven of his eleven years in the Army at school, at Oxford as a Rhodes Scholar, at West Point as an instructor, and at Princeton as a graduate student. Clearly it is not a typical career, yet Dawkins is the most highly regarded young officer in the Army, the surest bet there is for chief of staff in the nineteen-eighties. Not that he doesn't have his troubles with the establishment: "Pete Dawkins has got to get into the *system*," a recently-promoted brigadier said, "school is all well and good, but the Army is the *Army* . . ."*

*Army professionals talk about Dawkins as politicians talk about Ted Kennedy. He is one of the few career men with celebrity status. "If you see him," one disillusioned major told me, "tell him to get the hell out of the Army and run for the Senate from Michigan. That's where the action is."

There are a hundred routes upward, depending on the branch and the officer's MOS (military occupational specialty). Up to a few years ago, the wise infantryman became a paratrooper; there was no reason for this, except that a very large number of very high ranking officers were paratroopers. It is called, with sarcasm, the airborne club. At any event, what a man does not want as a senior captain or a junior major is a command in a stateside post, unless it is at the infantry school at Benning or, conceivably, XVIII Airborne Corps at Bragg. It is wise to stay away from the Special Forces, which are dismissed as "green beanies" by the Army establishment, and Pentagon duty is a disaster. The Pentagon is a disaster, that is, unless the job is special and sensitive or with the Joint Staff or the Army General Staff, in which case it is something of a plum. The experience of Major General Edward M. ("Fly") Flanagan is typical: "I was a young lieutenant colonel in the nineteen-fifties, doing fine, and Westy was working for the General Staff. He picked me to be secretary and it broadened my experience . . . introduced me to people I never would have met. I mean by that the senior generals." (Flanagan is now the commander of the Special Forces, which makes the point that it is fine to go in and out; what a man doesn't want is to be identified as a career Green Beret. I once made the error of identifying Dawkins as a Green Beret, and the general with whom I was talking brought me up short. "Pete Dawkins was never a goddam green beanie," he growled. "Never.")

There are any number of special assignments in the lower grades, among them service in the office of the Secretary of Defense or, much more common, service as a general's aide. Brigadier General Sidney Berry, now the assistant commander of the infantry school at Benning, is an example of the first (he has also been a fellow of the Council on Foreign Relations). Captain William S. Carpenter, the lonesome end of the West Point football teams of the early nineteen-sixties, an example of the second. After his spectacular fight in the highlands of Vietnam in 1966, Carpenter was reassigned to Saigon as an aide to Westmoreland. Carpenter, who liked commanding a company (he won a distinguished service medal, two silver stars, a bronze star, and two purple hearts in three years in the war zone), hated Saigon and did not care who knew it, including COMUSMACV.* Students of the Army system say that there is a direct relationship between appointment as an aide to a general officer and future advancement. Quite probably there is, although one otherwise critical colonel observes that it's difficult to know "whether these guys advance because they are general's aides, or because generals pick unusually able men as aides."

Selection for higher rank is made by a promotion board whose members change each time around. They are theoretically selected by the Secretary of the Army and approved by the Chief of Staff, but whatever the theory it is traditional that the civilian leadership does not interfere in the process (Air Force General Curtis LeMay once said, "as long as I am chief of staff of the Air Force I control the futures of these men . . ."). But that changed under the Kennedy Administration. When

*A word on Army acronyms. COMUSMACV is Commander of U.S. Military Assistance Command, Vietnam. COMUS-MACTHAI is ditto in Thailand. DCSPER, pronounced desper, is Deputy Chief of Staff for Personnel. It is crucial to understand the acronyms. When the civilian effort was merged with the military in Vietnam there were long discussions on what nomenclature to use. The military informed the embassy that whatever phrase was finally used, it had to contain the word "support." The reason had to do with budgetary procedures, and the Army couldn't fund the project unless it was acting in "support" of it. The name that was at length agreed on was Civil Operations, Revolutionary Development Support. That was later changed to Civil Operations, Rural Development Support. The acronym either way is CORDS.

Cyrus Vance became Secretary of the Army he chose the men to sit on the boards, concentrating particularly on the crucial promotion from colonel to brigadier general. Under the Laird regime, the machinery is back in the hands of the Army regulars. A number of astute civilians who have worked in the Pentagon are skeptical of the system: Paul Warnke, a former Assistant Secretary of Defense, would like to see one interservice board make all promotions, the better to reduce parochialism. By influencing the crucial selections, one influences in time the entire Army. Vance reckoned that he was successful up to a point, looking at the general officers list now and what it had been in 1961. The criteria for promotion are numerous, but they center around the efficiency report and the personal knowledge one man has of another; this last is composed of a hundred indefinables that would make a wonderful master's thesis for a major who did not care if he ever made lieutenant colonel.

Somewhere at senior major or junior lieutenant colonel (average age: 34.7 years; average length of service: 12 years) the ticketed officer is chosen to attend the Command and General Staff College at Fort Leavenworth, Kansas. C&GS is the first major weeding-out point. Selection depends on the efficiency report ratings, among the most important being whether a man has had a command and how well he did at it. In 1970, an extraordinary weight is placed on performance in the war zone. Those on the five per cent list (every promotion list recommends a certain number of younger officers for quick promotion) are certain of selection, and while the selectee can theoretically turn down the assignment, almost no one does; those few who do, pick it up the next time around. C&GS teaches doctrine and procedure for corps, army, and army group commands; that is, for the ranks of lieutenant general and above. It is information which the major will use twenty years thence if at all.

It is almost entirely a nuts and bolts school predicated on what has become known as "the good Leavenworth solution." That is, an agreed solution to any tactical or strategic eventuality. War is analyzed as a hard science.

At some point, usually after C&GS, a man must serve his time in the Pentagon. It is a billet which must appear somewhere on a man's record, and for most junior officers it means twelve-hour days and six-day weeks, shuffling paper, signing on and signing off. Endless studies and revisions of studies, all of them conforming to Army procedure, and all of them checked up and down the line. Personally it is a hardship, living off the civilian economy on a small salary, which means living in the military communities of Springfield or Vienna in suburban Virginia, worrying about the mortgage.

The Department of Defense is immense, a mountain of paper, a building of six million gross square feet, 435,000 cubic yards of concrete, a working population of 27,000. The system reaches its zenith at the Pentagon, a labyrinth of bureaus and offices, DA, DCSOPS, ACSFOR, CINFO, an organization chart gone berserk, with all the services in there together scrambling for the money, Army and Air Force and Marine colonels stuffed into offices beside Navy captains, and a parallel civilian structure, its lines winding down from the office of the Secretary of Defense through the service secretaries and the new apparatus like Systems Analysis. There is all of this, plus the connections overseas, to Europe and Korea and the MAAG missions in Latin America and Africa, quite apart from the war, MACV and USARV and CINCPAC, and those lines leading straight into the tank, the pastel war room of the Joint Chiefs of Staff. The Army officer, particularly if he is combat arms, endures it, lives with it, puts in his time and counts the days, looking at the white-haired senior colonels striding down the corridors, manila envelopes tucked under their arms. The place is a birdcage, the young major decides; the only thing to recommend it is that the Pentagon is where it happens, the place from which the decisions proceed. But it is no kind of life for anyone who likes action. In the Pentagon a man is pecked to death by ducks.

At lieutenant colonel and colonel there is a second elimination point, this one known as selection for the Army War College at Carlisle Barracks, Pennsylvania (or, less demanding intellectually, but more prestigious, the National War College in Washington). At the Army War College in 1970, about one third of the 184 students were West Point graduates (the percentage is usually 50 per cent), and selection is regarded as a virtual certainty that the officer is on his way to a star; only one-fifth of the C&GS graduates are selected for the war college, which is theoretically more theoretical than Leavenworth. Its course of instruction involves high strategy, civil-military relations, and the workings of the Joint Staff and senior commands like SHAPE. It is a touch more reflective than the other "colleges," but not much. To graduate, a man is obliged to write a thesis.

The avenues from war college are numerous. A man may go to Vietnam and command a brigade, or, if he has his star, may become an assistant division commander. Command of a military assistance advisory group used to be bad, but now it is good (and will become better, since Congress is in the process of cutting back military missions abroad). In today's atmosphere, almost anything having to do with "politics" is a valuable credential (there is some dispute on this point; not all Army men would agree). The obverse of that, also valuable, is a responsible point in Combat Development Command or Continental Army Command. But after the star, an officer's advancement is almost entirely a question of his record, his abilities as they are perceived by senior officers and, not least, who he knows or who knows him. It is there that the real mysteries begin, and there are very few generalities that are very useful. John J. Tolson III, now a lieutenant general commanding XVIII Airborne Corps at Bragg, thought his career was definitely sidetracked when as a brigadier he was made chief of the MAAG in Ethiopia; he does not think so now. The one constant is the desirability of a combat command, and a distinguished record while in it, including the appropriate badges. "A helluva war record" is a ticket like no other, although alone it will not take a man much beyond colonel.

At the highest levels the fog is impenetrable. When General Earle Wheeler was made chairman of the Joint Chiefs of Staff in 1964, there was a hot-eyed (and unseemly) scramble for Wheeler's vacant chair as Army chief of staff. The underground candidate was Creighton Abrams, then a lieutenant general and a Bostonian who was well and favorably known to Robert Kennedy, Robert McNamara, and Cyrus Vance. Abrams was understood to be "a Kennedy man," though with Lyndon Johnson in the White House no one spoke of it. Apart from being "known," Abrams had impressed everyone with his adroit handling of the Mississippi civil rights crisis as commanding general of the Third Armored Division. He had gone from that command to three stars and a corps command in Europe and from there to vice chief of staff, an abrupt and rapid rise. The former Secretary of the Army, Cyrus Vance, recalled: "He was not intellectually at the top of the heap, but he had a great capacity for leadership in tough spots. He was just damned good. We got to know him during the Mississippi civil rights trials. He was very sensitive to the problems of civilian leadership in government, and he was sympathetic to the problems of the Presidency. He would not knowingly keep anyone on his staff who was not giving it to him straight."

Those who thought the Army needed a shake-up believed that Abrams was the man to do it: widely admired among soldiers as a combat man (he led the relief col-

umn into Bastogne), he was no less respected by the
civilians for being "sensitive to the problems of civilian
leadership." One other candidate was the commander of
the Seventh Army in Europe, Lieutenant General William Quinn, but Quinn had been ruined by the lunatic
newspaper furor over his invitation to an old friend,
Presidential candidate Barry Goldwater, to his summer
retreat in the mountains of Bavaria. If Quinn had had a
villa in S'agaro or ski hutch in Gstaad there would have
been no trouble. But what he had was a hunting lodge in
Berchtesgaden, and when the newspapers got through
with him (Quinn was charged—wrongly—with leaking
classified documents to Goldwater, among other matters) his career was in a shambles. So Abrams was the
underground candidate, although not for long; the older
generals, especially Wheeler, thought that at fifty years
old he was too young. A very junior lieutenant general,
Abrams was put down on the basis of age. The civilians
(Robert McNamara apparently did not enter the controversy) did not feel they could push it, so in consultation
with the senior soldiers they named instead Harold K.
Johnson, who was two years older than Abrams and
therefore more seasoned. It was an appointment neither
hailed nor deplored. Johnson had survived the Bataan
death march and lived as a prisoner of the Japanese
from 1943 to 1945; there was some grumbling among the
brass that a man who had been "a *prisoner* should not be
chief of staff for the whole goddamned Army," but the
grumbling was not serious. Basically a staff man, Johnson had headed the Command and General Staff College
from 1960 to 1963. He had a reputation as something of
a moralist (he was deeply religious), and a capable technician. But what served him best was his position as
Deputy Chief of Staff for Operations (DCSOPS) when
Wheeler was chief of staff. A retired general explained it
this way: "Johnson is very capable, solid, humorless. No
foolishness about him, no comedy. What led to his suc-

cession was the direct and close relationship with Wheeler, and as the outgoing chief of staff Wheeler was the man they [the civilians] consulted. You see, they *fought the battles together in the tank* [the JCS war room]. If you are going to be chairman of the chiefs, who do you want as chief of staff of the Army, *your* service? What the hell, you want a man you can trust, who you know, who knows you, and who knows the most important job in the Army: operations. Don't misunderstand. Johnson is a good man, not a crony. But it was that association with Wheeler that got the job for him."

At the lower grades it sounds a bit bloodless, a man proceeding according to a computer printout. Provoke officers to reminisce about their times as majors or lieutenant colonels, and a different picture emerges. It is the continual struggle to subvert the system or, more charitably, to put it to work for you. Hovering over all of it is the efficiency report, a document resembling a high school multiple-choice quiz; a senior officer rates all the men in his command, on attitude, on obedience, on intelligence, on *ability to do the job*. It is meant to be an objective test, but it is not—can't be, since the judgments are human ones. At the lower grades, unless a man is something of a celebrity, the efficiency reports are the only things a selection board has to go by. If a man wants to get on, he goes along with his superior officer, which means making few waves. Matthew Ridgway once said that the highest duty of an Army officer was to protect the nonconformist, and sometimes that happens; more often, it does not. Colonel David Hackworth, one of the most outspoken and abrasive (as well as the most decorated) officers in the Army, puts it this way: "You can be difficult as hell until you are a full colonel. Until then, you can exist, within limits, on sheer talent. But you had better be damn sure you have got the talent. To go beyond bird, you need other things. Education and polish are two of them." Hackworth is adamantly opposed to the system of the efficiency report, which he sees as central to a system which produces yes-men. Given its priorities, it can produce little else, Hackworth argues, and mentioned a two-star general by way of illustration: "He wanted his star, which is all right, and he admitted to me once that he decided early in his career that he would have to yield, to compromise to achieve his end. He said to me that once he had three stars he would straighten it out, fix the system. And that's the irony, because you're a different man then. You become the guy who you started out to impersonate. And that's what's happened to him."

What they remember, the successful ones, is how a friend here in DCSPER or there in CONARC got an assignment changed, how General X helped Colonel Y around Regulation Z. What they remember, too, is the difficult son of a bitch at Leavenworth who left for the golf course every day at three-thirty and expected you to do all the work and cover for him, or the bitch wife of General A who roamed the post like the queen of Sheba. "Jesus, they sent around a mimeographed sheet to all the junior wives just before the reception," the major recalled, "and damned if one wife wasn't detailed to follow this broad around with an *ashtray*, I mean like a nubian slave or something . . ."

They reminisce about the times at Lewis and Benning, and the serenity of the peacetime Army. Serenity to some, boredom to others; or sometimes worse, the stateside tour at the beginning of a war. Every few months there is a new colonel's list or a BG list and over morning coffee, he and his wife read down it to see who made it; my God, *that bastard made it.* And checking over the list to see what it was that had gotten bird for him. Near the bottom of his class at the Academy ("Well, that's no barrier in this army"), no command, no people's hero badges. Ah, that's it. ADC/COMUSMACTHAI. General's aide. Someone was looking out after him all right, and then the thumb going down the list; all of it rational if you understood the system. Ninety per cent of the guys there had all the requirements, the command, the badges, the good assignments, the mentors; West Point, C&GS, the war college, a tour at DCSOPS, MA in business administration from Arizona State. *Battalion commander in South Vietnam.* And then, the list run out, the wife goes to the telephone to congratulate the fortunate wives. Next time around, her husband thinks. But it's tough to put a good face on it. In the American Army everyone learns about everything at the same time. A man could only hope that there wouldn't be a party like the one at Benning a few years ago. Some guy had made colonel and his wife had rented a room for a party at the officer's club and rigged up a throne and posted a sign, KING FOR A DAY.

You can get some of that out of your mind in the field, when you are actually fighting a war, but stateside it is what you think about. Promotion. If you screw up, it can take you years to recover and mostly you never do. One man who did said defiantly: "I can look myself in the face in the morning." Screwing up can become its own reward, if you are a certain type of man: take *me*, they'll say, I'm a rebel, never conformed, and I've paid for it. The best men in this Army are the colonels who never made general. But very seldom is there any real bitterness towards the Army itself, so strong are the institutional ties. Like an insecure college boy rejected by the best fraternity on campus, many of the men who drop behind secretly believe that the Army is probably right. Lieutenant Colonel Edward King, who hated the war in Vietnam and requested retirement after twenty years in the Army rather than serve in it, is another sort altogether, harshly critical. King, whose record is excellent, sent a memorandum to Stanley Resor, the Secretary of the

Army, and said what a number of his colleagues only think: "It is impossible to render honest, beneficial service to the nation or the Army in the atmosphere of fear, repression, injustice and selfish career promotion and advancement-seeking that flourishes within the command levels of the U.S. Army." King believes that it is morally and professionally repugnant for a man to lead troops in Vietnam simply because it is a valuable credential in DCSPER's dossier. For its part, the Army asked King to undergo a psychiatric examination.

The system seems to wear most men as smooth as a beach pebble. In an institution as complicated as that of the American Army, nothing is more excellent than sheer competence. The slogans reflect it: *No problems, zero defects*. The man who can make it work without making waves is a prize beyond value. It is a system of such rigid hierarchy that the young rebel must be consciously protected, taken under the wing of a senior man in order to survive. The Army will take its most talented battalion commanders and make them staff men in order to serve the system; it will insist that talented staff men command battalions, because a lieutenant colonel who has not been blooded is like a surgeon who has not operated. Thrust into a job, either at command or at staff, the officer is circumscribed by so many rules and regulations that he is rarely able to display either initiative or innovation. Innovation is not an OK word in the Army. The most thoughtful officers have a common complaint, in its most extreme form the heretical notion (as Dawkins once put it in an article) of "the freedom to fail."

In the finest tradition of the Harvard Business School (whose principles, Robert McNamara among others brought to the Pentagon) the Army has been corporatized. It has become something of a syndicate, a corporate state with its own laws and traditions and procedures. Its bureaucracy, even in the war zone (or perhaps most particularly in the war zone) is a swollen anachronism whose central function appears to be the rounding of hard edges. One is speaking now of procedure, and the cast of mind that succeeds. It was easily witnessed in Vietnam, where for the largest operations the planning overcame and transcended the objective. The machines were so wonderful, so dazzling to put into motion, that whatever it was the war was about was lost to view. The medium became the message, as any inquiry into Operation Junction City in 1966 or Operation Total Victory in Cambodia in 1970 will attest.

But the Army is not a college classroom, still less a debating society, and those who command must do so with certainty, with a grasp of the facts. Between ideas and facts, the wise officer chooses facts, because facts can be weighed and measured. Ideas are splendid, so long as they do not run counter to doctrine...

"No, that isn't right," the lieutenant colonel told the instructor at C&GS. The class had just been given a résumé of a battle in the Korean war. The class had been told to work out the right solution, and the lieutenant colonel had worked out a wrong one.

"Yes, it is," the instructor had said.

"No. I was there. I was at that battle. Your solution could not possibly have worked."

"Nevertheless, it is doctrine..."

An incalculable irony, then, that the sad science of warfare, the most uncertain and ambiguous science—art, craft, whatever—tends to produce in America the most rigid-minded men. They will set up a scenario at C&GS, this one a mock invasion of Rumania. They will install computers and work out the war game as close to reality as they can. All the units are there, and both sides have their doctrine. But the instructor admits that he can not allow for the lucky accident; nor for such factors as morale, brilliance, or unforeseen disaster. How close to the real world is it, the instructor is asked? Smiling: "About fifty per cent."

Reflection tends to produce doubt, and doubt is not the hallmark of the successful commander. Neither is irony. Who wants Jonathan Swift out there on point, mixing it up with the Cong?

There is a serious practical point to be made, and it is this: the process, beginning at West Point and proceeding through the efficiency reports to C&GS and the war college and particularly rooted in the requirements of combat, results in the virtual deification of general officers. The root of it is the combat Army, because orders under fire are meant to be obeyed without question and often without comment. The combat atmosphere has been made universal, and the underling, the colonel or lieutenant colonel or major, is frozen out of decision. It is an entirely different psychology than American business or the professions, which are also hierarchical in structure. The reason is that a young businessman or lawyer can quit if he strongly disapproves of policy or method; he can quit and go somewhere else, but an Army officer cannot. There is only one U.S. Army and a man either serves it or resigns from it. If he resigns, he goes into a new line of work. For the general officer, it is as if the route upward is so compromising that once there he is obliged to continue looking over his shoulder, wary at who might be gaining; surrender a sliver of authority and you are back at bird or below. Beyond that, the Army invests the system with a sense of infallibility. A general officer looks about him and understands that if he does it by the book, he cannot go wrong. There is that very neat command structure, and so long as everyone stays in place the machine will run. Responsibilities are very clear, and accumulate with rank. There is only one word to describe the aura: sanctity.

No wonder that the younger men are frustrated, because the system does not permit them a decisive voice.

A colonel relates a conversation with a four-star general: "It was Harold K. Johnson, and I really told him what we were doing wrong in Vietnam . . ." This is said with an extraordinary pride and sense of heavy moral courage, the military equivalent to banging on the corporation president's desk and demanding a change in company policy. But the longer the colonel spoke, the plainer it became that the conversation was muted; the critique (the colonel was a genuine expert on the war) was delivered with discretion and tact. You do not quarrel with generals, or tell them they are wrong. The response to it is either fury or the patronizing nod, the smile: Yes, *Colonel*, now to continue . . .

It produces an isolation of the highest ranks, an isolation both from the rank and file of the Army and from the rank and file of society. Respect for authority in the minor things, the saluting and the spit and polish and vernacular Yes, *sir*, becomes slavishness in the major things. It is not endemic to all armies, as anyone who has watched the British Army can attest. The British may have their problems, but excessive obedience is not one of them. Between officers and men there is a kind of jaunty familiarity which is instantly abandoned at the approach of serious danger. The reference is specifically to the troubles in Cyprus in 1964: performing an intolerable mission (interposition between Greek and Turkish Cypriotes), the British Army performed with extraordinary gallantry and discretion, even if during the worst of it the conversations, officers to men, sounded like something out of Evelyn Waugh.

Two aspects, then: the first an unhealthy climate of caste surrounding general officers, the second the inability of lower-ranking officers to use their most energetic years in productive work. There is a third side to the point, which is that the Army is compulsively anti-intellectual, as opposed to being anti-brains. Brains do not lock a man out, imagination does. The system does not yield to it, any more than it does to doubt; ideas are tested not in give and take, but in conformity to doctrine. And the doctrine, the *what* and *how* of military policy, is decided by these senior men, generals, who have laboriously made their way through the system; the truth is that many of them are excellent men, intelligent and honorable and skillful, but they have a personal and professional interest in the status quo, which is to say the past. Deny the status quo, and you deny your own career.

Much of the Army tradition in 1970 seems almost quaint, stemming as it does partly from the Southern military tradition in America. It is reflected now in a certain courtliness of manner among the Southern soldiers, of whom William Westmoreland is an excellent example. He once said in an interview that he had never thought (I think he meant schemed) about his career or how to advance in the system: "I just did my job to the best of my ability." When he was a major general commanding West Point, he refused a third star so he could stay on at the Academy a third year, "to finish what I had started." Westmoreland is a genuinely patriotic man whose virtues are scarcely believable, unless you know Westmoreland. He is representative of much of the best and some of the worst of the Army system, not at all the man to direct a war under the confusing conditions of Vietnam, which is possibly the highest compliment an American general can be paid. On the other side is George Patton, whose roots are also Southern, whom Ernest Hemingway claimed never told the truth; the Army is fond of remembering Patton as a knight errant.

The traditions wind back through the Army families, "the heads of the families" to use the mafioso term. They are Woodruffs, Stanleys, Echolses, Raymonds, Shattucks, Bonesteels, Stebbinses, Mileys, Paulses, Hewitts,

Armstrongs, Fosters, Donnells, Langus, Muirs, Marshalls, and Millers, and those are only some who date back three generations or more at West Point. Example: Captain Brink Miller, USMA '64, goes back five generations at the Academy. His father, Frank Miller, is presently a major general, and his grandfather retired a major general. His great-great-great grandfather graduated from West Point in 1836. The links by marriage are reminiscent of small New England towns: Lieutenant General Melvin Zais is Lieutenant General (Ret.) James Gavin's brother-in-law. In today's Army, there are twenty-two general sons of generals through the West Point connection alone; eliminate the factor of the Academy, and the list would doubtless double.* It appears that the tradition is not being carried forward into the present generation. Of those generals listed, only Bonesteel, Carter, and Boye have sons at West Point. At any event, probably only journalism, law, and medicine parallel the successful father-son syndrome in the American military. There is no equivalent in the U.S. government, with the possible exception of elective office in Massachusetts.

Having listed the names, it is difficult to know what to make of the list. Frank Clay, Lucius Clay's son, is adamant that his high-ranking father had no influence on his career. He said that his background played no part at all, either in his assignments or in his rapid promotions (rapid, but not so rapid as his brother, who at fifty-one is an Air Force lieutenant general). A Washington official confirmed Clay's statement: "That's probably right. Frank Clay is infantry and his old man was Corps of

They are Generals Bonesteel and Brown, Lieutenant Generals Carter and L. V. Clay, Jr., Major Generals Boye, Strong, Honeycutt, Surles, Mearne, Ryder, Shedd, and Richards, and Brigadier Generals Patton, Timothy, Frank Clay, L. V. Greene, Michael Greene, Crittenberger, Marshall, Cheadle, Walker, and McQuarrie.

Engineers. Those engineers, they're another thing altogether."

Still, a number of men identified as "real comers" in
the Army bear recognizable names. Clay. George Patton
III. Sam Walker (Walton Walker's son). Colonel Richard Gruenther. West Point plus family tree did nothing
for Colonel John Eisenhower, however; if anything, his
career was sidetracked because of it. But nine times out
of ten it will help, and sometimes deservedly so: General
Charles ("Tick") Bonesteel, the retired commander of
U.S. forces in Korea, a military don who graduated seventh in his class at West Point, was once described to
me as "the best general in the Army."

The importance of lineage often comes through in the
memoirs. Morris Janowitz quotes Mrs. Winefred A. Stilwell's introduction to her husband's papers. "General
Stilwell was descended from Nicholas Stillwell who
came to New Amsterdam in 1638. Records and family
documents carry the name back to 1456. Among those
Stilwells who followed Nicholas, there are many who
served this country as soldiers, so it was perhaps natural
that my husband chose a military career." General
George Marshall's biographer described the family tree
as follows: "With John Marshal of the Forest, the family
emerges from obscurity. Born in 1700, he became a large
planter, married the daughter of the sheriff of Westmoreland County, and sired nine children ..." Today, ten per
cent of the names listed in the Washington Social Register are military officers, but most of these are Navy,
supporting the contention (one supposes) that it is the
toniest of the four services.

Searching for support of conspiracy theories, one can
find them among the heads of the families, relentlessly
white, indomitably middle-class, usually Protestant, thoroughly traditional, and invariably socially and politically
conservative. The military dons set the tone and style of
the institution, for the insiders as well as the outsiders.

But the Army has grown too big for them to dominate it: too big and too rich and too significant, and so the elite, so-called, is a much more complicated matter than the fact that a man comes from a four-generation military family. It is obvious that there is something of a West Point conspiracy, elements of preference and privilege, all of it proceeding logically, more or less according to Karl Marx. Much more mysterious, and therefore interesting because they defy logic, are associations within the Army itself. The best example is the airborne club.

A very considerable mystique surrounds the paratrooper, who is a soldier trained to jump out of airplanes. When an airborne unit assembles in the shed to collect its parachutes, the commander stands in line along with everyone else and conspicuously takes an anonymous 'chute, "the next one on the pile." Aloft, he usually jumps first; he takes his chances along with the troops, and in a night drop his odds are no better than anyone else's against getting tangled in a tree. In the officer's club at Fort Bragg (the headquarters of XVIII Airborne Corps and the 82nd Airborne Division) there is a steady CRASH CRASH of boots hitting the floor; when a man arises from table, he bangs both feet on the floor to straighten out his trousers, the tops of which are tucked into highly-polished Corcoran boots. Airborne is strictly volunteer, and to those who take it seriously (and all paratroopers do) it is *prima facie* evidence of energy, initiative, and bravery. Major General Willard Pearson, now the commander of Fort Lewis, and as a brigadier the commander of a brigade of the 101st Airborne in Vietnam: "Now I have commanded Puerto Ricans, Filipinos, Negroes, Whites, and paratroopers and paratroopers are the best. If you want to select a group of people who are willing to fight, well, one of the best criteria I know is whether or not they will jump out of an airplane. Now that is not to say that some of the others *won't* fight, but sure as hell the airborne *will*."

The airborne club—you can call it a cult—began in the quiet years before World War Two. General James Gavin, the best known of the American paratroopers (he always jumped first), tells the story this way: "I graduated from West Point in '29, and rode horses a lot in the nineteen-thirties. A small group of cadets were invited to take equitation, and I thought then that there was no future in horses but, what the hell, it was romantic. I rode horses a lot in the nineteen-thirties. You've got to understand that the infantry was stuck in the mud and the Cav—well, in the Cav you had to make snap decisions. But the Cav was the one thing that was venturesome, and when the airborne came along, that was that. The paras were all former Cav men. The others had pot bellies. The paras had the challenge, and it was just like jumping horses. You come to a jump and that horse would be there, tense, and you'd ease him over the rail. Hell, you'd just ride him in. Well, the paratroopers were like that and I told the young officers of the 82nd Airborne that they were the future leadership of the Army. But it was a normal thing, nothing surprising. The paratroops were physically demanding, intellectually challenging . . ."

Nothing, then or now, provoked quite the aura of the romantic leader that Taylor, Gavin, McAuliffe, and Ridgway did. The historian and journalist S. L. A. Marshall wrote about the heroics in a book called *Night Drop*, an account of the airborne assault behind the lines on D-Day. Here is Marshall's description of Ridgway:

The reaction of Big Matt Ridgway to Ste. Mere's noontime tranquillity, growing out of the German recoil, could be only one way. As nature abhors a vacuum, Ridgway loathes inaction in the face of a possible offensive opportunity. His generalship has no room for the housemaidenly rule that there must always be a pause to tidy up the field; he keeps going. Hard on soldiers?

To the contrary, this perpetual drive, his habitual boring forward to the zone of personally aimed fire, his inquiring mind, and his persistent question to any subordinate, "Do you know anything that will help me right now?" are among the virtues that endear him to people on the foxhole line. Americans detest wasteful generalship and instinctively recognize it. But they need to know they are commanded by a Man—this above all!

To dig back into the records of the 82nd and 101st Airborne Divisions in World War Two is to find an astonishing number of young majors and colonels who in the nineteen-fifties and nineteen-sixties rose to general officer, and collectively ran the Army. The leaders set the tone and style. Maxwell Taylor, commander of the 101st Airborne Division, became superintendent of West Point directly after the war and rose to be chief of staff in the nineteen-fifties, and chairman of the Joint Chiefs of Staff and personal adviser to two presidents in the nineteen-sixties. Ridgway, airborne corps commander in World War Two, ran the war in Korea and after it became chief of staff (he preceded Taylor). Gavin, the commanding general of the 82nd Airborne Division in World War Two, rose to lieutenant general and in the mid-nineteen-fifties occupied the central position of chief of the Army's research and development in the middle and late nineteen-fifties.

The junior men, operating under the aegis of their seniors, fared just as well. Four of Taylor's protégés in the wartime 101st were Ewell, Cassidy, Michaelis, and Kinnard. Julian Ewell, successively a battalion and regimental commander of the 101st, is now at three stars and commanding a corps in South Vietnam; Patrick Cassidy, a battalion commander and regimental executive officer in the 101st, is now a lieutenant general and chairman of the board of engineers for rivers and harbors; John H. Michaelis, a battalion and regimental commander with the 101st, is now a four-star general commanding the Eighth U.S. Army in Korea; Harry Kinnard, as a lieutenant colonel the G-3 (operations) of Taylor's division, rose to three stars before he retired in 1969. Similarly, Gavin's 82nd Airborne. John Norton, the G-3 (operations) of the 82nd, is now a major general and presently deputy commander of Project MASSTER, the quiet but very high priority Army operation at Fort Hood. Reuben H. Tucker, commander of the 504th regiment of the 82nd Airborne, rose to major general and among other assignments the chief of the MAAG mission in Laos. Osmund Leahy, an 82nd battalion commander, is now a major general and commander of the Institute of Land Combat.

There are others. The late Robert F. Sink, a regimental commander of the 101st, rose to three stars and retired in 1961. Major William Desobry, who led a combat team into Bastogne, is now a major general commanding the 2nd Armored Division at Fort Hood. Gerald J. Higgins, a brigadier general at 35 and chief of staff of the 101st, retired in the mid-fifties, a major general. Thomas L. Sherburne, an artillery colonel with the 101st, rose to major general before he retired in 1960. John J. Tolson III, who commanded the 503rd Parachute Regiment during the war, is now a lieutenant general and commander of XVIII Airborne Corps at Fort Bragg.

Others joined the airborne (that is, became what they call jump-qualified—and one ought to keep in mind that all we are talking about is the ability to jump out of an airplane) after the war. They included: Francis W. Farrell, who commanded an artillery unit in the airborne during the war, became CG of the 82nd in the 1950s, and retired a lieutenant general; George Forsythe, who became chief of the 101st Division's planning group in 1956 and is now a lieutenant general and commanding the Army's Combat Developments Command; and Stanley R. ("Swede") Larsen, a regimental commander of the 82nd in the early nineteen-fifties and now a lieutenant general commanding the Sixth U.S. Army at the Presidio of San Francisco.

In the nineteen-fifties, Ridgway, Taylor, and Gavin were all at the height of their influence. Farrell was G-3 (operations) for the Army, Kinnard was running the airborne board, and a brigadier named William Westmoreland was the deputy G-1 (personnel) for the Army. Westmoreland was something of a protégé of both Taylor and Gavin (unusual, since Taylor and Gavin were rivals). Later, in the late nineteen-fifties and nineteen-sixties, a second group would center around Kinnard, who in Vietnam was the commander of the 1st Cavalry Division (Air Mobile). They were Generals Beatty, Roberts, Brown, and Moore. Roberts is currently the commander of the 1st Cav, and Moore, as a colonel, was one of Kinnard's most energetic brigade commanders. Of them all, Westmoreland was recognized as the chief of staff of the future.

Gavin recalls that he first met Westmoreland as a captain. ("One trooper would say to another, 'That guy is going to be chief of staff,' " Gavin said, and then smiled. "Well, they used to say that about me, too.") After the war, Westmoreland became a staff officer of Gavin's 82nd. He went on to the Army staff, and from there to the coveted command of the 101st Airborne Division in 1958, superintendent of West Point in 1960, COMUSMACV in 1964, and Army chief of staff in 1968. It is perhaps a bit much to add that the current vice chief of staff, Bruce Palmer Jr., was assistant commander of the 82nd Airborne in 1961. And perhaps more than a bit much to say that with the exception of only four men—General Forsythe, Lieutenant General Cassidy, Lieutenant General Zais, and Major General Desobry—all of the above-mentioned members of the airborne club are West Point graduates.

Cyrus Vance, the New York lawyer who was Secretary

of the Army in the early nineteen-sixties, and an excellent witness on these matters, remembers that the paratroopers quickly came to the notice of the Kennedy Administration. "People in the airborne had style, zeal, and motivation. They knew it, and knew where they wanted to go. They were strong, highly motivated, and walked into a power vacuum in 1960. The Army needed people to give it a thrust and it was a damn good thing that we had the airborne types there. The danger, of course, was that it would get out of hand." The irony is that the airborne concept had only barely proven itself in World War Two. The 82nd's jump behind the lines at Normandy was a near disaster, and the operation at Sicily scarcely better. Jumping out of airplanes, as a critic later put it, was romantic as hell but also dangerous and wasteful of lives; what it did was put a very high premium on bravery of a certain kind. Willard Pearson is not simply engaging in sentiment when he says that paratroopers are the best men to command. But it has nothing to do with the fact that they jump out of airplanes. It is that all paratroopers are volunteers, and the training is exceedingly rigorous. The units are tougher, and their commanders tend to be magnetic.

It is worthwhile delving a bit into the nineteen-fifties and the early 1960s, and the figure of Maxwell Taylor. Army chief of staff from 1955 to 1959, Taylor presided over a diminishing institution. The "New Look" defense strategy of the nineteen-fifties put the emphasis on atomic weapons and airplanes; the annual budget of the Air Force was habitually 46 per cent of the total in the fifties, with the Army struggling to maintain an 800,000-man force. It was Taylor who constructed the doctrine of Flexible Response as an alternative to Massive Retaliation, a formulation that was largely an effort to get the Army back into the game. His book, *The Uncertain Trumpet*, published in 1959, was the bible of the early McNamara regime. It is a central document for anyone interested in the intellectual roots of the American involvement in Vietnam. Taylor's idea was to build an army capable of going anywhere, anytime, to pursue any mission. This was his judgment on Indo-China:

> Indeed the ink was hardly dry on the New Look before the episode of the fall of Dien Bien Phu provided a practical test of the efficacy of the New Look strategy and exposed its weakness. The deteriorating situation of the French there in early 1954 led to discussions in the Pentagon and White House in April and May of the nature and degree of possible United States intervention. Although some exponents of air power urged intervention by aerial bombing, largely through General Ridgway's efforts the fact was eventually accepted that any intervention by that time would be either too late, too little, or of the wrong kind. In particular it was doubted that any air attack could be mounted on a sufficient scale to offer hope of success without, at the same time, endangering the French defenders. During these deliberations and hesitations, the need was apparent for ready military forces with conventional weapons to cope with this kind of limited-war situation. Unfortunately, such forces did not then exist in sufficient strength or in proper position to offer any hope of success ...

Taylor's anti-Communism was more rugged even than John Foster Dulles's, and in *The Uncertain Trumpet* he went a good deal beyond the military brief to posit Communist global strategy. "Since our disastrous demobilization in 1945," he wrote, "the Soviet advantage on the ground has steadily increased. . . . During recent years the Soviets have maintained an army of some two and a half million men, which they have completely reequipped since World War Two with the most modern conventional and atomic weapons. This army, more than the Soviet ballistic missiles, is the symbol of ruthless Communist power and a political weapon of tremendous value to the USSR." To riposte, Taylor wanted an American military establishment of more than two and a half million men, to meet the Soviets on the ground in Europe. He was very airborne in his insistence on American bases overseas: "Apart from their strictly military requirement, these overseas deployments have a very important psychological role to play. They exemplify to our allies the willingness of the United States to share with them the hazards of living under the Communist guns. There is no substitute for the personal sharing of the danger . . ."

That last line is crucial, and one of the reasons why the Kennedy Administration was enchanted with the paratroopers. James Gavin was sent to France as the American Ambassador, and by shifting General Lyman Lemnitzer to NATO in 1962, Kennedy was able to bring Taylor out of retirement to become chairman of the joint chiefs. The *sine qua non* of the heroic leader, Max Taylor *had written a book*. The intellectual warrior, president of the Lincoln Center for the Performing Arts in 1961, fourth in his class at West Point, a major general at forty-three, he spoke five—or was it seven, or nine?—languages, wore the distinguished service cross, a silver star, a legion of merit, unnumbered foreign decorations. Supernaturally handsome, Taylor played a smart game of tennis and could speak in a tongue the Kennedys understood. Robert Kennedy named one of his boys Maxwell; John F. Kennedy brought him into the White House as an adviser, put him on the Bay of Pigs inquiry, and finally (over strenuous objections of other military men) made him chairman of the JCS. Taylor was a member of the group centering around Robert Kennedy which initiated seminars on counter-insurgency, then a new word in Washington, but a highly appealing alternative to "the nuclear holocaust" (as it was invariably described). The idea, as clear as can be in *The Uncertain Trumpet*, was that American power was virtually limitless, there, waiting to be used. *There is no substitute for the personal sharing of the danger.* After Kennedy's death, Lyndon Johnson sent Taylor to Saigon as ambassador; but Taylor did not get on well with the South Vietnamese, and his tenure was brief. What was so magnetic about Max Taylor? A former official of the Kennedy and Johnson administrations gave this account:

"Well, he was a good soldier and the idea was that he would come to the White House to sort of interpret the military to Kennedy."

"How would he do that?"

"He spoke the language. He had, ah, a hell of a distinguished record." The official went on to say that Taylor was to act as a check on military ambitions.

"The civilians couldn't do that?"

Glumly: "The President liked him. He was a dashing, handsome guy and the President liked him. Max Taylor is a very, very talented man. A bit rigid, perhaps . . . well, rigid as hell. But he's an excellent soldier."

"And?"

Smiling: "It was personal, strictly personal. Kennedy liked to talk to him, that's all. They enjoyed each other's company."

Ditto the airborne: personal, strictly personal. In 1969, the proud 101st Airborne Division became the 101st Airborne Division (Air Mobile). Helicopters replaced parachutes, and now generals are learning to fly.

"My generation," Major General Jack Deane was saying, "my generation grew up in a period of pressure. We pressed beyond ourselves. I was commanding a battalion at age twenty-seven. We made up for the lack of experience with work. I didn't have time to play catch with my sons or go on camping trips." Deane, now the commander of the 82nd Airborne Division, looked straight

across the desk, as if to verify there would be no mis-
interpretation. "Anyway, now you've got unisex and the
boys wearing their hair like girls. But out there, out in
Vietnam, that same boy is charging with the rest of them.
He is so great, so great it makes tears come to your
eyes."

Deane is small of stature and looks Irish. Now he
smiled and said that his daughter had just married. They
held the wedding reception at Bragg and Deane arranged
for the Airborne Chorus to serenade the guests. "I didn't
want them to sing, goddammit, 'Porgy and Bess' or
'Black Is the Color of My True Love's Hair.' Instead, I
got them to sing 'This Is My Country,' 'The Battle
Hymn of the Republic,' and 'America the Beautiful.' Well,
we had seventy or eighty people there, people in their
seventies all the way down to the late teens or so. I have
never seen the chorus so well received. Never. The first
part of it, the audience was all choked up. I saw tears
streaming down people's faces."

Patriotism, he said. "It's *there* all right, the problem is
to bring it out." Then he began to talk about the leak
(I would call it a hemorrhage) of talented officers from
the Army. He said that pay was part of the problem,
although the worst of it was that the army officer wasn't
respected; not like he used to be, not like the old days.
What the hell, Deane said, he felt it and he was a major
general. But the money was part of it too. "I like to give
a little money to my kids' colleges, and give them a little
money from time to time. Get a car or . . . like that. I like
to go to St. Thomas in the Virgin Islands, myself. It
gives me a lot of pleasure." Deane paused for a moment.
We had been sitting in his office, and he excused himself
because he had to perform a promotion ceremony. He
had to pin captain's bars on his aide.

The new captain and his wife and her mother came
into the office, smiling self-consciously. A photographer
from the Public Information Office was there, and waited

a bit to one side while Deane got the captain's bars out and ready. He glanced around the room and talked for a minute about his aide, who he said was a fine young officer who had earned his promotion. On an impulse, Deane handed the bars to the captain's wife, a very pretty dark-haired girl in a miniskirt. She looked young enough to be in high school, and she approached her husband slowly and shyly. He was tall and blond and standing at attention in front of Deane's desk, nervous and looking dead ahead as his wife reached up to pin the silver bars on his epaulets. She had trouble getting them in place. Every one in the room was smiling, the general, the girl, the girl's mother. The camera clicked twice, and when the bars were finally in place the girl stood on tiptoe to kiss her husband, still standing at attention. There was an awkward moment after that, as they prepared to leave. Then there was conversation and laughter and handshakes all around, and when the general came back to his desk he had to clear his throat before proceeding with the interview.

One is surrounded by it. Reveille in the morning and taps in the evening, the words dimly remembered,

> Fades the light;
> And afar
> Goeth day,
> Cometh night;
> And a star,
> Leading all
> To their rest.

... the sound of aircraft overhead, sentences punctuated with *Sir!* A man's medals are reminders of where he has been, and what he has seen (the Purple Heart, Hackworth had said, "you can't fake *that* one"), his career laid out on his chest, and his rank in life signaled by bars or leaves or eagles or stars. And the post itself, not IBM or General Motors or any civilian town, but a military post; military police and olive-drab automobiles and orderlies, and the long row of brick houses, each identical with the other, except for the CG's house which has a tiny wing on it, a sunporch. Friends, one known first at the Pentagon, another at Leavenworth, a third overseas somewhere. Chapel on Sundays, a nondenominational creed so relentlessly military that the National Council of Churches once complained that the services were establishing a separate religion. There, on the parade ground now, recruits drilling, *hut, hoo, he, hoa.* All of it very tight, close, run by common rules and principles, and everyone subscribes. The Army. Love it or leave it.

Fort Bragg in late winter is a bleak place, but coming slowly into spring, a North Carolina promise. In a helicopter with Fly Flanagan that afternoon, one watched the land roll away to the west, dark green with wide marked places which were the drop zones for helicopter trainees. That was HALO.

"HALO?"

"High altitude, low opening," the general said.

The drop zones were all named for World War Two maneuvers of the 82nd Airborne: St. Mère Eglise, Sicily, the others. The chopachopachopachopa of the helicopter and the smell of electricity and fuel were heavily reminiscent of Vietnam, the land below resembling III Corps, Tay Ninh province west of Saigon. Flanagan was flying to Camp Mackall, to inspect the Special Forces training camp. Eat a few rattlesnakes, someone had joked, slit a few throats. The helicopter was making a wide turn, and Flanagan was looking down at the camp. We had been talking about generals, and he shook his head slowly. He said that a hell of a lot of generals' sons had been killed in Vietnam. It was really terrible, he said, and rattled off five or six names. He said that he thought what happened was that a boy tried to emulate his old man, the World War Two hero with stars on his shoulders and maybe a DSC or a silver star and v-buttons, and war stories deep in his memory. He hesitated then, and spoke briefly about family separations, the long periods in the field without family, and then admitted that he had not been able to spend as much time with his own sons as he had wished. But you went where the Army told you to go, and went without delay and sometimes the other things had to go by the boards. But it was a hell of a shame. I had learned that a number of general's sons had gone the other way, rejected all of it, everything their fathers stood for. I mentioned a few names to Flanagan and he nodded; the son of one man dropped out in Vermont somewhere, another leading antiwar demonstrations on the Coast, a third an embittered enlisted man, now in Vietnam and promising to join a commune later.

Flanagan shook his head glumly. The Army gave you something, he said. But took something away, too.

FIVE

Outsiders: One Major

Lying awake while the stove-light died redly in the corner of the room, I remembered the wine-faced Army commander with his rows of medal-ribbons, and how young Allgood and I had marched past him at the Army school last May, with the sun shining and the band playing. He had taken the salute from four hundred officers and N.C.O.s of his Army. How many of them had been killed since then, and how deeply was he responsible for their deaths? Did he know what he was doing, or was he merely a success-ful old cavalryman whose peacetime popularity had pushed him up to his present perch?
—Siegfried Sassoon, *Memoirs of an Infantry Officer*

The successful ones dominate the institution. Explain them and you explain the broad contours, and those are the contours of the regulars, the professionals who de-fine the Army. But there are others who fit into no cate-gory, who do not see the romance in commanding a battalion of infantry or firing a 152-mm. gun or driving

a Sheridan tank. The materials of war do not interest
them. They find no exhilaration in the mission. They tend
to question, to brood, to worry, to doubt, and one is left
to wonder what impelled them into the Army in the first
place. Inside it, they exist like beached fish.

Some of them went to military school, Culver or Shat-
tuck, and insist that the discipline and the style of the
institution got into their blood, "and it just went from
there," *there* being West Point or V.M.I. or a state university en route to the Regular Army. Others came from
military families, and found the continuity congenial,
and still others thought that the military life would be
unconventional, and therefore challenging. Some succeed inside it, most don't. The Army tolerates the outsider and very occasionally gives him encouragement; it
is a huge institution and a place—some place—can be
found for anyone. The very bright ones often are put into
oddball assignments, and some of those with real pa-
nache volunteer for the Special Forces; or did, because
even among the outsiders the Special Forces in 1970 has
lost much of its appeal. They are linguists or historians
or inventors or adventurers who have found themselves
inside the Army and endure in spite of it. A few are
authentic intellectuals, fascinated by the military process
and what makes it go; they are theorists, of history or of
American society or of war. What seems to attract them
is the symmetry and tradition of the institution, its
honor, and the conviction that some of society's best
ought to be soldiers. They take very seriously the military responsibility. The spirit is at root elitist, for which
no apologies are offered; if the best do not serve, it
leaves the institution to the mercies of the worst.

As Alexander Portnoy saw himself living in the middle
of a Jewish joke, the outsiders often see themselves in the
middle of a Hollywood war story, all tinsel and Cinema-
Scope and exhortation. *Peace is our profession.* Peck and
John Wayne and Widmark and Phil Silvers are all

around them, greater or lesser imitations of imitations, and the thing is on celluloid; it's a movie, *and all the roles are taken.* You have to hear some of the nicknames to believe them: the colonel known as rice paddy daddy, the sergeant called headhunter. Some are good, some bad. Some are dazzled by their rank, some not. *You stupid son of a bitch,* the colonel says to his aide, and stands in the doorway and reads the riot act before a dozen people, who look away embarrassed or bend over their papers. The aide, a young former Rhodes Scholar, stands stiffly at attention.

A few of them, neither best nor worst, are simply there. A sergeant interviewed at Bragg wanted to be a forest ranger, and to that end was enrolling in correspondence courses. He seemed to find in the Army that purity that eluded him in life, and that he sought in the woods; or that is how he explained it one night. The next night he said that the Army was not what he expected, not at all, and for that reason he would quit when his hitch was up. At Bragg, he was an orderly to a general. The sergeant explained that the Army was a place that he went to at seventeen, thinking he might stay for twenty years or more. It was a place like any other, although he had very strong religious convictions and did not like war. But there was evil in the world, most of it springing from Communism, which was a denial of the Christian ethic. He said he could escape most of it as a forest ranger. Meantime, he cooked and kept house for the general— who looked after him as a father would a son.

The sergeant could leave or stay with no implications at all for the Army. The Army would not miss him, there were thousands of others. More serious for the future are the officers, many of them young, who find the system intolerable not for any reason of ambition but for reason of personal style. There isn't much place in the

Army for a bookish or introspective officer, or anyone who is a loner or outsider by temperament; an outsider, in Army terms, is a critic and therefore an irritant. The institution wants (one suspects it *must have*) team players, men who can work in harmony and make the engine go.

Perhaps the reason for this is the Army's enormous reliance on machines, and therefore the necessity for sheer technical competence, and beyond that its size and the belief that war is an engineering problem. The impulse is not to make the Army safe for diversity, but to make diversity safe for the Army; the larger the institution becomes, the less tolerant it is. You don't find Guillaume Apollinaire or Edgar Allan Poe around the officer's club bar at Bragg; in 1970, you would not find U. S. Grant either. The outsider, like the West Point cadet who lives near Berkeley, walks on eggshells: "I'm home for thirty days and I'm dueling for thirty days," the cadet said. Stay away from criticism of the war or the general staff. They often conceal themselves under rough or silent exteriors, and finally at captain or major they say the hell with it and resign, tired of pretense, tired of keeping themselves screwed down. Tired of sterility, too, "the sterile, dull system"—a system that works beautifully on the surface, like the trappings surrounding an Episcopal church service. More: they find little sense of community in an organization so rigidly structured, whose tone and style so often resembles a men's locker room. The Army is so obvious—in 1970, who do they invite to make the commencement address at West Point? Spiro T. Agnew, who tells them naturally what they want to hear.

The outsiders look at kindred spirits among the older officers and what they see is compromise. Compromised men who have found a neat, noncontroversial niche and have tucked themselves away in it, remote in a way that prep school masters are remote. Distant and sardonic, cultivating half-smiles, indicating by their attitude, *I really am better than this.* It is an easy matter then to be witty about it or to rationalize, and conclude that a military career was a mistake from the beginning; an aberration, a man can say, crazy from the outset. But it takes a definite act of will to shed the uniform, because if you are a professional you know that you are shedding responsibility as well; and now, in 1970, the service is under attack. A man never quits under fire. Beyond that: a man who doesn't fit in must somehow explain those who do, and it is doubly difficult when the military mystique is so wrapped up in images of masculinity, balls.

—Allrightyoumen it's gonna be tough, and we'll find out which ones can hack it and which ones can't. Who's man enough to stand it. Who's hard.

With or without the outsiders there are remarkable men enough, so perhaps it doesn't matter. There is no inherent reason why the U.S. Army should be as diverse as, say, the Congress of the United States or the Philadelphia Phillies or the United Auto Workers. But there is no reason why it should be as exclusive as the D.A.R. or S.D.S. or the Presidium of the Supreme Soviet. It wasn't always true: Ridgway said a cardinal duty of a commander was to protect the nonconformist. But the leveling process, in the Army as in the rest of society, is relentless: for the outsider inside, it means working to no effect, and the root of the discontent is not anything so grand as philosophy or motivation, hawkishness or dovishness, or in 1970 whether the Vietnam war is good or bad and the precise degree to which an Army officer is an accomplice to it. Much more interesting than any of these questions are the Army's institutional characteristics, so what a man comes down to are details, personal matters. *Will I be a desiccated staff lieutenant colonel at forty?* The Vietnam war is there, good or bad, moral or immoral, wise or foolish; the officer, any officer, sees the war as a collective responsibility. A man is thirty or thirty-five, came to maturity during the Eisenhower years, and dimly remembers the victorious dispatches from the Second World War, the stability and order represented by George C. Marshall, the soldier's soldier, at the elbow of F.D.R. and Harry Truman. In 1970, he is caught between that impulse and the irrational murderous impulse of the nineteen-sixties: Kennedy, Vietnam, King, another Kennedy. And friends. Any Army officer has friends now dead. Nostalgia and reality, and where do a man's primary loyalties lie now? The formulation is a trite one now: reform from within, or bore from without? An Army officer, having taken an oath to serve the nation, stands under the volcano in a way that the rest of us do not. At thirty or thirty-five the loner has become a compulsive outsider and then it is a matter of personal honor to stay honest. To resist or resign, the Army and the society being what they are. There is that, and the state of a man's conscience.

You can analyze it that way, or you can say (as most regulars would): The Army is no place for a neurotic. Make your choice. Fish or cut bait. Either way, the foregoing was a composite picture, a generality, and it is wise to avoid composites and generalities. How many outsiders are there in the Army? Who can say? The major whose Vietnam diary appears below is an outsider who appears every inch the professional soldier, a man whose record is excellent and who has proceeded inside the system. He is beautifully educated, almost scholarly once you talk to him, a man fascinated by the witlessness of history and by novels like *The Charterhouse of Parma*. A complicated, cultivated mind, in other words. Read the diary for an appreciation of isolation, darkness at high noon.

11 January. It's all so sad. Can I put up with this sort of

thing until I have sufficient rank to avoid it? Or is it
everywhere in the Army? And if I stick with it, will I
be a desiccated staff lieutenant colonel at forty, per-
petuating the sterile, dull system . . .
3 February. Another "accident." I would wager we lost
(in the unit) an average of one man a week killed or
badly wounded because of accidents. Today a young
soldier almost blew off his right hand with a blasting
cap. It was a horrible wound, what remained of it,
purple-black, torn apart, pouring blood, while the
young soldier looked at it dumbfounded, his lips
mumbling. A pathetic sight. As a measure of my em-
pathy, I thought of Chopin.
9 February. I slept very late after a night of hard, but
'busy' work and then went to lunch . . . AFVN Radio
was broadcasting a speech of Senator [Edward] Kennedy's in which that man, mouthing the intelligent
conclusions of his staff, was passionately declaiming
against the present Vietnam strategy . . . not very pro-
foundly. Suddenly a lieutenant at our table, feeling the
sympathy he knew he was about to enlist from everyone there, burst out feelingly: "I am ashamed to admit
that man is senator from my home state." Another
officer, taking his cue, said: "We've got the solution.
Right here" (meaning the military solution not, apparently, to be applied very surgically). There were hard
murmurs of assent all around.
11 March . . . because knowing is probably the most
important thing in life, and the source of all action.
Because it is essential that I never lapse into that most
tragic denial of the possibilities of human thought:
"The military mind." The mind with all its parameters
and limits ingrained through years of constant failure
to aim beyond the "feasible" and "allowable," the
"probable." I read *Timon of Athens* today . . .
12 March [A general had come for lunch.] A captain
came up and asked me something about a report—and
suddenly a lieutenant colonel, a common-looking man
with a pompadour hair 'style,' veins popping out of his
neck, said, "You never carry on a conversation in the

presence of generals!" Our conversation, such as it was, ended . . .

17 April. Long conversations last night with my young friends. They do me the honor of wondering why (how could you?) I am in the Army. I was hard-pressed to answer. The roads are beginning to diverge in the woods, I am afraid. And though they may run parallel for another three years I can scarcely hope to straddle them both beyond that time. Once I was sure that whoever would be a good soldier must be an educated man. I mean this subtly . . . slowly I shift from that conviction. An "educated man"—in my terms—becomes disenchanted with an enterprise which cannot truly enlist his abilities, his experience, what he has in his heart of hearts . . . I cannot read Clausewitz without irony.

SIX

Machines

The machine stood on a vacant knoll, its foreshortened gun pointed north. There were deep ruts in the rocky earth, and the land fell away and then came up steeply in a rise two miles distant. This was Fort Hood in east Texas, and the machine was a Sheridan tank.

The sergeant was brisk. He was explaining the machine, how it worked, what the equipment did and how it did it. He touched and patted the machine as he spoke, pointing to the huge treads and kicking them, and then looking at the gun and smiling, patting the armor plate. There was no trouble with this vehicle, Sergeant Rosario said; it was the best vehicle he had had in twenty years in the Army. We looked at it, dark green against the sandy earth, squat and lethal, permanent as a Sphinx or some other rough beast. The sergeant opened a flap at the front end and extracted a canvas cover, then unhooked other flaps to show how the canvas could be deployed so that the machine could float, move through the water like a fish. But it was not really meant for water warfare because the gun did not work well in water. It was designed to act in support of the cavalry scouts, the armored personnel carriers; the Cav was the spearhead, the reconnaissance element of an armored or mechanized division. Of course classic infantry doctrine permitted the cavalry element to work in support of troops as well, covering the rear and the flanks, capable of suppressive fire in case of heavy engagement. More than that, Sergeant Rosario said, this was a vehicle capable of accompanying paratroopers, floating to earth on the end of a parachute and landing undamaged. That was what made it special; that, and the swimming component and the main weapon, the Shillelagh missile. Now the airborne had a real armored element. The main gun could hit a dime on edge at two thousand meters, and it was no lucky accident. That is what it did at a demonstration for members of Congress: hit a dime on edge at two thousand meters and balloons at five hundred meters. Of course the real range of the main gun was closer to ten thousand meters. The exact distance was classified information.

Back in the public information office there were pictures of those who had driven it, Congressman Poage, General Westmoreland, the faces not amused under steel pots with the flash of the division on the pot: the 1st Armored Division ("Old Ironsides"), the 2nd Armored Division ("Hell on Wheels"). Anyone could drive it, it was a machine designed for simple operation. It was there to act in support of troops, a reconnaissance vehicle, you understand, not precisely a tank. It only weighed seventeen tons and nothing that light could properly be called a tank; the M-60, the American main battle tank, weighed in at more than fifty tons. So it is wrong, really, to call it a tank even though it looked like a tank and behaved like one. It is a reconnaissance assault vehicle. That's clear isn't it?

Inside now, the sergeant has a rag in his hand and absent-mindedly passes it over the metal. The hatch looks to be a manhole cover, heavy, rounded, thick metal, and the sergeant is pointing at the dials and the switches, the guidance systems for the Shillelagh missile and the 152-mm. gun. He calibrates the sight, and focuses it, and offers it for viewing. The optics are wonderful, the hill two miles away coming into sharp focus, the depth of field intimate; it's like looking through a camera with a long lens. One twists the dials and they mesh silently and the scope moves left, right, up, down, and the sergeant explains that when you are firing the gun, it is the turret that will move. The machine is headed in one direction while you are firing in another; there is no limit to the field of fire. The sight is so clean you can see little particles of lint, an anomaly but true as you look through it. The sergeant explains about the dials and switches, which operate as an aircraft dashboard operates. You have to go through checkouts before the missile or the gun will fire, and if there is a malfunction anywhere a light will blink on.

So look here, the sergeant says, and points to the ammunition containers. The machine is capable of carrying 10 Shillelaghs and 20 rounds of 152-mm. artillery shells. In addition, there are 9,000 rounds of 7.62-caliber ammunition for the M-60 machine gun. There are God knows how many rounds for the brutal .50-caliber machine gun which is mounted on the cupola, fired by hand. What firepower that is, the sergeant marvels. Do you see what the destructive capability is? The guns can be fired more or less simultaneously, except of course the big main gun which could fire in tandem both the missile and the artillery round. And what is new about *that* is that the artillery shells, the cartridges in the main gun, self-destruct. They are burned and destroyed *inside the breech*. It takes less than a minute, and then you can fire again. Fire and keep firing, and how simple that is compared to the old tank where you had to unload by hand and drop the hot shell casings on the floor of the vehicle. Now they jet CO_2 into the breech to cool it off, and it takes just sixty seconds or less. Beyond that, the sergeant goes on, there is a full complement of smoke grenades to lay down a smoke screen and make good an escape. And of course there is the XM-44 Light. That goddam wonderful Light that is set to move with the gun, so you can fix a man or another machine in its beam and therefore fight at night. It has a twenty-four-hour, round-the-clock fighting capability.

"I think he wants to drive it," the PIO man said to the sergeant.

"Come on and drive it," the sergeant said. He was a Latino, very friendly now because I was listening with care to his explanations and not asking very many questions.

"No," I said. "You drive it." I regretted saying that right away, and Sergeant Rosario shrugged and put on his helmet and spoke into the tiny microphone fitted on to his helmet so it came out and touched his lips. I looked down and realized for the first time that someone else was in the machine. It was the driver, hidden in the bowels up front, his head just visible. The sergeant had explained that each tank had a four-man crew, the commander (himself), the driver, the gunner, and the loader. There are three tanks to a platoon, and three platoons to a troop. There are three troops to a squadron, which is commanded by a lieutenant colonel.

So we drove off, the engine releasing a high whine. The tank drove like a Buick, accelerating smoothly and powerfully, turning in a second and moving now up a hill. The machine could climb a sixty-five-degree angle, and while the speedometer said it could do sixty miles an hour, the best this particular tank had ever done was forty-three miles an hour. It would be devastating in desert warfare, the Sahara perhaps, or the Gobi. I focused the gunsight as we drove, calibrating the azimuth, and pretended I was firing at the small shed at the base of the rise. The shed moved around in the sight and then I had it fixed. I fired four missiles and three shells, pulling the trigger on the pistol-grip and watching them move to the target, correcting them in flight, and hitting it bang on, exploding the wood into a thousand fragments with the first missile, and then hitting it again and again, and lobbing the artillery shells back of the shed to catch the Japs or Krauts or VC or whoever, *Comanches*, as they fled the fortified position. The enemies exploded along with the shed. Then I watched the infantry come up from behind and secure the objective, mop it up and report back that the place was *taken*, now the rest of the division could come through the pass. Yes, colonel, your squadron did it, routed the Boche . . .

The sergeant had said that you could guide the missile while it was in flight, watch it even as it arched out of the gun and turned, a bird of prey seeking its target. You could sometimes miss with the artillery shell, which was fired like a rifle. But you never missed with the Shillelagh—oh, well, occasionally. But not if you knew what you were doing.

Sergeant Rosario had given me a helmet equipped with the radio, and now I pushed the button that turned it on. The static was ominous in the background as we chatted back and forth, the tank charging up and down small hills. Rosario said you could fire while underway, and there wasn't much kick at all; that was the idea, in fact, to fire while moving.

. . . and aiming again with that marvelous scope, looking through it like a cinematographer, seeing it with Antonioni's eyes, watching the land bounce and jiggle in slow motion with the movement of the tank. I came away from the glass and looked out the turret. I still had the helmet on, and I put away the clipboard and forgot about notes and looked at the land rushing by. If you had a tank like this, you could do damn near anything, do what Patton did and wheel an army ninety degrees, run a hundred miles in thirty-six hours and relieve the airborne at Bastogne. It was a machine built for exploits, invulnerable, safe, a world to itself, this one tank with the firepower of a platoon of men, and more dependable; a damn sight more dependable with the armament and the Shillelagh.

Rosario was giving instructions to the driver, who peeped through an aperture in the front. He said that the range of the tank was three-five-three miles. Carried one-five-eight gallons of gasoline, suitable for any day's run unless you're going from here to Hanoi.

... hell, more than a platoon. More firepower than a company, when you counted everything, the missiles along with the artillery, the big .50 mounted on the cupola and the .30 bound coaxially with the main gun, that to keep the bastards honest, keep their heads down. And maneuverable, fast, through a river or up a steep hill. You could hide behind that hill and just lob the shells over it, so much firepower there that even if you couldn't see what you were doing you would hit *something.* Stand off and hit and keep hitting, and when it was tough, when your ass was in a crack, and you were up against the real Commies, the Russian T-54 or T-55 or T-62, the big babies, well, you just high-tailed it out of there at forty-three miles an hour. You got out, and you were fast enough to do it because the machine was smart, damned smart, and knew what to do. If you got out of the sights of the T-62 you would be all right. Live to fight another day. (And Oh God if the Reds were looking the other way for just sixty seconds, you could put a Shillelagh on them, home the missile in on that fat ugly armor plate, blasting it to smithereens ...)

We came back to the knoll and they shut the machine down, its engine moaning as it died. There was complete silence on the hill as the sergeant smiled and looked at the tank. What else was there that I wanted to know? Some of the electronics were classified, but the rest of it was open information. Fine vehicle, Sergeant Rosario said, wonderful vehicle. I had been a fan of the infantry, always; tanks were coffins (what was that movie? *Sahara*, Bogart was in it, and Hemingway wrote in *Across the River* that tank commanders had the mentality of bullies). But that machine, so sleek and unforgiving, hard as a good welterweight, lean, fast, nimble; it was a machine of the nineteen-seventies, technology neatly blended with the traditional *fighting spirit* of the American soldier. Thank God the American Army had tanks. There wasn't anything a man couldn't do with a squadron of tanks. Uh, armored reconnaissance assault vehicles. Nothing.

There are still a few Sheridan tanks in Vietnam, but not very many. The command there did not ask for them, but when they were sent accepted them with good grace; they were machines, after all, and therefore useful. The Department of the Army wanted the tanks in the best possible hands, and so it was no accident that the first shipment was consigned to the Eleventh Cavalry Regiment, whose commander was Colonel George Patton III. A carbon copy of his old man, Colonel (now Brigadier General) Patton ran what was known as a very tough outfit, the regiment's motto was *Find the Bastards and Pile On!** There was no fixed doctrine for the Sheri-

A note on Patton and his regiment. Dr. Gordon S. Livingston, a West Pointer and Army major, was returned to the United States from Vietnam as an "embarrassment to the command" after an incident at the change of command ceremonies for Patton. General Creighton Abrams was there, pinning a Legion of Merit on Patton and commending him as "one of my finest young commanders." Livingston was a medic with Patton's unit, and used the ceremonies to distribute a prayer he had written. It reads:

God, our heavenly Father, hear our prayers. We acknowledge our shortcomings and ask thy help in being better soldiers for thee. Grant us, O Lord, those

dan in Vietnam, so Patton's men had to decide what to
do with the machine now that they had it. Classic cavalry doctrine calls for the Sheridan to operate in support
(protection) of reconnaissance patrols, that is, to protect armored personnel carriers against enemy tanks or
artillery. But there were no enemy tanks in Vietnam (or
none that faced the Americans, anyway), so the Sheridan could be used in assault, pure and simple. The
classic Cav troop is nine vehicles, so Patton's people
decided to sprinkle the Sheridans in amongst the APCs.
Reconnoitering a road, then, the formation would look
like this:

APC S APC APC S APC S APC APC

Or, moving through a wood, on line:

---

*things we need to do our work more effectively. Give
us this day a gun that will fire 10,000 rounds a minute,
a napalm which will burn for a week. Help us to bring
death and destruction wherever we go, for we do it in
thy name and therefore it is meet and just. We thank
thee for this war, fully mindful that while it is not the
best of all wars, it is better than no war at all. We
remember that Christ said, 'I came not to send peace
but a sword,' and we pledge ourselves in all our works
to be like Him. Forget not the least of thy children, as
they hide from us in the jungles; bring them under our
merciful hand that we may end their suffering. In all
things, O God, assist us, for we do our noble work in
the knowledge that only with thy help can we avoid
the catastrophe of peace which threatens us ever. All
of which we ask in the name of thy son, George Patton.
Amen.*

*The reaction, according to Dr. Livingston, was swift. He
was relieved of his duties, confined to a trailer for forty-
eight hours, given a psychiatric examination, and sent
home. He received what is called a general discharge, and
is now practicing medicine at The Johns Hopkins
University.*

```
              APC
           APC
        APC
          S
          S
          S
        APC
           APC
              APC
```

It was lethally symmetrical. In Vietnam, the Sheridan could operate as a main battle tank, and in Vietnam the record of the Sheridan was very mixed. Some (not many) have used the word catastrophe. The Army contends, perhaps rightly, that the problems with the Sheridan were no greater than those with any new weapons system. And the Sheridan was a "weapons system" as surely as the scout cavalry of Genghis Khan was a weapons system. This tank, the Sheridan, was the latest, most elaborate refinement of a military tactic dating to Biblical times. Any dedicated armor commander can quote the line from Judges 1:19, "And the Lord was with Judah, and he drove out the inhabitants of the mountains; but he could not drive out the inhabitants of the valley because they had chariots of iron." What else was it but a chariot of iron? There was the Shillelagh missile and the 152-mm. gun and the airborne and swimming capabilities; but at root, now as then, it was an iron chariot. And the Army called it a weapons system, like the ABM or the Polaris.

The first time around in South Vietnam, the performance marks were not high, and the reasons had nothing to do with the Shillelagh, which was not deployed to Vietnam. It had to do with the highly sophisticated mechanisms. The first official report lists 16 major equipment failures, 123 circuit failures, 41 weapons misfires, 140 ammunition ruptures, 25 engine replacements, and persistent failure of the 152-mm. main gun. Sixty-four Sheridans were sent to Vietnam in February, 1969, and after the breakdowns were reported to the authorities in Washington, a new set of instructions was sent to the squadron commanders. Performance improved thereafter, as the men in the field made frequent checks for fuel spillage and vegetation-clogged air intakes, kept a high stockage level of spare periscopes, and were very, very careful in loading the highly flammable 152-mm. ammunition. Those were four of the new procedures detailed in a long list.

In partial explanation of the failures, the Army would cite the vehicle's long and complicated history. Development of the Sheridan was initiated in 1959, long before substantial American involvement in Vietnam. Indeed, it was not intended for a tropical environment at all. It was intended (in the Army's ominous phrase) for "the plains of Europe." This was the Army's rationale:

> A significant and immediate increase in mobile protected firepower is required to offset the quantitative and, perhaps, qualitative superiority of Soviet armored vehicles. Since tank gun development appears to be reaching the point of diminishing returns and a new parallel approach is essential, the potential of the guided missile should be exploited in order that a direct-fire, armored vehicle-mounted missile system can be available for operational use at the earliest possible date.

The operational requirements, the "roles and missions" in Army jargon, were written in 1958. There was then on the drawing board a machine called the T-92, the fruit of an armored board that assembled after World War Two to devise a means of protecting lightly armored scout vehicles. The role of these scouts was not to fight, but to reconnoiter; but in a tough spot, the board believed, they must have some means to protect themselves. The requirement was difficult because the value of the armored scout was (first) speed and (second) mobility. In World War Two, the scouts were often nothing more than a jeep equipped with a light machine gun; casualties were extremely high. So the idea was to reinforce the reconnaissance element, replace jeeps with well-armed tracked armored personnel carriers (APCs) supported by some kind of scout vehicle with a heavy gun. But to be effective, the latter had to accompany the former; no good, in other words, if the machine with the heavy gun had to stay behind as the APC swam the stream. In 1958, it was clear that with the T-92 the Army had just another conventional light tank. It wouldn't do. The doctrine now was very clear, and what the Army required was an armored reconnaissance *assault* vehicle.

In 1958 and 1959, as the Army contemplated a holocaust on the plains of Europe, there were four very tempting possibilities, and if they were realized it would revolutionize the utility of the cavalry. In short order, the four possibilities became requirements. First, the machine would have to be able to swim—"not the goddam Rhine," as Lieutenant Colonel Joseph Ameel, a systems staff officer in ACSFOR, later put it, "but a stream, a small river, and not at full flood . . . " In World War Two, the machines had frequently been obliged to wait for the bridge-builders before they could proceed; operations were delayed, opportunities missed. Second, to complement the airborne, the machine would have to be air-droppable by parachute. General Maxwell Taylor was chief of staff of the Army in 1958 and 1959, and Lieutenant General James Gavin was chief of research and development; both men were dedicated paratroopers and charter members of the airborne club. Partly for budgetary reasons, partly for sentiment, the Army was being "airbornized" to aid in quick deployment of troops. Taylor and Gavin, among others, saw the Sheridan as the chance to finally get an armored component for the paratroopers. Third, the development of guided

missiles was proceeding apace, and only a fool could
overlook the application to tanks—or, in the case of
what was to become the Sheridan, armored reconnaissance assault vehicles. Fourth, although this was to come
along a bit later, the bane of tankers since the invention
of the tank has been disposal of the artillery shells.
They were heavy (made of brass), expensive, and dangerous—fire-hot when ejected, and hazardous rolling
around the inside of a tank. In addition, the fumes gave
off an ammonia-like aroma, nearly noxious, which seriously reduced the combat effectiveness of the tank crew.
Further, because the brass was so expensive, on firing
ranges the casings were collected and sent back to the
factory for re-use, a complicated and inefficient practice.
So to eliminate these traditional disadvantages, the
Army would sponsor the development of a combustible
cartridge case which would self-destruct inside the tube;
no fuss, no muss, no bother. (The combustible cartridge
case, due to its developmental difficulties, now has a bad
name so with its genius for nomenclature the Army has
renamed it the non-metallic cartridge case.) As a collateral development to all this, the main gun would em-
brace Robert McNamara's principle of commonality.
It would fire both the missile and the 152-mm. artillery
round, and it would be called The Universal Combat
Vehicle Missile System, and if it worked it could be
fitted to all the tanks of the future.

It was a major enterprise, and encompassed a number
of companion developments. So promising was the Sheridan that the tankers took to the drawing board to re-
design the entire cavalry fleet. Work began on the M-113,
which was the classic armored personnel carrier, and
the M-114, which was the scout, both of which would
act in concert with the M-551, which was the Sheridan.
Therefore, there was one type of vehicle for point reconnaissance, one to ferry troops, and the third (the
Sheridan) for fire support. In each troop, moreover,
there would be a fourth vehicle containing a 4.2-inch

mortar. If you were a tank man, the possibilities were dazzling. Compared to World War Two—well, there was no comparison. And best of all was the Sheridan, equipped with the long-range, high-hit capability of the Shillelagh. It could defend the recon elements against enemy armor anywhere. Or it could as long as it got in the first shot. The Russian tank of the 1950s was the T-55, and the Sheridan could not stand up to it; neither could it stand against 50-caliber machine guns at short range. But if it got in its licks first with the Shillelagh or the 152-mm. main gun, the Sheridan would hold its own.

So it was designed as an air-ferried assault vehicle with a gun-launcher, capable of firing both the Shillelagh (itself still in the research and development phase) and the 152-mm. artillery shell, "the only one of its kind in any army in the world," a HEAT (high explosive, anti-tank) shell capable of penetrating any known armor. Packed into the gun would be highly sophisticated fire control and guidance equipment. There was also under development the high explosive multi-purpose round, the grim XM-409, whose objective was to provide a so-called soft target capability—people, unarmored vehicles, flimsy structures, and the like. In Vietnam, there was added yet a third shell, the cannister round, a blunt-nosed bullet which exploded on impact and distributed 9,800 "fleshettes," which look like little roofing nails with barbs on the end; the cannister round was for use against people, or personnel.* Perhaps more important,

---

*Armored officers speak very highly of the cannister round. One of them described a battle in Vietnam in which cannisters were used, and after the fight nine men were found dead in one bunker, all of them eliminated by one burst. On another occasion a Communist was found dying and no one could determine the cause. An autopsy was performed and a single fleshette was found in a vital organ. Of 9,800 fleshettes, one had hit its mark. There are officers in Vietnam who believe that cannister rounds are worth a platoon or more of infantry.

and another legacy from World War Two, was the tank's night-fighting ability. A high-power searchlight had been developed, but tankers were understandably reluctant to use it. So the engineers invented the ambient scope, which acquired light from the stars or the moon and concentrated it, and to augment that there was the Xenon searchlight, which, with a pink filter, is exceedingly powerful and difficult to spot from afar. It gave the Cav an around-the-clock fighting ability.

There was a continuing problem with soft targets, so the Army produced a white phosphorus round, the XM-410, which was meant to be employed for screening, marking, and fire-making. But it is also useful against troops: when white phosphorus touches flesh it burns non-stop. There was, in addition, a target-practice training round, the XM-411, which was developed as a cheaper alternative to the XM-409 and the XM-410. Nor was that all. Development of three more ammunition rounds was initiated in the mid-1960s, among them a grenade launcher which would dispense smoke. So to recapitulate, the Sheridan would bring to bear against its enemies a missile, a heavy gun (with its different types of shells), a 50-caliber machine gun, a 7.62-caliber machine gun, the white phosphorus, and the grenade launcher, plus the scopes to see at night. It was a machine of seventeen tons, capable of being dropped from the air and, once dropped, of swimming on a lake (if it was placid) or a river (so long as the current did not exceed 3.8 knots).

The Army contends that there are eleven different state-of-the-art improvements in the Sheridan, a vehicle that would do for the cavalry what *Madame Bovary* did for the novel. Not least of these was the Shillelagh missile, which early on acquired an independent life of its own. Shillelagh, lethal, eye-guided, was considered so promising that the Army developers wrote its specifications into Dream Tank, the MBT-70, the American main battle tank scheduled for the 1970s, if the American economy can support its deployment (the cost is $700,-000 a tank) and the MBT currently in use, the M-60, and work on that proceeded in 1964 and is still proceeding. One mentions it at all to make clear that the Shillelagh was an instrument apart from the Sheridan, and indeed in terms of priorities it may have been (for a time, anyway) the more important of the two.

The development of a weapons system is a highly complex matter, and the more requirements there are, the more complex it becomes. This is quite apart from technology. The addition of one requirement can reduce the effectiveness of another, and what is supposed to happen is that all the requirements are brought into balance. This in turn requires a very stern sense of priorities, and a precise understanding of what the machine is meant to do. Everyone must understand the roles and missions. The classic example of a weapons failure is the badly fudged TFX airplane (now the F-111), the fighter-bomber-reconnaissance aircraft which McNamara insisted be made compatible to both the Navy and the Air Force, both of which had different missions for the plane and different environments from which it flew (carriers in the one case, airfields in the other). So it was with the Sheridan. The troubles began when the Army added the airborne requirement. To be dropped from a C-130 transport aircraft on a parachute, the tank had to be light; but to withstand the shock on the ground, it had to be rugged.

In 1965, when the Army commenced to test the Sheridan, it was observed that the flywheel on the engine was fluttering. It was not equal to the load because it was made from aluminum, which is lighter than steel. But when it operated under heavy pressure, it began to warp and eventually to fail. (In Vietnam, the aluminum flywheel was junked altogether.) At the third airdrop test at Fort Knox, when the tank hit the ground, the floor dropped out. So the floor was taken out altogether and the bottom was cross reinforced: the machine was lightened by a few pounds, but at some cost to the safety of the crew. In 1959, when Sheridan doctrine was written, Army planners envisaged a war in Europe; it was decided that there was little need for armored protection on the floor because the scouts, not the Sheridans, would be out in front, in effect clearing the way of land mines. But in Vietnam, it was the Sheridans which were out in front and mines proved to be the principal enemy. So when the machines were sent to Vietnam, 1,000 pounds of armor was added to the floor, an improvement which had the effect of ruining the airdrop capability. Other concessions were made to increase the freeboard for floating. As one might expect, there were dead ends: in the beginning, the turret was constructed of aluminum, until the engineers discovered that so much aluminum was required to reach the desired protective levels that the turret ended up heavier than it would have been with steel.

What is gained by the swimming capability?

"Well," Colonel Ameel said, "it means that you don't have to build a bridge."

How disadvantageous is it to compromise the air-droppability?

"The airborne is less crucial now than it used to be," Colonel Ameel said.

In 1970, the cost leveled off at about $335,000 a tank, a sum rationalized largely on the basis that it is about three-quarters of a million dollars less than a helicopter. But the Sheridan's armor can be penetrated by a B-40 rocket (the type used by the enemy in Vietnam) or by a 50-caliber machine gun. It cannot stand against any of the big Russian tanks in a head-to-head, and its complex, often jittery mechanisms make it difficult to use in places like jungles or deserts, where on the one hand the engine exhausts become clogged and overheated and on the other the combination of sand and heat make it intolerable to operate. It has been tested in Alaska and found wanting, and the specifications warn that the speed over water is but 3.8 knots. Two requirements established in 1959 have been waived. One of these was silence, obviously a critical element in a reconnaissance vehicle. Tests in Panama disclosed that the whine of the engine could be heard three miles away and the "signature" of the rooster tail (exhaust smoke) was definite and unique.

There were technical troubles from the beginning. The Shillelagh with its 17,000 parts was satisfactory, but there were continuing troubles with the artillery cartridges. Because they burned inside the tube, they were highly vulnerable outside it; that is, because the shell was not encased in brass it was sensitive to shocks and heat, results of the sort of accidents that are commonplace in combat. Tankers insist that the brass-encased shell is even more dangerous in the event of a direct hit, but is not as volatile otherwise. Apart from that, the Army testing agencies found that the destruct mechanism, while excellent, was not quite excellent enough. Small bits of smoldering residue often remained inside the tube, and when another shell was inserted that shell tended to explode. Compared with these matters, problems with toxic fumes and flashbacks were as nothing. The Army devised a scavenger system to eliminate the residue, and modified the breech in order to accommodate the scavenger. As late as 1967, eight years after conception, the Army considered junking the gun and remaking it to accept conventional rounds. But partly on a hint from the Navy (which has a similar apparatus on its own big guns) the scavenger system was devised and installed and now after each firing jets of CO_2 gas are directed through the muzzle.

The gun is operable, but it requires a good deal of care, and problems remain. As the Army elaborated:

"Sensing at ranges of less than 1,000 meters is difficult due to firing shock, vehicle displacement and smoke obscuration." There is a bit of uncertainty remaining with the marvelous night light (the gunner is blinded by the flash of the gun reflected into the light), and there are safety measures hard to maintain in combat. For example: No foot soldier must be within five hundred yards of the tanks in a forty-five degree arc when the missile is fired. It is sometimes subject to shortfall. Due to carbon monoxide released by the missile, the Army recommends that there be no more than four firings a day; more would be dangerous to the health of the crew.

Colonel Merritte W. Ireland, Patton's chief of staff in the 11th Cavalry Regiment, accurately points out that nothing is invulnerable in warfare. The perfect tank does not exist. There is nothing that cannot be got at, and that includes the Sheridan. For himself, he is satisfied with the performance. But both the project officer, Ameel, and Ireland agree that maintenance, particularly in a combat environment more difficult than Vietnam (where a unit may go weeks without a contact), will be a continuing problem. The Sheridan is fully computerized and "boxed." That is, when something goes wrong a light flashes and the commander takes out one box and replaces it with another. It's called modular construction, but in combat—heavy use with high wear-and-tear —repairs are going to have to be made in the field. Each black box is more complex than a television set. It takes fourteen months for the Army to train a warrant officer to repair the missile system alone. Ameel: "Where are these guys going to come from in the future?" The ordinary buck sergeant can't be trained in a system as complex as the Sheridan. It is easy to operate, as Ameel says, but hellishly difficult to fix. In the future, the Sheridan will be filled with sensing devices, electronic target-acquisition gear, and all the rest of the exotica now under development by Army R&D. Who is going to maintain all of it?

But the Army felt the Sheridan was one hell of a tank. All of that is clear enough—clear, as they say, to the meanest intelligence. It was, and is, somewhat less clear precisely what the mission of the Sheridan was to be, and how significant that mission was. It was clearly not a machine crucial to the waging of guerrilla warfare, so its utility lay in what is described as conventional war. But it could not do battle with the Soviet main battle tank, unless it could fire first. While the Sheridan was fast at forty-three miles an hour, it was not *that* fast and no faster, in any case, than the best Soviet tanks (or British tanks, for that matter). It was maneuverable and light, it swam and could be dropped from the air, but in reality it was neither a pure reconnaissance vehicle nor a pure assault vehicle nor a pure heavy weapons carrier. It was reminiscent of the automobile they called the "hard-top convertible." Definitions were troublesome, but Colonel Paul A. Simpson, the project manager for the Sheridan in the late nineteen-sixties, had a go at it before Representative Samuel Stratton's armed services investigating subcommittee: "It is not a tank," the colonel said. "It is a lightweight armored vehicle. We have no other vehicle, that is a combat vehicle, that is air-droppable." He might have added, but did not, that no other nation did either; the Sheridan is unique in the history of warfare, armored or otherwise. When Colonel Simpson went on to explain the mission, the ambiguities and inconsistencies grew along with the explanation. The machine was oriented towards Europe, in part to replace the M-60 main battle tank supporting American cavalry regiments along the Czechoslovakian border. But by the Army's logic, the Sheridan was not a tank. How could it replace one? Colonel Simpson told the subcommittee that the M-60s were there in the first place only because the Cav did not have reconnaissance ve-

hicles; the TO&E, the table of organization and equipment, called for recon vehicles, not tanks. More than
that, as Major General W. C. Gribble, the deputy assistant chief of staff for force development (ACSFOR), told
the subcommittee: "I think it is worth emphasizing that
all the important decisions that have been made during
the progress of the tank programs have been made in
the general environment of an ominous threat . . . "
That is, a Soviet threat, on the plains of Europe. More
plainly: a Soviet invasion, but one bolder (apparently)
than accomplished in Czechoslovakia in 1968.

Simpson had made the essential, breathtakingly simple point: the United States did not have a reconnaissance vehicle as required in cavalry doctrine; if you have
the M-113 and the M-114, you must then have the M-551
(Sheridan), and no matter which preceded which; to do
otherwise would be like having cruisers and destroyers
without battleships or Wynken and Blynken without
Nod. There is a symmetry to armored warfare which
must be understood and obeyed. The United States did
not have a reconnaissance vehicle as required in Cav
doctrine, and it is immaterial that no other nation did
either. What is important is that the requirement was
there, and because it was there it was imperative that it
be satisfied. Gribble: "The Army does not today have a
vehicle which is specifically designed to meet the doc-
trinal requirements of the armored cavalry. The Sheridan is that system. In the absence of the Sheridan,
armored cavalry units have been equipped with tanks.
As a result there are tank battalions which do not have
modern tanks. The situation is justified at the particular
moment because the armored cavalry regiments are stationed in Europe. The armored divisions are in training.
But it is a situation which we are very anxious to correct."*

*Interesting argument. The "urgent" (the word appears
elsewhere in the testimony) need for rapid deployment of*

The saga of the Sheridan is not ended. Eleven years after conception, the machine has cost the American government something over one billion dollars. Estimates range from $1.2 billion to $1.5 billion, and this for a "weapons system" which was supposed to be fielded in 1964 and is not entirely satisfactory today. In the complex of weapons in the American arsenal—ships, aircraft, vehicles, men—the Sheridan played, by any estimate, a minor supporting role, and the heart of the matter is that it is of very limited utility, even granting the proposition that tanks have any tactical role at all in post-1970 warfare. At any event, the Sheridan is precisely what an anonymous Pentagon official said it was: "The Rolls-Royce of tanks."**

The limitations of the Sheridan were known to segments of the Army, notably the Army Material Command Technical Committee (TECOM) and the Army Munitions Command (MUCOM). TECOM, in fact, recommended a slowdown in development and all along the line looked at the Sheridan with a skeptical eye. Or, no, not a skeptical eye: As the tester, it wanted to be certain that the vehicle and its components were combat-ready and safe. This was no simple matter, because of the eleven different state-of-the-art improvements, all of which were proceeding more or less concurrently, and all the time the tankers themselves were marvelling at the machine which was unique in any arsenal. MUCOM, as the devel-

---

the Sheridan, according to Gribble and others, was the necessity to return the M-60 tanks to the armored divisions. The M-60s had been doing double duty and now it was time to straighten it out; there were not enough M-60s to go around. But, as a matter of fact, at the time the Army was selling M-60s to Austria. So there was no urgent need at all. The argument is witless.

**I have called it a Buick. The Pentagon man called it a Rolls. In fact, it was built by the Cadillac Division of General Motors.

oper and the arm spending the money, was anxious to get the Sheridan out of the shop and into the field. There were other developments coming along, and the Sheridan was becoming an embarrassment. The House subcommittee chaired by Representative Stratton looked into the development of the Sheridan and concluded: "The facts as developed by this subcommittee make almost unavoidable the conclusion that so much time and money had been spent in developing the Sheridan/ Shillelagh system that the developers felt irrevocably committed to production. Under such circumstances, the project manager became more a captive than a manager of the project, and might understandably feel that a failure of the project to reach fruition could be interpreted as demonstrating his own lack of managerial skills and thus affect his Army career. Such a condition must inevitably result in management of doubtful quality and questionable management concepts."

Of course the subcommittee was correct. Weapons systems tend to acquire a life of their own. The ingenuity of American industry is so great that the odds on solving seemingly insoluble technical problems are very favorable. The theory is that if you wait it out, the solution will in time present itself. Add to that the extraordinary sums of money available to the military for research, development, and procurement and it is, or ought to be, no mystery why a Sheridan system proceeds, and proceeds at the rate of $100 million a year. It is very difficult, once the contracts are let and the development begins, to drop out of the game—particularly in the instance of the Sheridan, where the crucial question is not whether a tank with a self-destructing combustible cartridge case is useful, but whether it is needed and how great that need is. Priorities never seem to enter into it, except in the case of monstrously expensive weapons like the nuclear airplane or the Cheyenne helicopter (and the Cheyenne may not be dead yet). The defense apparatus is so complicated and so rich that, as Vice Admiral Hyman Rickover once observed, it is literally impossible to put an accurate price tag on weapons. TECOMs merge with MUCOMs, material commands with combat development commands, Army project managers with civilian auditors, the joint staff with systems analysis, users with producers, soldiers with civilians, and politicians all wound up together in a welter of conflicting loyalties and responsibilities. Gilbert W. Fitzhugh, the board chairman of Metropolitan Life, who headed up the Nixon Administration's commission to study the Pentagon, put it excellently: "Everybody is somewhat responsible for everything and nobody is completely responsible for anything. So there's no way of assuming authority, responsibility or accountability. There is nobody you can point your finger to if anything goes wrong, and there is nobody you can pin a medal on if it goes right, because everything is everybody's business. . . . They spend their time coordinating with each other and shuffling paper back and forth and that's what causes all the red tape and big staffs in the department. Nobody can do anything without checking with seven other people."

The common interest of all of them is to *get the project out*, get it running, get it out of the plant and into the field, because there are all the new projects coming along. Keep the General Accounting Office and Bureau of the Budget off your back, and keep running. The nation needs its defense. The soldier wants perfect safety, or something as close to perfect safety as he can reach, and that is the reason for the complexity of the process; that, and the abundance of money. No soldier will voluntarily eliminate a weapons system because *you never know;* you never know what might make the difference.

The technological revolution affects the Army as it affects the rest of society. While it may be logical to say that the tank occupies the same position as the horse in World War Two, no tank man will believe it. Give up armor? While the Soviets still have the T-34? The guns become larger, the armor plate thicker, the mechanics more complicated, and costs rise. Put a missile on it, and a sensing system to complement the missile. *Stay in the game.*

"Look," said the colonel as we walked back from an interview at the Pentagon. "You've got to understand that none of this happens in a vacuum. We aren't just doing this to *do* it, I mean for our own amusement or anything."

"No," I said.

"You've got to estimate the *threat*."

"Of course," I said.

"And the fact is, there is a threat."

"Right," I said.

"I mean, you know."

"What's that?"

"The Soviets are working on the same damn things."

So the tank survives, fighting a rear-guard action now but prevailing. Obsolete, really; too costly, and bound to be replaced in time by helicopters. If you describe an armed helicopter as an airborne tank, what do you call the tank? A land-bound helicopter? At a time of budgetary restraint, the tankers are going to lose the game; the civilians won't go along with the MBT-70 and Sheridan has been an embarrassment. There are those voices, but you will not find them in the armor branch.

"Nothing in the last twenty-five years has replaced anything else," Colonel Ameel said, smiling. "We do not eliminate weapons, we improve them. Let me tell you something: if you are going to occupy *ground*, you are going to need a tank. I don't know of a war yet that we've won by"—the smile again, hands moving across the tabletop—"backing up."

But they say that helicopters will replace tanks. Much faster, more maneuverable . . .

"If you want to *take* and *occupy* a position," Ameel said, "you are not going to do it with a helicopter. Hell, I can demonstrate the value of tanks over helicopters on cost-effective grounds alone. Look, a chopper costs one point two million, right? A Sheridan only costs three . . . hundred . . . thousand! Well, I can go in there and make a hell of a case on those grounds alone. A hell of a case. And when we get finished *improving* the Sheridan . . ."

Improving?

"Huh! We've got a hell of a lot of new stuff coming along. Ever heard of the beehive missile? Well, we're working on a mechanism for *command detonation*."

The budget of the Defense Department is an extraordinary document, an inch thick and a pound or so in weight, and in 1970 it was accompanied by a handy précis containing the views of the new Secretary, the former Wisconsin Congressman, Melvin Laird. Still, no one—not even an accountant, or perhaps particularly an accountant—can read the budget and gain anything from it, so serpentine and fleecy are the contents. The numbers are meaningless except as guideposts to the order of magnitude; more interesting is the rationale.*

A note on the military-industrial-academic complex. There are 22,000 major corporate defense contractors in the United States, and 100,000 subcontractors. There are defense plants or installations in 363 of the 435 Congressional districts, some of which depend absolutely for their livelihood on the war business. The best known example is the South Carolina constituency of L. Mendel Rivers, the chairman of the House Armed Services Committee. It contained, at last count, the Charleston Army Depot, the Charleston Naval Hospital, the Charleston Shipyard, the

The Defense Department lives in a world of menace, and the least of it in Southeast Asia. The principal menace is International Communism, on land, at sea, and in

---

Charleston Naval Station, the Beaufort Naval Hospital, the Charleston Naval Supply Center, the Charleston Naval Weapons Station, the Charleston Fleet Ballistics Missile Submarine Training Center, the Charleston Polaris Missile Facility, Atlantic; the Marine Corps Air Station, the Marine Corps Recruit Depot (Parris Island), and Charleston Air Force Base. During the five years since Rivers became committee chairman, factories have been built by General Electric, Avco, Lockheed, McDonnell Douglas, and J. P. Stevens. United Aircraft is waiting in the wings with a helicopter plant, and all in all (according to a report in Look *Magazine) some fifty-five per cent of the region's payrolls are federal dollars, either military or industrial.*

Retired military officers are a very helpful tool to the industrialists. Senator Proxmire has disclosed the relevant data: more than 2,000 retired senior officers (Army colonel, Navy captain, and above) employed by the 100 largest defense contractors. It is nothing new. In 1959, Senator Paul Douglas assembled a list of 768 former senior officers in similar employ. Following World War Two and the Korean war, MacArthur went to Remington Rand, Bedell Smith to American Machine and Foundry, Bradley to Bulova, and Bull Halsey to International Standard Electric. These men lent prestige to the corporations, among other things. The other things which might make a high-ranking military officer valuable to civilian industry was described with uncommon candor by Owen D. Young of the Radio Corporation of America, in a memo written after World War One. Young was looking for a suitable chairman of RCA.

"1st. He should be well-known both nationally and internationally and he should have made such a place for himself as would enable him to speak with authority either to foreign governments or to our own government.

"2nd. He should not have been previously identified with politics because that would mean party alignment and partisan reaction.

"3rd. He should not have been identified with Wall Street or the money interests because it is important that the American people should accept the Radio Corporation as

the air; at home and abroad. There is a strategic nuclear
threat, a general purpose forces threat, and an insurgency threat, all of them coming under the general cate-

---

*an organization of service to American interests at home
and abroad rather than as an organization primarily to
make a profit for Wall Street interests.*

*"4th. He should have had administrative experience and
if possible business experience.*

*"5th. He should be well-known in Washington and in a
position to appear before committees of Congress and
before the Department and have his statements of fact
accepted without question. It is particularly important in
this connection that no one should be able to question his
Americanism, such as they have done in several instances
in the case of our international bankers.*

*"6th. He should be a man of public position whom to
attack would be bad politics rather than good politics."*

*That is truly a seminal statement (it appears in Gleason
D. Archer's book,* The History of Radio to 1926, *and is cited
by the political scientist Samuel Huntington among
others), as clear as crystal; it was written in the days
before public relations. It is doubtful today if a corporation like RCA would think of hiring a man like Earle
Wheeler or William Westmoreland. A Texas oil company
or a right-wing newspaper chain might, but not any large
corporation whose image was one of . . . neutrality. Where
is there a general who could speak before Congress and
"have his statements of fact accepted without question"?
In 1970, generals and colonels who go to work for defense
contractors work as inside men, not outside; their presence
is required in the conference room or over the luncheon
table, not before committees of Congress.*

*The enormous quantities of federal money that have
been pumped into defense industries have had a debilitating effect, like feeding sweets to a diabetic. Companies like
Lockheed and North American are economic dinosaurs,
sluggish and with their competitive edge gone. This is the
judgment of Ernest Fitzgerald, the civilian accountant fired
by the Air Force after his close inquiries into defense contracts. The federal money has bloated and swollen companies like Lockheed; they survive as clients of the defense
department, and will be forced to reorganize or go bankrupt.*

gory of THE THREAT TO NATIONAL SECURITY. Lately, the
soldiers have identified an internal threat as well, and
true to their style they have written a doctrine and set
up an office in the Pentagon to deal with it. Under
pressure (they say) from civilians in the Justice Department, the Army has assembled data on dangerous characters and put it on the computers at Fort Holabird, an
aerie in Maryland outside Washington, D.C. Theoreti-
cians at the Command and General Staff College at Leavenworth have devised courses that deal (gingerly, as far
as one can tell) with the homegrown revolutionaries.
There was a cry of alarm when the Holabird operation
was disclosed, and Congressional investigators learned
that the data banks there were something of a gargan-
tuan dossier on all sorts of citizens: S.D.S. leaders, black
militants, journalists, Quakers, "peaceniks," and (re-
portedly) a few Congressmen. It should have surprised
no one: the Army is bureaucratically and temperamen-
tally incapable of small and tidy activities (even granting
that the Holabird operation is properly a military mission, which it assuredly is not). The Army has too much
money and too many men and its definition of "suffi-
ciency" is always generous. Army officers have said that
they wanted nothing to do with monitoring civilian
activities, but when urban and student riots began and
national guard units (and in the case of the Detroit
riot, the regular airborne) were called, they felt they
had to have their own intelligence net. At Fort Lewis,
for example, Army agents are "penetrating" the antiwar
movement, which centers around a coffee shop called
The Shelter Half. The Army has argued that its communications are in a language—presumably Army jargon—
that only its own people can understand, both literally
and figuratively; by this analysis, FBI reports are useless and local police inept anyway. The G-2 (intelligence)
for the 82nd Airborne wants his information in a military context. The civilians pushed them into it, went

the argument, and therefore with civilan backing they threw out the dragnet. The Army claims it is dismantling the civilian dossiers at Holabird, but if Congress is wise it will continue its investigations; military activites are rarely dismantled altogether.

"The first requirement we faced upon assuming office was to reappraise the spectrum of threats that exist in the world today," Secretary Laird told the Senate Armed Services Committee early in 1970. "These threats dictate to a large degree how we should implement our basic policies in conjunction with our allies." The quintessence of menace, as any reader of Poe or Pinter knows very well, is mystery. The unknown is more ominous than the known, and in analyzing world-wide threats to the peace and security of the United States a man need only point to the mysterious purposes of both the Soviet Union and Communist China. Hostility is taken for granted; what one is after is intent. The Chinese are an exquisite example, the equivalent of Harold Pinter's silent, glowering breakfast-table figure, a presence with no past nor future, just a menacing immediacy. With the Chinese, it is very difficult to know at any given time who is running the country and therefore what impulses govern. What is the Chinese national interest? It appears to be an easy matter to accurately calculate weapons capacities, bombs and their delivery systems. What if the Chinese, collectively, are *insane*? What if Mao Tsetung, as Joseph Alsop has suggested, is paranoid? So lurking in the background of all the estimates of enemy intentions (you need read no further than Marx and Lenin to grasp the general drift) is inscrutable China —armed, as they say, and dangerous.

It is interesting in reading the Laird document to observe that while U.S. programs are often delayed and misfired, the Soviet programs are usually moving ahead very nicely. There are no TFXs in the Soviet arsenal, or, if there are, we do not know of them. Laird: "The Soviet strategic threat is impressive and it is growing. We now estimate the number of SS-9 Intercontinental Ballistics Missiles deployed or under construction to be over 275, rather than the 230 as I reported publicly less than a year ago. The number of SS-11 ICBMs has also increased significantly. The Soviets continue to test improvements in offensive weapons . . . " The technological threat? "In the long term, one of the most serious threats confronting the United States is the large and growing research and development effort of the Soviet Union." Why? "The implications of this Soviet effort for our future security cannot be clearly foreseen at this time. Because the Soviet Union is a closed society, they can conduct their military research and development programs behind a thick veil of secrecy, making it difficult for us to assess their programs in a timely manner. However, we have seen evidence of this technology in the new systems they are deploying, including the Foxbat Interceptor Aircraft, nuclear power ballistics and attack submarines, and other impressive evidence."

We have seen evidence. The point is that it is a threat all the way around the box. Polaris submarines? The Soviets have prototypes, and are building more. Minuteman Missiles? The Soviets have the SS-9 and are going to the SS-11. Aircraft? Flagon is at least as good as the F-111 and behind Flagon there is Foxbat and behind Foxbat—what?—Foxbat II. The infantry? "At the present time all of the Soviet Union ground divisions deployed in eastern Europe are combat-ready. A considerable number of divisions in the Soviet Union, including several airborne divisions, are also considered to be fully ready or in a state that would permit very rapid mobilization. . . . A high density of tanks, many of which are over fifteen years old, provides the Soviets on all fronts with heavy direct fire support in place of conventional artillery . . . " But if one takes comfort from that, one would be wrong. "Recent changes have resulted in a substantial increase in the number of artillery tubes available to the Soviet ground forces." And the Soviets are not the end of it. The secretary speaks next of East Europe, and the threat there, and then goes on to the Far East: "North Korea is a militarily strong country that has demonstrated a dangerous aggressiveness and hostility toward South Korea and the U.S. It has some 350,000 troops and an effective air force of more than 500 combat aircraft . . . "

Lord Salisbury: "If you believe the doctors, nothing is wholesome; if you believe the theologians, nothing is innocent; if you believe the soldiers, nothing is safe." When estimating a potential threat, which in the American system means defending a budget, the style is deep pessimism. In estimating more or less danger, the tilt will always be to more; the military man wants all the support he can get, and then he wants more. In 1970, accordingly, the proposed budget was $77 billion to meet the entire spectrum of threats, and you could divvy those up any way you wanted: put one way, it was $7 billion for strategic forces, $27 billion for general purpose forces, $5 billion for intelligence and communications; put another way, there was $24 billion for the Army, $22 billion for the Navy, and $24 billion for the Air Force; put yet a third way, there was $22 billion for military personnel, $21 billion for operations and maintenance, $20 billion for procurement, and $7 billion for research and development, test and evaluation. And none of the figures add up.

Where is the corrective? Paul Warnke, the brilliant and original lawyer who served as the assistant secretary of defense for international security affairs in the Johnson Administration, thinks the answer lies in stronger, more tough-minded civilians. Warnke does not believe there is very much wrong with the present system, or the soldiers who run it. "They are really remarkable men," he said not long ago. "They have extraordinary dedication to the country and to the uniform and it is their job to find threats. What else do we expect them to find?" Before the battle they are natural pessimists, during it dedicated optimists, and either way responsible for the country's security. Any military man can find a use for an object of war. Warnke was (and is) bemused by revelations of deficiencies in the TFX airplane and the Sheridan tank, events which revealed in his opinion nothing of very great importance. The point about both machines was not that they wouldn't work (given enough money, American industry can in time make anything work) but that they weren't needed. Warnke supplied a Naval metaphor: the Soviets penetrate the Mediterranean with their fleet, and the U.S. Navy counters with a proposal to send its own at flank speed. "Well, what do we do then?" Warnke asked. "Hold a regatta?"

The mechanism for control is there. What has happened, according to Warnke and others, is that the civilians have declined to use it. Military men, very adroit at Congressional liaison and with an annual budget of $27 million to spend on public relations, have dictated tactics and interpreted strategy; civilians have never taken hold of the weapons development process, with the result that the military dominates that, too. I cannot produce the document to prove it, but my suspicion is that weapons priorities are fought out within branches of one service, not between the services themselves; the result of that is a procurement process which ignores *national* defense. In the Army, an infantry or armored officer reckons that it is his branch and his branch alone that stands between the country and Armageddon. But it is the civilians who should be called to account, because it is the civilians who permitted the process to spin out of control.

Today, the military appears to lag behind in its thinking, as it has always lagged behind. It is still preparing for the world of John F. Kennedy, when the United States was prepared to "pay any price, bear any burden" in defense of "the free world." The military takes its key from civilian leaders, and throughout the nineteen-sixties those leaders have cited the Communist menace as the engine driving American foreign policy. Richard Nixon declares that the United States will not accept defeat in Vietnam, a statement fully consistent with those of Johnson and Kennedy before him. Elsewhere, in the State Department and in Henry Kissinger's workshop, there are other voices offering other definitions. But that is not policy. There is a Nixon Doctrine, but it is ambiguous enough to yield three different interpretations from three general officers queried on its meaning. "So what do you expect of a soldier?" Warnke said. "He bases his judgments on what he considers to be national policy." In other words, he follows the Constitution to the letter. What separates the military man from the rest of us is that the military man still believes what he hears from the White House and from the Vice President: to wit, Communism is a menace and the United States has the right and the duty to oppose it. The world is chancy, and the American Army can make it stable, rational.

In ten years of war in Indo-China the military man has sought victory as it was defined (or not defined) by the civilians. Lacking firm control in the essentials, the soldiers supplied their own war aims and the means of achieving them. In the early nineteen-sixties, while Robert McNamara struggled with the Joint Chiefs of Staff to persuade them to testify in favor of the nuclear test ban treaty, the Vietnam war enlarged and grew under rules of engagement that were not monitored. McNamara's effort with the chiefs sprang from noble motives but as a practical matter was feckless, an enterprise which expended his own valuable credits and diverted attention from the war, whose really important issues— small details in another context—were decided by military men. A former Pentagon official and admirer of Mc-Namara put the proposition this way: "All Bob had to do was *tell* those guys to go up to the Hill and testify [on the test-ban treaty]. McNamara tried to persuade them of something they really didn't believe, that the treaty was a plus for American security. They wanted to be told, and told not only by McNamara but by the President. They wanted to be told, 'This is national policy.' The fact of the matter is that civilian control was largely a problem in McNamara's mind." It sounds a little too pat, supposing too much discipline on the part of a soldier, and minimizing the often hypnotic effect senior military men have on the American population. But as a hard kernel of fact, it is probably accurate. In the nineteen-sixties, by this analysis, the eyes of the civilians were on the wrong sparrows. Political timidity inhibited the wisest of them, and military influence was permitted to grow unchecked. Under the American system, the civilians have to control the military because there is no mechanism for the military to control themselves.

SEVEN

Futures

The war will end and the Army will endure, a volunteer force if necessary, a citizen army if possible. The central question now is the definition of the mission of the Army, which is to say the future of counter-revolutionary warfare. Does the Army organize itself to fight a land war in Europe, or does it envisage (as John F. Kennedy evidently did) a series of brushfire wars, local insurgencies in which American military power is brought to bear on the side of whoever appears friendliest to the U.S. interest. This central question turns on the lessons learned in Vietnam.

The war and its meaning dominate the Army today, dividing it along many lines, but primarily according to age and rank. Older, senior officers tend to look upon Vietnam as a historical deviation not to be repeated, a mistake better forgotten. "I will be damned if I will permit the U.S. Army, its institutions, its doctrine and its traditions to be destroyed just to win this lousy war," was the way a senior American general in Vietnam put it. Younger men believe that Vietnam is the face of the future, and the Army must deal with it or perish. The subject is extremely complicated in their minds. While many of the older men regard the war as an aberration, they often add that if the Army had been permitted to fight it properly, then it could have been won—"Just two divisions in Laos, two lousy divisions." They mean by that a total national commitment, and a policy encouraging the allies to carry the struggle to the homeland of the enemy (by this analysis, most of Cambodia, Laos, and North Vietnam). Many of the younger professionals view it precisely the other way around: the United States could have won by carrying the fight to the guerrilla, by attacking the roots of the tree (in one colonel's phrase), not the branches. For the older men, the villains tend to be timorous civilians and the left-wing press; for the younger men, they are the tradition-bound senior generals and the craven press. For one group, it is the arrogance of McNamara; for the other, the rigidity of Westmoreland. Only the genuine radicals, few in number and not organized, see the war as a fundamentally impossible mission for the United States. One man reads Mao, Giap, and Che and insists they contain the blueprint for American success; another man reads the same books and concludes the United States can't win.

The central lesson? For the professional soldier it is not that the war was unwinnable, but that American power was not applied at the right time in the right places, either by bombing the North or by shifting to a guerrilla strategy. The war was not in either case intractable, merely difficult and made more so by the foolishness of those who were managing it. There were other difficulties as well. William Westmoreland, in a bitter speech at the Lincoln Academy of Illinois, said early in 1970:

The armed forces of the United States have never failed our country on the field of battle. Starting with our own

revolution, we have never lost a war. I ask you in all
humility, and yet with a deep sense of pride, "What
more could you ask of your soldiers?" Your Army can
accomplish for an extended period only those missions
that are accepted by our citizenry for whom the Army
exists to support. . . . The strength and vitality of a
democratic society depends on an enlightened elec-
torate. . . . But because national security is everyone's
concern, most everyone joins in the loud debate. Some
speak from knowledge; others do not. Yet all proclaim
authority. *Military leaders, however, are singularly*
qualified by education, experience, and profession as a
group to address military aspects of national security
problems thoroughly, competently, and without equivo-
cation. And that is their responsibility under law.
[Italics added]

Westmoreland is not Douglas MacArthur, either by
temperament or intellect; he is not a genius as a field
commander, and the principles of Leavenworth are deep
in his bones ("without equivocation"). But he has a very
strong streak of decency, and an even stronger one of
responsibility. No special insight is needed to see what
Westmoreland is getting at, and no surprise to learn that,
as he looks at it in retrospect, he would have resigned his
command on the issue of the management, or mismanage-
ment, of the war—he would have resigned, he says now,
if he had been in overall charge of the military effort
in Vietnam. But he was not. The ambassador had the
political war and Admiral Sharp had the air war and
the Vietnamese had their sovereignty and what COMUS-
MACV had was control of American ground forces and
the advisory effort to Saigon's army. With the war divided, the White House ruled; or thought it did. Westmoreland put the thesis with care and considerable cir-
cumspection to an interviewer from *U.S. News & World*
Report: "One of the interesting things about this war is
that responsibility has been divided. . . . No U.S. authority short of the President had cognizance over the entire

conflict. Therefore, the President had to get into all
sorts of details. And he had many pressures brought to
bear on him . . . "

Now senior military men want to lay down new rules,
a new definition of the role of the Army. No more Vietnams, where the armed forces carry the can for civilian
stupidities. The next war is going to be directed by the
military, so "those who sacrifice the most" (in Westmoreland's phrase) will not be abandoned to politicians
or journalists. If you believe, as soldiers do, that the
institution of the Army is singular in American society,
then the implications are very ominous indeed. A theory of stab-in-the-back (which is what it is coming to)
is followed logically by savior politics: a man on horse-
back. Westmoreland is not that man, and personally
he would be mortified at the suggestion. But it is a
notion which proceeds inescapably from the Vietnam
tragedy, and what will surely become a search for scapegoats. Who is responsible?

Soldiers fasten on the civilians. A Rand Corporation
analyst (and a former soldier) believes the major civilian failure was the failure to supply war aims. "What
isn't understood is that we do not have a German General Staff. To the Americans, all wars are defensive wars
—done in response to someone else's thrust. We don't
move first. And in Vietnam, we mistook exhortation for
policy. There was still something very romantic about
the American Army—*Roll those tanks through the Michelin Plantation!* These things were entirely irrelevant to
winning the Vietnam war. Saigon was characterized by
reactive planning, second-strike mentality, and contingency plans for every conceivable contingency." In
Vietnam, the operations were the strategy but there was
no end point. There was no objective, in the Clause-
witzian sense, because the civilians in the White House
and the Pentagon did not know what it was they wanted,
beyond an independent anti-Communist (later non-

Communist and in 1970 partially-Communist) South Vietnam. There was no point at which a soldier could look about him and say, Mission Accomplished; not as long as there were still Vietnamese in Vietnam. Beyond that, the civilian leadership did not rally the country round the war; it insisted on both guns and butter, a short-term, short-sighted formulation that created awful psychological dilemmas, among both those who served and those who did not. Among them was the inequality of sacrifice. It was a bankrupt policy, fundamentally immoral and essentially divisive.

But when historians look into it, they will find that the civilians did not control the war in its most crucial aspects. First among these were ground combat operations, which set the tone of the war and ultimately turned the American public against it, beginning with Ben Suc and ending with My Lai. Was it the policy of successive American administrations to leave the rules of engagement to the military? A very senior official, with the war from the beginning, speaking slowly and somberly, explained: "We controlled the air war, all right. I mean, whether you bomb and where. But you can't control operations of battalions and regiments. We would have controlled it if we could, and we sure as hell —in retrospect—should have made the attempt. Search and destroy was wrong. Wrong. Wrong. It was a mistake. I couldn't get into the tactics. I was in the war [World War Two], but I never had one of these"—the official pointed sardonically to his chest, meaning the Combat Infantryman's Badge—"How could you go in there and talk to those guys who had been on the battlefield, *who had seen it when you hadn't seen it?*" The official shook his head. "No way."

The civilians, dovish now, believe they did not control enough; the soldiers, wounded and angry, believe they controlled too much. Or, more complicated than that: they believe the civilians controlled the strategy, and inhibited the tactics. To the civilians, the problem was seen as tactical; to the soldiers, it was strategic. So the soldier sees himself as used, then discarded, finally blamed. Congress hates the war, so it cuts the military budget; the press hates the war, so it exhumes My Lai; the students hate the war, so they foment revolution in the barracks.

This is the atmosphere in which the general staff is plotting the curve into the nineteen-seventies. What is happening at the Pentagon and elsewhere is that they are re-fighting the Vietnam war, reckoning where it went wrong and why, and certain in their bones that the Communists have one, two, many Vietnams in reserve. If so, how does the Army organize itself? What is the definition of national security? Where are the vital interests of the nation? Europe is there, and Europe is important; so is the Middle East. But what of the world's soft underbelly, South Asia, South America, and Africa? Most military men insist the responsibility for world order is still America's. That is the reason the Army fought in World War Two and Korea and Vietnam, and if you deny those imperatives, then what was the point of all the dead? Have Americans died in three wars for nothing? "The threat to Latin America is both real and apparent," said a senior general, and the Army intends to deal with that. One way or another.

They have erected a great stone statue at Fort Bragg, the heroic pose of the Green Beret, his eyes clear, his backbone straight, his index finger not on the trigger of the M-16 but on the safety catch. *We will pay any price, bear any burden, support any friend, oppose any foe, to assure the survival and success of liberty. . . .* The lyrics are John F. Kennedy's, and they are graven in brass in the lobby of the John F. Kennedy Special Warfare School (in 1969 the name was changed to the Institute for Military Assistance). The building is modern, low-slung; walk through the corridors in full light and the Green Berets are coming from class, huddled over a coffee talking about Oswald Spengler and Bernard Fall and Joe Namath. There are other nationalities present: Vietnamese, Laotians, Indonesians, British, Argentinians, Portuguese, Iranians, Greeks. The flavor is cosmopolitan.

Fort Bragg accommodates a number of commands: it is the headquarters of XVIII Airborne Corps, the 82nd Airborne Division, the Special Forces, and now a new program called the Military Assistance Officers Program (MAOP). MAOP is not literally connected with the Green Berets, although it is run by them; neither students nor faculty wear the beret, and the objective appears to be to minimize the connection. It is a program that has barely begun, but after intensive lobbying it appears to have won the endorsement of William Westmoreland and Westmoreland's staff. Its sponsors are quick to admit that the instruction is not all that it might be, and the doctrine is barely comprehensible. There are the usual problems, in other words, but officials at the JFK Center insist that these are being handled. MAOP, according to the official Army prospectus, is "a highly selective program which will carefully train officers, already qualified in their basic branch, in the broad and complex fields of economic, social, political and psychological endeavor which confront senior military commanders and staff officers in their overseas assignments. . . . Objectives of the program are to develop officers who can assist foreign countries with internal security problems and can perform functions having socio-political impact on military operations." Internal security problems, of course, means revolution; "functions having socio-political impact" means civic action and military advice.

It must be understood clearly that this mission represents a sharp departure from most of the traditions of the pre-Vietnam U.S. Army. The Americans had military missions in the Philippines, the Marines occupied Haiti for a time, and General Joe Stilwell headed an elaborate advisory effort to the Chinese in the nineteen-thirties and nineteen-forties. If there is a model, it is Stilwell's operation, but in 1970 there are new twists, and it is worthwhile pursuing in detail the Army's view of the world and its own role in it, that is, its *doctrine*, which to an Army officer is as the catechism to a Catholic. The Internal Defense Development Planning Guide (internal defense is a euphemism for counterinsurgency, itself a euphemism for counterrevolution) issued by the Special Warfare School in December 1967, states in its preface:*

> In the years since World War Two, international Communism has won a succession of victories in its struggle for world domination unequalled since its existence. During this period, nearly 700 million people and 5 million square miles—about one-tenth of the total land areas of the world and about one-quarter of its population—have been brought under the control of Communist regimes.
>
> While occupying the attention of the free world through pressure and threat of overt military action along the periphery of the 'iron' and the 'bamboo' curtains, the Communists have concentrated their efforts on the seizure of power in target nations through internal means. These target nations presently constitute a major portion of South and Southeast Asia, the middle east, Africa and Latin America. Using their established worldwide subversive apparatus to manipulate Communist party cadres, the Communists have exploited a wide variety of techniques ranging from psychological and political action to civil war, revolution, terrorism, and guerrilla warfare to achieve

---

*The euphemisms, in ascending order of candor, run like this: stability operations, internal defense, internal security, counterinsurgency, counterrevolution.

established goals. Allying themselves with budding national independence movements in colonial areas, and popular front governments in former dictatorships, the Communists have scored notable successes and gained considerable support through promises of material betterment and achievement of nationalistic aspirations in a wide variety of situations and areas.

The primary and ultimate objective of the Communists has been and will remain the total subversion and seizure of governments in all target nations. This includes the replacement of governments with totalitarian Communist dictatorships.

The document goes on:

. . . The primary responsibility for conducting ID/D must rest with the local government. Insurgent warfare, by its nature, is an intimate affair normally fought between antagonists of similar ethnic backgrounds. The application of force by a foreign power, *unless carefully applied through the medium of the local government*, can have a debilitating effect on the government's power to control the affairs of its own nation. [Italics added]

And later still, in discussing the role of the defenders:

. . . Other . . . harassing operations are reconnaissance patrolling, combat patrolling, raids, ambushes, aerial surveillance, 'hunter-killer' operations, 'eagle flights,' mining probable guerrilla routes, *artillery fires, tactical air strikes, 'search and clear' operations,* stay-behind patrols, 'snooper flights,' 'lightning bug,' 'snipe hunt,' *chemical defoliation, crop destruction and any other suitable tactic or technique that serves to harass the guerrilla.* [Italics added]

And finally, in defining the underdeveloped countries and their regimes, the document asserts:

. . . the officers in most cases exceed their civilian counterparts in administrative skill. *In many nations, military officers are used to establish new government administrative agencies or to revamp inefficient organizations.*

. . . the level of technical skill usually is greater among professional military personnel than among the population as a whole. They have been exposed to technology, logistics, and training in modern organizations. *This training gives the military man a modern outlook which is not often an outstanding characteristic of the civilian elite.*

. . . the military, since it represents a force in being, is *responsive to the direction of the national government and can be employed in remote areas where it would be extremely difficult to recruit a civilian organization.*

. . . *the military provides direct representation by the national government, and the use of uniformed military personnel portrays to the people the interest of the national government.* [Italics added]

The document is dated 1967 and it is doctrine, in use today. There is no evidence that the Army's estimate of the situation now is any different than it was then. The director of the military assistance school, of which MAOP is one part, and the commander of U.S. Special Forces is Major General Edward M. ("Fly") Flanagan, a professional, West Point '43. With charts and bar graphs, Flanagan ran through the history briefing (the Army has doctrine for everything, including history): 6 coups a year for the first 40 years of the twentieth century, and since then it's gotten worse. There have been 300 coups since World War Two, "so it's fair," General Flanagan said, "to call this the age of insurgency." Of the 149 insurgencies the Army has identified as "serious," only 58 have involved the Communists—"it's well to remember that," Flanagan said—and right now, there are 38 good insurgencies, ranging from Bolivia and Guatemala to Laos, Malasia, Uruguay, and Malawi.

Since World War Two, the general went on, eighty-seven per cent of the countries the World Bank describes as "very poor" have had significant conflict. Only one of the rich nations has had one (France, in Algeria). The four causes of revolution, or insurgency, according to the Army, are national independence (Algeria), relief from oppression (the U.S. in 1776, Cuba in 1958), elimination of foreign domination (Indo-China), and a simple desire for change. No example was supplied for the last. Flanagan was doing all this with small charts and graphs. It ended in a fifteen-point program, which included the observations that not all insurgencies were bad and some military governments were good. Tanks were useless; the military establishment is the prime source of power in developing nations; and "unhappy people are ripe for the Communist Big Lie."

"We must develop institutions," Flanagan said. "Not the great ones like universities, but the small ones like dams, roads, culverts, school houses, dispensaries, and so forth." He looked worried, and said that "there are ninety-three nations in the world which are underdeveloped, and so we have a serious problem." The U.S. Army, he went on, was the only instrument capable of *action*, the only instrument with men and money enough to contain the ninety-three potential revolutions. He had said that insurgencies would continue, but America must be careful to back the proper horses. I thought I sensed a contradiction: either there would be no more Vietnams or many more Vietnams; and Fly Flanagan did not seem any more precise on the matter than Richard Nixon. At any event, there could not be both. Of course the contradiction could center around the definition of Vietnam. What was "a Vietnam?" Flanagan had acknowledged that the United States was no longer the gendarme of the world, "but we have some responsibility for and interest in these nations." He concluded: "The Communist threat has not gone away. In the coming era, it

falls to the lot of the military-assistance types to further
the foreign policy objectives of the United States. That
is what we are about now. That is where the action is."

  The objectives, not to put too fine a point on it, are
in considerable state of flux as this is written: the Nixon
Doctrine is not precise, so all there is to go on is intuition
and a fair-minded man's intuition would indicate a very
conservative foreign policy in the future; conservative,
in this case, meaning non-adventurous. Lacking any firm
understanding of what the future holds, the Army is
preparing a number of policies. MAOP is the spearhead
of one of them, and to round out the *Weltanschauung*
it is necessary to listen to Colonel Samuel V. Wilson,
Flanagan's deputy and a career Army man of considerable, and controversial, style. Wilson was a Merrill's
Marauder at seventeen (he still wears the arm patch),
and after that went to Hollywood to help write the screen-
play and act in the inevitable movie. He is an unusual
inner-and-outer, in the early nineteen-fifties attached to
C.I.A. in Europe, in the late fifties and early sixties back at
Bragg working with the Special Forces. In successive
towns in Vietnam, he was on loan to the American embassy, first as associate director for field operations of
the aid program, second as embassy coordinator (with
the rank of minister-counsellor) and finally as chief of
Long An Special District, a priority pacification project
south of Saigon in the Vietnamese delta. Well-read, ambitious, highly articulate (Wilson and Major General William Knowlton, now the superintendent at West Point,
are said to be the best briefers in the Army), Wilson's
extracurricular activities have done him no good with
the regulars who staff the promotion boards. He was
passed over twice for brigadier general (he finally made
it in the May 1970 list, one of a token two officers whose
careers were, by Army standards, eccentric), a fact
that can be shrugged off until you think about some of
the people who have made it with no trouble. Wilson's
reputation is mixed, inside the Army and out of it. He is

sophisticated and (very rare for an Army officer) has a shrewd understanding of the civilian bureaucracy, specifically the lunacies of the State Department. To the extent that there are fathers of the MAOP program, they are Wilson and the young West Point lieutenant colonel, John H. Johns, who wrote many of the original papers. More interesting still, Wilson understands the implications of the MAOP program at Bragg, and does not try to slide or slip them.

With some embarrassment, he brought out the charts and bar graphs (they are the essential tools of military briefings; in Vietnam there is a Saigon bureau which does nothing but prepare charts and graphs to order) and proceeded to explain the world as seen from Bragg: "The old style was cold war, limited war, and general war"—the pointer tapping at the words on the chart—"and it isn't that way any more. What we are now involved in is low-intensity conflict, limited conventional warfare, and nuclear warfare." (Wilson was getting the nomenclature right, like a professor defining terms.) "The area in which conflict is demonstrably more likely now is the mid-limited conventional warfare back through the low-intensity conflict. This middle"—he tapped at the CONVENTIONAL WAR part of the chart—"is what we are best at. But an element of the American Army must be well prepared to participate in low-intensity warfare, the characteristics of which are now in the field manuals. The point is this: we haven't learned how to wage that which will be the most likely form of war in the coming decades." It was one of the reasons for the name change at the Center (from special warfare to military assistance). Wilson went on to mention that Westmoreland, General Richard Stilwell, and General Bruce Palmer "are now saying that the adviser's role is just as important as the command and general staff role.

"We are going to turn out a man who can act as an adviser at the lower end of the scale, and a staff officer at the upper end." That is, an adviser to a foreign army at the lower end and to, say, the American Joint Chiefs of Staff at the upper end. "I am hoping that this guy . . . well, in the final analysis we are talking about a soldier-statesman, MacArthur in Japan, Bruce Palmer in the Dominican Republic . . . "

No fanfare and no luxuries, Wilson was saying; no air conditioners, huge supply depots, sprawling staffs. MAOP men would go lean and mean, the idea to act truly *in support* of "the host government." Wilson mentioned the phrase "soldier-statesman" several times, and as he talked it became clear that combat operations were the least of it. What he was propounding was a soldier in primarily a civilian role. And why was that? Was he suggesting, for example, a civilian failure in South Vietnam? "Look," Wilson said, "it was the record of civilians that they . . . ah, had little discipline, were looser and less structured. They had less training and less experience. The civilian agencies do not *motivate.*" Others had expanded the point, which was simply that the civilians had neither the money nor the talent, mostly the money, to undertake sustained advisory operations. In Vietnam, the civilian-run U.S. Operations Mission (USOM) was a disaster and USAID scarcely better. When the civilian effort was merged with the military and called CORDS (Civil Operations, Rural Development Support), matters brightened a bit—because the military had the equipment—the aircraft, the vehicles, and the manpower—to do whatever it was that had to be done: distribute rice, move a village, build a dam, repair a road, in short do all the things that needed doing due to the devastation caused by the war—the ground war initiated by the Americans. The Army was tops both ways, in destruction and reconstruction; it was more efficient than any civilian operation, and in the long run probably cheaper. In the future, Wilson said, it would be even more difficult for civilians to do what needs to be done: "We will be operating in a dangerous environment, and the civilian might get shot at. He's not trained for that sort of thing, and we are." Wilson was quick to say that the lines must be kept straight, and he did not want to see a civilianized Army. "There must be a clear-cut dividing line where the military man cannot move with propriety. You have got to be extremely sensitive to these problems ... "

At Bragg, they are thinking of developing a soldier-statesman at both the general officer level and at the major and lieutenant colonel level. They want the officer of the future to be part soldier, part secret agent, part engineer, part diplomat, and part political adviser, equipped with languages, advanced history degrees and other academic impedimenta. Wilson acknowledged that the Regular Army (he meant the military establishment) was not unreservedly enthusiastic over MAOP (pronounce that May-op), because of the feeling among the senior men that a soldier ought to be a soldier and not something else. "We must sell ourselves to the Army," he said, "which is extremely hostile to an elite." He might have added that it is also extremely hostile to commingling with civilians.*

*The Special Forces is the case in point. They were orga-nized in the early 1950s, and were originally detailed to CIA in Europe and eventually went to Vietnam as advisers. In Vietnam in the early 1960s, the Green Berets worked very closely with the CIA, which supplied some of the money and often exercised operational control. Sometime in the mid-nineteen-sixties the Department of Defense severed the for-mal link with the agency, the better (they thought) to bring the Berets back into the military family. When John F. Ken-nedy was killed, the Green Berets lost their staunchest champion; in 1960–63, the Berets got all the money and encouragement they wanted—indeed, the brigades ex-panded so rapidly that quality was sacrificed to quantity. The civilian-military problem of control has never been sorted out. After the Bay of Pigs, there was a National Secur-ity Council Memorandum (NSCM 57) which attempted to define the dividing line between the civilians and the military

There was one final point, and it was perhaps the most important of all. It is that at Bragg the MAOP officer will be taught specifically to deal with the military forces of the host country. Wilson: "The military in the United States is very circumscribed. I am an apolitical servant of the body politic. But this is not so in the developing nations. We must understand the difference in the role of the military in the United States and in the poor countries." Very often the armed forces are the only functioning institution in a developing nation; often it is the government itself. It is therefore the only institution with which the U.S. Army can *deal*, push a button and have something happen. Wilson: "Are you going to restrict our military? Are you going to deny us the charter to advance the aims of American foreign policy? Either way, by God, you have got to educate them . . . "

U.S. Army doctrine defines Special Forces operations in this manner: "Unconventional warfare consists of mili-

---

in clandestine operations. But definition or no, the area is still vague; military officers are often detailed to the CIA and (more rarely) vice versa. It wasn't clear then and isn't clear now where the two break out. The lines of accountability are also vague. In Laos, the military runs some spook operations and the CIA others; in Vietnam, there is still a link between the Special Forces and CIA. Before so many of them were killed in Vietnam, the Green Berets probably had more sheer talent than any unit in the American armed forces—Army, Navy, or Air Force. Many of them were European emigrés, who combined sharp motivation with specialized skills like languages and medical degrees. Some Green Berets are convinced that the arrest of Colonel Rheault and his associates over the killing of a Vietnamese double-agent was a calculated effort by the Army to discredit all of them. In the Pentagon now there are hints that the Special Forces will be discontinued altogether. But don't count on it. Their new commander, Brigadier General Henry Emerson, is one of the most highly regarded officers in the Army.

tary, political, psychological or economic actions of a
covert, clandestine or overt nature within areas under
the actual or potential control or influence of a force or
state whose interests and objectives are inimical to
those of the United States. *These actions are conducted
unilaterally by United States resources or in conjunction with indigenous assets, and avoid formal military
confrontation.*" (Italics added.) For all the emphasis—
at least in public statements—on advisory efforts and
permitting the "host country" to do it, the Army does
not think that way. Or the regular Army officer does
not, and never mind that master's degree acquired at
age thirty-five. He is action-oriented, a problem-solver
("We are interested in the 'doer,'" Major General Koster
had said, "not the thinker.") As a type, there is very
little about him that is analytical, which is one of the
reasons the Vietnam estimates were so inaccurate. A
diplomat is trained to observe and report, and he is not
responsible for the course of events; his career is not
entangled in his reports, unless he seriously misjudges
what is happening. The diplomat represents his country,
proffers advice when it is asked, and otherwise watches
events. It is the reverse for a military man. The principal
reason why military reporting from Vietnamese districts
and provinces was so poor was that a young major or
lieutenant colonel could scarcely write of a deteriorating
situation when, as a military adviser, his superiors would
hold him to account for it. All well and good to say that
Binh Chanh district was disintegrating under Communist pressure, not so good when the commanding officer
wrote the efficiency report that described events going
from bad to worse when Major X was in charge. How
could a man receive a decent ER when his area of operations was crumbling? The answer was, he could not;
so everything in Vietnam was always on the upswing,
things were always getting better, the ARVN improving,
the Communists collapsing, the advisory effort "real

fine." Given the Army system, there was no other way. Only a masochist participates in his own destruction. Colonel Harry Jackson, who is in effect the head of the academic board for MAOP, observes: "Soldiers are positivists. They are opposed to relativity. They say, 'Can Do!' They tell us all the time in class, 'All we ever hear about are problems. Questions. We want answers.' "

There is a cheap shot and a debating point to be made in criticism of the MAOP curriculum, which isn't much. Nineteen weeks, and most of those in vague survey seminars of Nigeria or Bolivia or Malaysia. MAOP follows the case-study method: an analysis of a Vietnamese district, the Columbian "internal defense" plan, the JCS Operation Exotic Dancers (a contingency plan for a Caribbean crisis à la the Dominican Republic), a conventional war on the Korean model, and a nuclear exchange. Talented instructors are difficult to find, and the doctrine even tougher. "We are just beginning," as Wilson said, and it seems fair to grant them that. It also seems fair to assume that with more money the curriculum and the instructors will improve, the nineteen weeks become thirty-nine, and before another twelve months pass there will be a full-fledged school at Bragg. Dealing with ideas, not facts; a political school. MAOP will become Army doctrine, and with the right people behind it—Westmoreland, Stilwell, and Palmer will do for openers—the program will proceed. Already the men in charge are casting about for help from the outside.*

*An interesting example of the military-academic complex at work. One the places Wilson went was the Center for Rural Development at Harvard University. George Lodge, a trustee of the Center, and Christopher Russell, the executive director, were called in for comment on the MAOP program. Among other observations, according to the Army report of the conversation, Lodge contended that the U.S. "must lose its 'naive idealism' that is often represented in programs which ultimately result in what he termed 'the crime of civil action,' programs whose results

There is no lack of it from the inside. One of the many documents that the JFK Center has on file (it came to me from an outside source) is from a lieutenant colonel who fancies himself an expert in counterinsurgency. His attitudes toward the program are extremely complex. He wrote that "the only effective and lasting answer to Communist revolutionary ideology and practice is a concept that is equally revolutionary . . . we are faced with the task of directing change, not preventing or countering it." How? "The pragmatic application of power to direct change is the only principal that has relevance." The military man "does not have the background to effectively manipulate those formal or informal or government and non-government institutions that underpin nation-building." Moreover: "The concerted and obvious effort to exhume a justifiably defunct counterinsurgency course and the equally forceful attempt to use 'off the shelf' PSYOP [psychological operations] . . . courses are, to my mind, simplistic solutions to an extremely complex problem. This is nothing more or less than an at-

---

are often scandalous (e.g., utilize forced labor) and perpetuate the status quo (e.g., the power behind the military in a foreign nation). Rhetorically, Lodge asked if you needed one million dead in Mexico to make a nation or the impending threat of World War III to make Cuba a nation . . ." Further, paraphrasing the report, Lodge questioned the notion of promoting both stability and change, as envisaged by MAOP proponents; it had to be one or the other, Lodge said. He "quipped"—according to the report—that MA officers would best serve by giving every Jesuit missionary a quarter-ton truck and call it, "Nation Building—The Contribution of the Army." Lodge and Russell concluded that they would be delighted to undertake studies for the Army, in light of the fact that the Center for Rural Development was "one of only three organizations of its kind that deals with problems of rural development . . . and institution-building in various environments around the world." At this writing, however, there is no contract. Harvard is sensitive about these matters.

tempt to reduce the . . . officer to a psychological opera-
tor with civil affairs training or vice versa." And finally:
"The elimination of evil, if taken as a basic or fundamental mission of the military, would require a rather
radical shift in both our current foreign policy and the
military's present role in support of this policy." The
lieutenant colonel did not last long at the JFK Center.

There are now 480 slots for MAOP-trained field-grade
officers, some of them in military missions abroad,
others in the office of the Joint Chiefs of Staff and the
Bureau of International Security Affairs in the Pentagon,
and others in the State Department (at State, there is a
civilian office whose sole role is to "liase" with the
military). All but twenty of these positions call for a
graduate degree in addition to the nineteen weeks of
MAOP. Officials at Bragg said early in 1970 that they
would graduate 170 men that year and increase the
number in 1971 if the budget grew. But as it turned out,
only about 120 men will be graduated, a reflection
partly of the difficulty of finding "qualified" candidates,
partly the resistance of qualified candidates to sign up
for the program. "We are going to train them to operate
at any level and at any environment, with probably
seventy-five per cent of the emphasis on low-intensity
activity," according to Jackson. The thrust of it will be
techniques of working with the foreign military. Jackson
echoes Wilson: "In an underdeveloped country, Latin
America say, the military is the most important relationship. Because the military is the only functioning institution in the country. It is the only cohesive part of
the society."

Elaboration on the point came from Colonel Louis
Waple, one of Flanagan's two deputies, a career man
who retired from the Army in mid-1970. Waple is not a
man who likes euphemisms, and he laid out the MAOP
program in direct form:

"The object is to get the military into the political," he

said. "Whether an operation is GO or NO-GO is as often
as not a political decision. You cannot separate the two.
We work within the constraints of foreign and domestic
political considerations."

What will change?

"Take for example an Army battalion. As it is now in
Vietnam, there are various civilians attached to it—
State, CIA, AID, or whatever, and that is artificial. What
you want, and what we are going to have, is a MAOP man
advising that battalion commander. With the civilians,
the commander does not have control. The civilian is not
in the chain of command and does not appreciate
the realities."

Waple was thinking specifically of Vietnam, where
various civilians are often attached to military units.
But they are not, in the formal sense, under the Army's
discipline. Waple's objective was to tidy up the organization, put it back into the system and have a direct *military*
chain of command, each link with its own responsibilities. Waple went on to stress a point Wilson had
made: AID or State or CIA or any of the civilian agencies
were not by nature operational, but analytical. They
were not managers, either of men or of funds or of
materials. "The MAOP concept is forced on us by
default," he said. "The decision to employ or not to
employ weapons is compromised, victimized [if civilians
are in the command chain]. The military commander
must have charge of the entire environment. The profession of arms is too demanding and not equal to this
[division of responsibility]."

Waple: "There is a communications gap between the
military and the civilians, and the reason is that both are
talking from different perspectives. The thing that under-
lies a military man's life is *discipline*. When you mix the
civilians into it there is an absence of common understanding, and there is no joint doctrine, and that is very
goddammed important."

Why does the Army—or the country—need a "politi-
cized" officer?

"There is in 1970 no purely military decision. At one
time there was, but that was conditioned by the fact that
we had never lost a war." Waple paused there, letting the
implications of the thought disperse. "A national course
of action is poly-directional: a military offering which is
strictly military in nature is misleading."

Then, in a low, bitter voice:

"We are victimized. We are called upon to take abuse
from the press and the public for decisions in which we
have taken no part. So we must have men on *our staffs*
who have got all the tickets, who are going to make
recommendations in military terms and the other terms,
too. I mean the political terms. *We want a voice in our
own destiny.* We want a reasonable concern that we will
be used in a place where it is reasonable to use us, and
not improvise policy as we go."

Waple paused for a moment, and concluded:

"Hell, our destiny is the country's destiny. We want to
be where we can best contribute solutions to problems."
Then, again: *"We are the ones who are victimized by the
lack of political direction."*

I said then that he seemed to be thinking about an
entirely different relationship between the politicians
and the soldiers in the United States, and he shrugged
at that.

"If we were reserved just for the deployment of arms,
perhaps we could justify that," he said, "but we are not."
He added, obscurely, "even platoon leaders have more
responsibility than that."

But what Colonel Waple was saying, and what he
conceded when I asked him directly, is that somewhere
in the White House there must be a piece of paper listing
caveats of the joint chiefs of staff. He meant Vietnam.
In other words, when the decision is made the military

has its own political estimate; it has *on paper* its own judgment of the political difficulties, and what the military will require to overcome them. So if the thing is not supported, and begins to fail, and the press gets into an uproar and the hunting for scapegoats begins, a piece of paper is there; it outlines the military estimate of the situation, and what the military expects of the civilians. And if it comes to that, the paper can be brought out and published. When the witch hunt begins, the Army would have its own record.

I said that was an old bureaucratic principle, widely known as CYA—cover your ass. No, it wasn't just that, Waple said; then he smiled and said he understood the principle, though. "The Army is an indispensable part of our national system. And we must do better," he added.

Wouldn't the MAOP man take just as many chances as the civilian, probably more chances because he is operations-oriented?

Waple shook his head. "He is *not* going to take chances. He is going to make sure that our military involvement in Country X is a realistic involvement."

I was accompanied by an escort officer during this interview, a lieutenant colonel who became increasingly anxious as Waple's conversation became progressively interesting. He now observed, in a strangled voice, "the MAOP man is a uh conflict manager, he is concerned with more than the terrain and the weather. . . . We cannot be content at Bragg with letting it grow like Topsy. We uh have got to bring all this along very carefully, not let it get out of hand because, hell, there are no restraints. No one is really looking at this program, no one from the White House and no one from State.

"MAOP will never end, I think," the lieutenant colonel said.

The conversation had wound down, and Waple was talking now about the difficulty of bringing the young talent of the Army into the program. The first indication of success will be when a MAOP man becomes a general officer (Wilson's promotion to brigadier general will help), and then it will be raised from the level of a crusade to the level of a program. "This will take time," Waple said, "and for a very practical reason: careers are based not only on management of men and materials, but on other factors, and one of the most important of them is barely understood today. That is, how can you accomplish a mission with a minimum of political and psychological fallout?"

Put another way: Can you fight a Vietnam *sub rosa?* We were just chatting now, and I had put my notebook away. I wondered aloud if there was any place in the world where the American Army ought to be. It seemed to me that the record was mixed, Indonesia deposing Sukarno with no American help at all (although, as knowledgable officers tended to remind me whenever I made the point, two of the five key coup-makers had spent a year at C&GS at Leavenworth, and in Djakarta they had been supplied with American arms . . .), and 550,000 American troops had not been victorious in Vietnam. The Green Berets had succeeded in Bolivia and failed in Laos. What could you make of it? Where was the record?

The lieutenant colonel was horrified. "Why, that is like saying that children ought to grow up without parents!"

A very American judgment, that. If the lieutenant colonel wanted to believe that Americans were to Vietnamese as parents were to children, it was all right with me. But I realized then how much of the MAOP program was founded on just such a premise, "a man never stands so tall as when he stoops to help a child." Now Waple was talking of the Vietnam experience, of the benefits, and I was reminded again of American optimism; slap an advanced degree over it, and it doubles and redoubles. In Asia, a man bends with the wind, accommodates himself to it, and in so doing becomes in harmony with the universe; in America, you fight it, believing that progress comes only through struggle, believing in the perfectability of man or the American dream. Never underestimate the optimism of the Army officer, either; no situation so disastrous that something cannot be salvaged (Westmoreland once told me that the Russian general staff was envious of the Americans in Vietnam, "all the experience we're gaining over here . . . their general staff wishes their army was being trained in air mobility tactics.") Michael Herr, the best war correspondent there was in Saigon, once wrote that Vietnam was what we had instead of happy childhoods.

At any event, Waple was saying, "the Vietnam experience is educating us as we could get education in no other way . . ."

I said: "Except that no one ever stayed in one job long enough to understand it." I quoted John Paul Vann's* famous remark: "We don't have twelve years' experience in this country. We have one year's experience twelve times."

"No," Waple said, and he was definite. "If you didn't have Vietnam you wouldn't have all those fellows who had six-month tours as advisers, getting all that good experience at the rice roots . . ."

Dazzled by that, I croaked in reply: "But while you were getting all that good experience, YOU WERE LOSING THE GODDAMMED WAR!"

*One of the legendary American officials in Vietnam. Vann was an Army lieutenant colonel in the early 1960s, when his disagreements over American policy led him to resign. He returned to Vietnam as a civilian, where his cranky, virile, sometimes eccentric, often brilliant, talent is at work in the Delta.

Waple smiled thinly, and the interview broke up.
Then, leaving, I thought of a remark MAOP's Harry
Jackson had made. We had been talking of the altiplano
of Peru and Bolivia, and the insurgency (or what passes
for an insurgency) there, and Jackson was saying that
Peru wouldn't have been nearly as tough as Vietnam.
Not nearly. "Oh look," he said, smiling and leaning
across the desk. "Look. Get in there early, get in there
very early and really analyze the situation. Analyze
the revolution. Find out all about it, the people, the
methods, the particulars. Get in there early and form it,
shape it . . ."

However zealous they may be at Bragg, it is at the Pentagon where the program will succeed or fail, because the
Pentagon is where the money is. From the Army establishment there is some skepticism—principally because
MAOP violates so many ancient Army traditions. But
compared to missiles and tanks it is very cheap, and the
Army is entering a period of what to them is severe
austerity. That is, severe austerity at $24 billion or so.
A reasonable guess is that the Army establishment will
play along with MAOP to see what develops. Lieutenant
General William DePuy is in the middle of these matters
as assistant vice chief of staff. His estimate is this: "We
are already seeing a strong feeling against anything like
Vietnam. We're finding out as a nation that it's not
worth the effort in terms of the central effect. The
second thing is that it's a lot tougher than we thought to
win. In the early 1960s, when counterinsurgency was a
household word around here, it was not thought out.
By any of us. We thought we could do it, and Kennedy
and McNamara backed us. But they didn't understand it,
or its implications, either. Counterinsurgency really is a
catch phrase, you know; a slogan. The Army spent its
time trying to figure out what it meant." DePuy was

talking of this in a very detached manner, almost as if he were an historian reviewing the century before. But he was one of those who was in the middle of it, who went to Vietnam in the early nineteen-sixties and reported back that the war was winnable (in an admirable admission, an admission comparable to a newspaper reporter admitting a botched quotation, DePuy indicated that he didn't know enough about the situation to know how little he knew). What the Army thought it could do, he said, was win the Vietnam war quite cheaply, a few advisers and some arms, demonstrating to the Communists that wars of national liberation wouldn't work. "The Green Berets made sense, in some of their activities," he said. "But our psywar never made any sense, and still doesn't. It's a mechanized capability only.* We're really talking about political warfare here, and we wouldn't admit that. If you're talking Vietnam it's Ky versus Thieu, and if you're talking Bolivia it's Barrientos versus Ovando. And I am not sure the Army is the best instrument for that. The Army shouldn't be so quick to get into the problems of insurgency."

DePuy is currently preoccupied with the limitations of the institution. "Nixon says we'll help allies with technical assistance, spare parts, and so forth, but we're going to be very reluctant with our infantry and we're looking at the outer bounds of what we are going to do. We do have certain commitments: Korea could be a full-fledged fight. But don't look for the Army to get mixed up in Latin America or Africa." DePuy, like most

---

*He is so right. At Bragg, the psywar department is hopeless, a grabbag of highly sophisticated instruments to, as they say, "use communications to influence the behavior of the target area." To that end, psyops operatives at Bragg are studying the world's religions, "group dynamics," and "the social system." It is sociology gone berserk. "Rumors," one of the psyops colonels said quite seriously, "the problem is how you utilize rumors."

of his senior colleagues, is Europe-oriented, and that means weaponry. "Those of us who fought in Vietnam have a different image of the nineteen-seventies than those who did not. We think about air mobility, target acquisition, the role of the helicopter."

"What about advisers?" I asked.

"Well, the advisory thing is fine and works OK sometimes," DePuy said. "As long as you have got a [Peter] Dawkins or a [Lieutenant Colonel Robert] Schweitzer advising. But what if you have only Major Glotz? He is not a Rhodes Scholar and he does not have a PhD degree and a skyhigh IQ. The institution, dammit, has its limitations . . ."

It is an irony. Many of the older generals want to shy away from adventures in counterinsurgency, and many of the younger ones do not. It has little to do with the perception of the Communist threat, it has to do with the traditions of the Army. Burned in Vietnam, many of the senior men want to get back to the comfortable pre-insurgency mission—the protection of the United States. The younger men, looking for the action in the next decade, see themselves at command posts in the Andes; some, not all. One of the bright young men of the Pentagon, a lieutenant colonel, says he would not touch MAOP with a ten-foot pole. "It's a non-program," he said, "and will do nothing for a man's career."

The older men are wary, none more so than the commander of Fort Bragg and XVIII Airborne Corps, Lieutenant General John J. Tolson III. Tolson is rugged and grandfatherly, and speaks in a soft southern accent. To me he embodies most if not all of the decent traditions of the Army. In Vietnam, he had the reputation as a division commander of being careful with his men, and at Bragg he was instrumental in establishing an advanced clinic for drug addicts. Tolson is not at all sure of the utility of placing the Army in political/civil/military roles in foreign countries. Particularly underdeveloped countries.

"They sent me to Ethiopia in 1961," he said. "I was a brigadier general and I figured it was a career-busting tour. I saw the Peace Corps in Ethiopia, and it was great and all that. But you know, we might have more to do in our own country, maybe we could use a few of those here at home . . .

"Until we get our own social structure straightened out, we are not going to be successful elsewhere. You know, my generation, we thought we were 'It.' But we've got young people who don't think so. This is a great young generation, they are *thinking*. But we are in a very precarious thing, we've got a heavy psychological price we are paying." Tolson meant the Army, and he went on: "There is definitely a reaction against the Army. There are a lot of people worried about 'the military.' . . . Other things, too. I have established racial seminars here, and we have got to get on with the process. There are the same racial tensions in the Army as there are in society as a whole."

I asked Tolson about nation-building as an appropriate role for the Army.

"Well, based on my limited experience in Vietnam and Ethiopia, you don't want that to be military. You can't hack it that way. Look, we have got to improve our own society, not its quantity but the quality. Maybe . . . hell, maybe we could build a few dams or bridges here rather than in Latin America.

"The main mission of the Army is as a part of the defense team. Protecting the country, and that is second to nation-building or anything else."

The main mission of the army. But at the Pentagon they are thinking of other possible missions, wondering about new forms of CCC camps and plans by which the Army would rebuild the United States. It is the only institution in the country that is capable of it (that is, with sufficient men and money), and when the war has ended and the recriminations begun, there the Army will be: well dressed up and no place to go. Talent to burn, and no match to light it. A peacetime mission of high priority is not only desirable; from a professional officer's point of view, it is very nearly mandatory. And it might take some of the sting from the Vietnam postmortem. If the Army could build, rather than destroy . . .

It is a plan under consideration at highest levels, but at the lower ones the eyes are on the main business: security. Incipient insurgencies everywhere, and how is the Army to deal with them unless it has the capability, the understanding. Aggressive Russians and unpredictable Chinese and their surrogates. So the Army must devise the doctrine and acquire the know-how. On the other side of Bragg from Tolson's office, the young MAOP students and Special Forces work at it. The Green Berets study Laotian and Haitian and Portuguese, and a dozen other languages. They are learning more about what it means to go 'lean and mean,' establish small camps in the mountains and work outwards, either with the government in power or with the insurgents, either way. The Special Forces A-Team: communications experts, demolition experts, medics, language officers, and quick killers. The A-team in the mountains, and the MAOP man in the capital. Or in the future, MAOP men in the mountains, in the capital, and at the elbow of Henry Kissinger in the White House. The handbook: "*A major objective of U.S. policy is to thwart further Communist inroads into non-Communist areas by safe-guarding and assisting the less-developed nations in fulfilling their aspirations to remain free to fashion ways of life independent from Communism or other external domination or control.*

The civilians can't do it, Sam Wilson had said, and anyone who had observed them in Vietnam for any length of time would have to agree. Too loose, not disciplined enough—but most of all, no resources, no men or money or chain of command; no *doctrine*. That is what the Army has. It has all the money and all the talent, and what are you going to do with it? Let it go to waste? "Are you going to deny us the opportunity of furthering the objectives of American foreign policy?"

And lying back of all of it, a palpable presence, the notion that it could have been done in Vietnam. If we knew then what we know now, none of it need have happened. Oh it was difficult, all right; no one is saying it was easy, and hindsight is always treacherous. But from the beginning, *if* you had set limits on what you expected from the Saigon government, *if* you had understood the politics of South Vietnam and therefore the strength of the revolution, *if* you had known the language and the customs. Maybe then you would not have gone in at all. What the MAOP program may do is *prevent* future Vietnams, *prevent* American quagmires—and do this on the basis of the facts. If you can estimate the factors accurately, then you can make a rational judgment: no good saying this or that adventure is not in the American tradition, or beyond the capacities of the government in Washington; leave that sort of thing to the theorists, historians or social scientists or journalists. You put a smart Army officer in that country, *on the ground*, and . . . Look, the MAOP man will have the tools to estimate the threat, the strength of the insurgents, the will of the defenders, so it will be a protection for Americans as well as an opportunity. Either do that, or surrender the battleground to the Communist enemy; no middle ground. But the point, as Lou Waple said, was that the MAOP man may look at the challenge and refuse it, declare the situation hopeless, beyond solution.

But when did an American Army officer ever declare anything hopeless?

The Bragg program is infinitesimal by Pentagon standards, a budget of $5,000,000 for the institute and the JFK Center (excluding the Special Forces brigades). The budget for MAOP is only about $100,000, very very petty cash. Fly Flanagan had posited the obvious, that training men is a much less expensive proposition than buying all the new machines; and in the nineteen-seventies, he was convinced, it was a question of men more than machines. So the program at Bragg goes forward, watched closely by a few officials, some of whom are alarmed but most of whom are not. At the Pentagon and elsewhere, the major effort is concentrated on weapons and the structure of the institution, as the budget plunges and the Army melts into the background of society. A central concern now is the steady leak of talented officers, most of them young captains, majors, and lieutenant colonels. A study is underway to find the causes, but the most sensitive Army officers already know them. They are four: the repeated Vietnam tours, the anti-military atmosphere in the country, the low pay, and (for the younger men) the anachronistic spit and polish, the Mickey Mouse. Women's liberation has come to the Army, and now wives are telling their husbands, one tour and no more; when the second tour comes around, it is Vietnam or me. This is true not only for the officer corps, but for the career non-com as well. Sergeant Gillis, the "lifer" interviewed at Bragg, said he was puzzled: "These young guys can't seem to control their wives any more, and the wives don't seem to understand that a soldier's job is to fight."*

*Potentially more explosive than any of it is the problem of the blacks, which I have not addressed in detail. Only a black can write it now. The outlines are obvious, however. The blacks, many of them, do not feel a part of the Army any more than they feel a part of society in general. There are exceptions (see Chapter Three). The Army is integrated, but many blacks do not care to become officers so most of the officers are white. About one percent of the officer corps is black. Blacks have carried a disporportionate share of the burden in South Vietnam, sustaining casualties out of all relation to their numbers—both in America

"I was going back for my third tour," the young airborne major said, "and my wife and I had it out and I agreed, the hell with it. Your number is bound to come up sometime. It has to: percentages. I was in this business for good, but what with the fucking public . . . What do they know about it? I decided I might as well go to work and make some money."

Or the retired lieutenant colonel, a PhD, largely self-educated, now a librarian in Kansas City because his career ended . . . why? Who knows? His friends, all regular Army men, say he was a first-class combat leader and smart in the bargain. But he was old when he enlisted, and kept getting older, and finally he got the message he would never make bird colonel. Rough, very abrasive, outspoken—too uneven a gem for the Army in the era of professional managers. So now he is a librarian, but those who know him well say that he would have been one of the best brigade or division commanders in the Army.

Your wife, I asked the young airborne major, apart from Vietnam, did she like the Army? Like Army life, post life?

"No," he said. "She really didn't. I think she found it dull." The major shrugged, puzzled by it.

Major General John Norton's wife, the daughter of a colonel, had told me a little of the Army life at Riley and Leavenworth in the nineteen-twenties and thirties. It was a graceful life, almost sensuous, with polo ponies and tea in the afternoons in the large houses on post.

and in the Army. They gravitate to the elite units like the airborne, where they tend to make sergeant and stop. The black problem in the Army is not much different from the problem in American society, and the same results are evident: separatism, black nationalism, and rage. From the perspective of a professional soldier of either race, the prospect is a melancholy one, because for men to fight well there must be common respect and affection. That is not present now. Not in America. Not in the Army.

As a young officer finishing a short tour, F. Scott Fitzgerald wrote part of *This Side of Paradise* at Leavenworth. If you were a youngster, you got instruction in equitation; the women, military wives, were brought together by the Army as the men were, "Rosie O'Grady and the general's lady." You lived well, if you were a field-grade officer; it was not Greenwich or Grosse Pointe but it was nice enough, and the Army was respectable. Just before the second war, some of the old colonels tried to get the horse cavalry reinstated. The Army had a charm and an ease of manner about it; the conventions were good. The tours abroad were fun, the exotic places such as the ones Nancy Shea described in a book called *The Army Wife*, first published in 1941 and then as now something of a bible for the professionals: "Dine on the porch or in the garden, if practicable. If the porch is screened, you will enjoy your meals wherever there is a cool spot and an attractive view. Serve the coolest food you can imagine. If your imagination deserts you, then the next time you dine at the Manila Hotel, the Condado or the Washington Hotel, ask if you can take one of their menus . . ."

It was quiet and relaxed, as the country was. The civilians tended to snipe, but it didn't matter; the Army was like a family then, close and small. But the United States is different now, a volcanic economy and the tensions everywhere, and some of those tensions centering on the Army itself, the Army as an institution. The kids and the blacks, the students, Vietnam . . .

"When my girls were growing up, I had to tell them that because their father was an officer that didn't make him different from the other people on the base," the general's wife said. She was showing me her children's bedrooms, the walls covered with gaudy posters, peace symbols. "Now, because of the war and what you read and hear, I have to . . . *defend* who he is and what he does."

At the bar of a Bachelor Officers' Quarters at Leavenworth, the men trickled in after a day at class, a day analyzing battles from World War Two and Korea, and sat and stared sullenly at Walter Cronkite. Cronkite was talking about the war, and the picture leapt off the screen—how many times have you seen it?—a burning hut and a crying kid and a dead gook. Some town you couldn't even pronounce the name of, and a curly-headed television reporter mourning the *gooks*. Then back to Washington for a few more cracks against soldiers.

So the world penetrates an Army base in a way that it didn't thirty years ago: there are directives to the senior officers to mingle with the civilians, to invite them to the base and accept return invitations; get to know the local newspaper publisher, and, after a suitable period of time, give him a plaque for services rendered. The ban on pictures in the society pages continues, but harmonious relations are important now. The life is less quiet and less graceful than it used to be, but for the young wife it is too quiet, separated as it is from the mainstream of American life. Columbus, Georgia. Fayetteville, North Carolina. Killeen, Texas. And the quarters of a captain are less, very much less than those of a colonel.

General DePuy had said that with feeling running the way it was, the Army would have to draw its talent from the small towns of the Midwest and the South and the mountain states. But what is clear now is that no part of America is further than five or six years away from any other part. Berkeley in 1965 is Kent State in 1970, and while some of the senior officers shrug off the loss of R.O.T.C. programs (Westmoreland is not among them: "Extremely important to the Army," he said in 1970), many of the serious-minded junior officers do not. There are still 281 R.O.T.C. chapters at American colleges and universities, and 41 applications pending, but these are not the front-line schools. In 1970 three of those which were lost were Boston University, Dartmouth, and

Harvard. Three of those gained were Weber State College in Utah, Southern Oregon College, and East Central State College in Oklahoma. R.O.T.C. over the years has given the Army its leaven, broadened it with men whose perspectives were wider than West Point and whose sense of the institution was drawn more from society than from the professional perspective of arms. More than that, there was a sheer practical reason: the Army needs more officers than West Point or Officers' Candidate School can supply. It needs educated men, even in a buttoned-down peacetime situation (some officials in the Pentagon are talking of a 750,000-man Army post-Vietnam, a smaller Army by 100,000 than existed when Eisenhower left the presidency). But anyone who has been around colleges and universities lately knows that R.O.T.C. is in trouble. In time, there will be trouble even at Weber State College.

A brigadier general came to Boston College in January 1970 to speak to the R.O.T.C. students there.* The lieutenant colonel in charge of the program had told me that the ranks were thinning at B.C., that students figured they could beat the draft and therefore have no need for an officer's commission. The general, there to talk in a general way about the Army, is a highly regarded man at Harvard, where he occasionally attends seminars. Deeply concerned about the state of the Army, apprehensive of the public attacks on it, worried about morale, the general initiated several thoughtful reforms in his command; there was a committee established to hear black grievances, and the general's telephone number was published in the post newspaper. If a man had a grievance he could ring up the general and talk about it.

"Be seated," he said commandingly, and the thirty or so students in the auditorium sat down quickly. They

*Boston College announced termination of R.O.T.C. late the same year.

were well-scrubbed and neatly groomed and all of them were white.

The general stood easily at the lectern, and began with a small joke. "It is a pleasure to meet our customers," he said. "I'll try to tell you about a career as an officer."

The general said that his own father was an infantry officer. He said that he thought his father's career was uninteresting and . . . slow to proceed. At age 42, he was still a captain. But then World War Two came and his father ended up a brigadier general, an assistant division commander. After the Second World War, the general said, he assumed there would be twenty-five years of peace. He graduated from West Point after the war and chose the Corps of Engineers, and then went to M.I.T. and got an engineering degree. But something happened, he said, "and I decided to go where the real mission of the Army is, the infantry. I went to transfer and the personnel officer looked at me and said, 'What's wrong with your record?'" The general was making the point that no one ever volunteers for the infantry.

"But it is the guts of the Army," he said. "We need signals and engineers, roads"—he paused for a moment, thinking about it—"and bridges built and so on. We need adjutants and MPs, artillery. But the infantry is the heart of it . . .

"This is a tough time for the Army. Anybody who reads the papers or watches the television knows that the issues that divide us are great. You will hear people tell you that during the Mexican War and the Civil War it was the same situation—but, really, this is unique now. And when you say 'the military' you mean the Army. The controversy over the all-volunteer Army ties into the draft, the cost, the military-industrial complex, the war in Vietnam, racial tensions . . ." He seemed to lose the thread here. ". . . drug abuse, other things. These impact directly on the Army. The Army is and always has been a part of society, but now it is caught up in a deeper sense than it ever was.

"How many generals are there in the Army? There are about 500. I am senior in rank to about seventy-five of them, and no one is typical. I'll tell you my own views. I see the scene as very troublesome, the problems severe. I went to the West Coast last month, and people say there is nothing new. There were military and civilians that I was talking to. But I think they were wrong. I think the problems are more severe now and if you are not worried, friend, then you don't understand the situation.

"The times call for very high, exceptionally high, performance. Truly superlative. And that is what is requested of you when you put on that soldier suit."

The general was talking conversationally, leaning casually against the lectern. He is a dark-haired, handsome man, with a quick smile and a youthful face, but he had what soldiers call command presence so the students sat at attention and listened carefully.

"I don't know what will happen next year or in the year 1990. I say that the Army can be a very interesting life. There is a variety and a . . . ah, spectrum. Those of us who have had responsibility are looking for young men to take this responsibility from us. It is tough. The profession of arms is not as highly esteemed as it was in the past, particularly among this age group (he nodded at the students), and this is partly due to Vietnam, and may be wholly due to Vietnam. It is appropriate, then, for me to give you a justification.

"We live in a world of nations. Maybe in the future people won't organize themselves that way, but now they do. The U.S.A. is unique because of its power, and its ideals. All men are created equal, the government derives its authority from the consent of the governed. With international conflicts, with politics, you have . . . force. As you do in all politics. It is not irrevocable or inevitable, but when it is needed, you have to have an army. Society needs an army, but the ways to which an army is put is not decided by the army but by political magistrates duly elected by the people. . . . We assume that the magistrates have chosen a just war. When war comes, freedom is in the balance, and lives are in the balance. There are no easy solutions, no simple answers."

He paused for a moment. "So you do it, you fight at minimum cost with maximum skill. You use insight. I know of no profession that is so fraught with responsibility. Leaders are responsible for the lives of their own men, the enemy, and noncombatants. Insight. Management. Integrity. Skill. You need all that, when the stakes are so high." He smiled thinly, and leaned forward.

"The military profession is also one of considerable enjoyment, although it has not seemed so in the past few years with the frequency of Vietnam tours. Hopefully, the U.S. will not find itself at war full-time. What you have in the Army is companionship, post life, travel . . . a friend of mine, a general, used to say that Army life was fine until someone screwed up and got us into a war.

"If you come to my command, I believe in dealing with problems, the manifold turbulence and the challenge of the outside world. It is there all around us. Near my command are nineteen SDS chapters, underground newspapers, something like two hundred thousand college students, peace groups—all of them looking for a target, and that's me. So that's the message, gentlemen. I like the life, the comradeship . . ."

The general mentioned a letter he received from a retired sergeant major when his name appeared in the local paper. The letter arrived on the general's birthday, and the sergeant major asked if he was related to the officer, the captain, who served in China in the nineteen-twenties, in Tientsin. He mentioned the baseball games they used to play in Peking. Yes, and the old man—the officer—had a baby boy at that post and if that was you,

Happy Birthday. "That fine sergeant remembered that," the general said, "and what does that story point out? Well, that the Army is a fine life."

He said that he would be happy to answer questions. But there were none. There was silence.

"Would you like to ask me a question about the Vietnam war?"

Nothing.

"Would you like to ask a question about My Lai?"

After a few moments, a boy raised his hand and said that he "would like to" ask a question about My Lai. The question was not a specific one. It was just My Lai.

"Well," the general said. "You might say that I have given you a nice theory so far, but what about My Lai? Something very bad happened at My Lai. If what they say happened did happen then it was an abomination. It went against all the instructions." Then the general said that he commanded a brigade in Vietnam and observed that he was obliged to fight in villages, where the people were.

"The way you do it is to have good leaders, squad, platoon and company, battalion leaders. The man who comes into the Army must have a reverence for life. He must realize that lives would have to be spent but . . . a reverence for life. Whatever malfeasance led to that incident [My Lai] will be dealt with. If I were not sure of that, believe me, I would not want to be a member of this institution."

Question: What about regimentation in the military?

The general: "I consider myself to be a nonconformist. I angered a lot of people, and here you have before you a general officer. A friend wrote me, when I got my star, that he was pleased that the 'burr under the saddle' guys could make it. You have got to make waves, and that is all there is to it. You have got to be careful about your revolutionary zeal, but if you're intelligent, you'll get by. The Army is changing, and the question is: How are we going to adapt? They [the old men] want to see it all go away, the student unrest, the black unrest. I don't think the Army will survive unless it loosens up."

He talked a little then of Afro haircuts, and said the Army is uptight about the haircut policy. He used the word 'uptight' four times. He said that uptight outfits like IBM and Sears, Roebuck don't allow hair as long as he, a brigadier general, does; he meant that a junior executive at IBM had to be more circumspect about haircuts than a sergeant in the general's command. It had been fifty-five minutes, and the students were restive now. The general ended on a positive note: "The profession has been around for a long time and will be here a lot longer."

The students left right away, and the general stood talking to the four R.O.T.C. instructors. He said that perhaps he had gone too soft on the War Is Hell theme. Sherman was right, the general said; war was a terrible, miserable business. A young black major agreed with him, and added that the Army's recruitment advertising was a mistake. *The New Army. Learn A New Skill.* No one was going into the infantry now, and the quality was dangerously low. It was dangerously low in Vietnam, and anyone who had been there commanding troops knew that. Someone else said that misleading advertising never did any good, in the last analysis.

The general nodded, agreeing. War is hell, he said again. "I should have mentioned that."

The Army is giving up its R.O.T.C. chapters without much of a struggle, and if anything is certain this year, it is that the Army will live to regret it. In February 1970, the sources of Army officers were these: West Point supplied five per cent, Officer's Candidate School thirty-three per cent, R.O.T.C. forty-one per cent, and direct commissions fifteen per cent. By the summer of 1970, the

Army had all but closed down O.C.S., and was doing everything it could to discourage men from entering. The officer corps is now too large for the declining ranks, and there is a collateral problem: the most talented men are not entering the Army, and some of the best men already there are leaving it. The Pentagon puts a good face on this, drawing comparisons to the wind-down of other wars. Given the embattled psychology of the professionals, many of them feel good riddance. William Westmoreland is one of these: "You always expect it," he said. "The highly motivated officers are staying with us. They always do. Ike and Bradley did after World War Two. Although many officers are resigning for perfectly legitimate reasons, the number resigning because they cannot stand the heat is considerably larger than usual."

Preliminary returns from a study of the West Point class of 1965 (the class which in 1970 was ending its last year of obligatory military service) support Westmoreland. Officials explain that they can dig through the 201 files of those who are resigning and find indications of unsuitability: "We will find unfavorable reports." But it is a classic self-fulfilling analysis, and all but useless because the resignee as often as not leaves in the first place because of dissatisfaction with the system, and naturally his file would reflect that. Anyone who believes that the system is correct as it is now operating could derive considerable comfort from the statistics. A few senior officials have said privately that they would like to do away with the efficiency report but are at a loss (or say they are) to find a substitute, a better way to judge a man's capacities. How do you estimate talent? There are 46,000 field-grade officers in the U.S. Army and how can you know which ones are the standouts?

What the Army has truly not come to grips with is the recommendation for a professional army, an all-volunteer force. No one likes the idea, principally for philosophical reasons—"a bunch of mercenaries is not in the American tradition," one senior general said, "and the strength of the Army is in its citizen character."* Beyond that, both military and civilian officials at the Department of the Army contend that the quality of enlistee would not be high enough to operate and maintain the machines of the nineteen-seventies and nineteen-eighties. By this analysis, the Army must have a civilian draft in order to secure men bright enough to work the gear, to drive the Sheridans and service the Shillelaghs, and program the computers and read the maps. Thomas S. Gates, the Chairman of the President's Commission on an All-Volunteer Force, estimated that it would cost $3.5 billion for a two-and-a-half million man force; the Pentagon strongly disagrees, and puts the figure at twice that. Regular officers do not like to contemplate an army which would (they reckon) be mostly black, mostly uneducated, and—by its nature, they say—separated from society. Bad, bad, bad, one general said, shaking his head and summoning recollections of American valor at Omaha Beach and Argonne. It is contended that if the draft calls went down to five thousand a month, the Army would be able to secure the men it needs. By General DePuy's estimate, there will be enough of these outside the eastern and western seaboards. But take all the facts away, and the objection is basically rooted in a soldier's reading of American history: volunteers or mercenaries,

As a matter of fact, the all-volunteer army is in the American tradition. There was conscription only in times of clear danger, the Civil War, World War One, and World War Two. Between the wars, the Army all but disbanded, accepting only volunteers. What is different now is that war or no war the nation's standing army is very large, too large to rely on volunteers alone. The military budget has continued to grow, war or no war, or, in the case of Vietnam, undeclared war. But still, mercenaries—or, in the euphemism, volunteers—do not seem in the American grain. The suspicion is that, again, it is a fascination with innocence. Of a certain kind.

or whatever you want to call them, are simply not in the tradition of the country. America's military men do not like to think of themselves as hired guns. And no good arguing (as the Gates Commission did) that policemen, firemen, and U.S. marshals are volunteers. They don't have to fight in wars, at the direction of the state; on foreign soil, pursuing the national destiny.

So the professional soldier tends to dismiss the professional army. The real problem, he says, is "the tiger problem." That is the phrase of a lieutenant colonel now analyzing the data from studies of men who left the Army. "How do you get an innovative, aggressive man through the middle management of the Army, where life can be very, very dull?" It is difficult for a man to take a year or eighteen months at Fort Bliss without cracking in the process, without saying the hell with it and resigning. The examples are everywhere: the young (and by all accounts brilliant) Army scientist and inventor who was made an adviser to the Vietnamese military academy, the tough and aggressive battalion commander sent to staff, the colonel "selected for retention in grade" as a not-so-oblique put-down because he spent so much time working for civilians in Saigon. Officials at the Department of the Army concede that many of those who leave blame the organization. Other resignees skip it, reporting only that they have "a different career goal." (It is worth mentioning that in 1970 a number of those who resigned had serious second thoughts; life on the outside, in a period of economic recession, proved more difficult than advertised.)

It's impossible to know whether My Lai has accelerated the resignations. It was common knowledge in Vietnam that men coming from Officer's Candidate School (Lieutenant Calley was an O.C.S. man) were not the Army's best quality. One senior officer said with some heat: "Why are we short-handed? Because the bastards at Harvard [Harvard is shorthand for any student who refuses the war] wouldn't fight, wouldn't step up to their responsibilities. They got their deferments and left the war to the least competent people. They are the ones to blame . . ." By this analysis, the men who perpetrated My Lai were not badly trained or badly motivated but just bad. Bad apples, likely to turn up anywhere, and doubly likely given the junior officer requirements in 1966 and 1967 and 1968. The best young Americans were evading the draft, which left the management of the war to the worst; it is an argument with hypnotic appeal to professional soldiers.

These matters worry the Army, and worry it more than senior men are prepared to admit (it should come as no surprise that the Department of the Army has commissioned a study on what makes a hero). But the central preoccupation now is money: how to make it stretch, what to choose, what will fit the requirements in 1975 or 1980. The days of geometric progression are over. The Army's budget was $3.9 billion in 1950, $9.3 billion in 1960, and $24.4 billion in 1970. For probably the first time in American history, the military establishment faces a genuine necessity for choice. The budget is going down, and everyone knows it, but what has happened in the Army is precisely what has happened in American industry, a technological revolution out of control—in Toffler's phrase, "future shock." The problem is both inter-service—that is, the classic struggle among the Navy's carriers, the Air Force's planes, and the Army's infantry—and, for the Army itself, inter-branch. There appears to be almost no one who cultivates detachment and introspection: armored officers want tanks, the infantry wants helicopters, the signal corps wants laser beams. The Army is an institution of adversaries, and the prejudice of the branch carries straight to the top—a "general officer" is that in name only. But the general staff has apparently made its choice, and it is probably no accident that the choice is

one in which all branches will share. It is STANO—
Surveillance, Target Acquisition, and Night Observation.
More broadly, it is what Westmoreland once called "the
automated battlefield," and its premises proceed directly
from the Vietnam experience.

Or, if you will, the Vietnam effect. There are several of
them, but the one most carefully considered in the Pentagon is the extraordinary waste. The Vietnam war is
simply not cost-effective and the problem there, as they
see it, is that weaponry is adequate but the means of
finding the enemy are not. One heard it a thousand
times in Vietnam: *If we can only find the little bastard,
we can kill him, but half the time we don't find him; and
sometimes we find him and don't know it.* The artillery
strategy, called in Vietnam "harassment and interdic-
tion," is illustrative of the dilemma. H&I fire was
directed indiscriminately at trails, "suspected troop con-
centrations," and "suspected enemy base camps." In one
year, the Army fired more than one million rounds of
artillery in H&I (at $100-plus a round); surely some-
where there is a classified document reporting on the
effectiveness. Whatever that document says, the men in
the field were skeptical, as anyone with a sense of logic
and probability would be. What the Americans in Vietnam were faced with was the luxury of absolute weapons
superiority—air, artillery, heavy weapons—and with the
helicopters, absolute mobility. But they were unable to
prevail, and the only plausible reason could be a failure
to find the enemy. There could be no other reason, at
least there could be none if you regarded the war as
strictly a military operation, "an engineering problem."
If you could devise a way to find the Communist, then
you could fix him; and having fixed him, then you could
kill him. STANO.

The technological revolutions are basically two, mini-
aturization and computation. The Army is developing
sensors that can track a column of men, and indicate

whether or not they carry weapons. They are working on
chemical detectors, sound detectors, heat detectors, and
light detectors. Under development now is infra-red
radar, "discreet and accurate," as the planners describe
it; magnetic devices, people-sniffing devices. One Army
colonel in ACSFOR sees a future in which a platoon of
men is little more than a reconnaissance force, each man
with individual radar meant to find and fix the enemy.
Individual impulses are fed back to a computer at the
command post, and the computer tells the artillery
where to fire. In its finest flower, the infantryman need
no longer carry a weapon; all of it will be done by
remote control, and be done twenty-four hours a day.
The dispatch didn't appear in *The New York Times* or
the Washington *Post*, but in the Killeen *Daily Telegram*,
inserted on page one so as not to alarm the natives.
There were tests being conducted at Fort Hood, the Army
news release said, and

> The sky will glow every ten minutes for approximately
> three minutes every night, all night long. The device
> being used to cause this will be an airborne searchlight,
> a light with the brightness of 1.9 million candlepower.
> The lights will be mounted on helicopters and will be
> turned on at altitudes of 2,500 to 10,000 feet. According
> to Major Raymond G. Andrews at Project MASSTER,
> there is absolutely no danger involved. However,
> Andrews cautions advisers [sic] not to stare directly
> into the light as this might cause some discomfort, as
> would staring into the sun . . .

Along with the Vietnam effect, or really part of it, is
what the Army identifies as the population explosion.
Bluntly put, the Army cannot destroy the countryside as
it did in France or as it is doing in Vietnam. A staff man
in the Pentagon said, "But the commander has got to go
into the city much more often than he had to do in the
past, because there are more cities and more people. So

you have got to discriminate in how much fire power you use, and where you use it." The prospects are dazzling. "If you go into a city, on a block, can you target *one man*? Or burn down *one house*? There are very stringent ground instructions on soldiers now, and these will become more stringent not less."

The computerized command post, as Cyrus Vance observed, has been kicking around for a decade. But it now seems technologically feasible. It seems feasible now to commence to develop systems which will eliminate human error. At I-CAS (Institute for Combined Arms Studies) at Leavenworth they are working on it, thinking about a progression of computers: a small one on a man's back, a little larger one for the platoon leader, larger still at the company CP, and still larger at battalion and brigade and division. All of these are linked to one another, so programmed to eliminate trivia along the way. And the computers are linked to the big guns and to the aircraft, so once the target is acquired the machinery capable of destroying it can be zeroed in. And none of it, in the ultimate, is touched by human hands.

The problems are enormous, not least among them the expense (no one in the Army seems seized by the irony). Second, as Colonel Ireland observed in connection with the Sheridan, is maintenance. At Leavenworth, they speak of "ruggedizing" the equipment. The Pentagon colonel preferred the phrase "make it idiot proof." But at both locations, men are worrying about the talent needed to operate such sophisticated gear. "The battalion commander of the future better damn well know ADP [automatic data processing]," one soldier-scientist said. The computer is essential because with the new devices, information will overwhelm the commanders. To a degree, that has already happened with captured enemy documents in Vietnam. There is so much paper it cannot be collated. It will require a computer to separate wheat from chaff. Already the computer is calculating logistics, both in supply and in men, a process which has resulted in a man "in the pipeline" from fort to field (or vice versa) in only forty-eight hours, compared to two or three weeks in World War Two.

Regression analysis, they say. *Functionalize the threat.* This appears to mean a method of analyzing precisely, by function, the nature of the various threats presented to America. In order to diversify the Army (if that is the word), there are a number of proposals which would do away with either the corps command or the division command or both. Lieutenant General George Forsythe, now the head of the Army Combat Developments Command, would like to break down the Army into brigades. By this theory, the division at fifteen thousand men is an inefficient instrument; much better to organize in brigades, each independently targetable (as they say about the MIRV missile), and if time comes to move in a division formation simply put a tactical commander at its head. They are thinking, too, of new definitions—is riverine warfare a function of the Army or the Navy? Is "the beach" or "the beachhead" five hundred yards or five miles? And, crucially, what of the helicopter? Hugely expensive, successful in Vietnam, but how successful in Europe? Or the Sahara? Is it best as a troop carrier, or is it really an airborne tank? Or both? And how vulnerable, in a combat environment where the enemy is both more ubiquitous and better armed than in Vietnam? Helicopter partisans are not unduly concerned with attacks on their machine, because its STANO uses are obvious. Ditto the Sheridan tank and the APC, which could resemble a computer when the scientists are finished touching it up.

"The money crunch has never been greater," said the Army colonel. "Anything that looks promising, we investigate. And then we investigate it some more. We are getting into the early stages, testing for mobility, fire control—*field testing* that is; we are not going straight to procurement, because that is what costs the money . . ."

Much of the testing is being conducted at Fort Hood, along the lines suggested in the following document. One hesitates to summarize it. Better to read it in full. (MASSTER stands for Mobile Army Sensor Systems Test and Evaluation Resources.)

STANO-MASSTER DECATHLON

Take the most explosive technology (electronics);

Combine it with experimentation in the most sensitive combat functions (intelligence and control);

And faced with the greatest proliferation of new R&D material;

Test and evaluate this new material, along with new concepts, with precision adequate to measure combat effectiveness (Benefits vs. burdens);

And systematically document and test the land combat process;

And drastically improve the design and procedures of the command post;

And conduct, for the first time, integrated (CDC, AMC, CONARC, ASA) tests with integrated inputs and integrated outputs;

And test critical items, particularly DCPG itself, in record time—with the equipment on hand sixty days or less;

And complete deployment within the same sixty-day period;

And, finally, recruit and assemble the necessary test organization in face of rapidly declining Army, manpower, budget and other resources.

Without detailing every new weapon in the arsenal, it is clear where this is leading. It is the final depersonalization of warfare, the ultimate separation of the killer from the killed. It is mechanization of responsibility as well, taking judgment farther and farther from the minds, and therefore the ethics, of men. Some fine old quotations also go into limbo: "It is well that war is so terrible," Robert E. Lee said, "lest men grow too fond of it." It is the information explosion, they will tell you: communications. Warfare in the global village. "We can do away with wire, and use an electromagnetic spectrum instead. The computers can talk to the sensors, and vice versa." One of the wonders of it all, the colonel said, is the breakthrough in storage of energy; no problem with that now—and the computers acquire the ability of infantrymen. The words are precision and discretion, which a computer can do better than a man—how can that be denied? The man can't assimilate the information that the computers are feeding him. The information is too unwieldy, there is too much of it, from too many different perspectives. The man can control the environment *through the machine*. A machine is nothing more than the creation of a man, anyway; and it's *war*, and you do what you must in a war.

Hopelessly out of touch, this journalist, but he asked the colonel if he really wanted to give machines that kind of authority. What kind of men do you get to run them?

A fatherly denial, stern and direct: the computer will never replace the man. It all depends on that grunt with the rifle, has since the time of Solomon. Warfare still depends on man's judgment.

Pointless to pursue it further. One can see where it springs from, this desperation of soldiers to *know what is happening*. War: so imprecise, confused, lunatic. And so much at stake. Bring a logic to the asylum, something that can be made sense of. Remember Ridgway's insistent question: "Do you know anything that will help me right now?" A fact that will last from today to tomorrow.

Technology has changed and will continue to change the perspective. The Army is gazing straight into a non-linear future; the revolution began in the Second World War, and is now all but out of control. Who understands the aesthetics of revolution? When do two and two make four, and when do they make five?

In November of 1967, William Westmoreland returned from the war zone, troubled (as any commander is) but highly confident. He conferred with Lyndon Johnson at the White House, and later with the press. It was part of the Administration's fall offensive to convince the American public that the war was going well, on its way to being won, in fact; the public was not unreceptive to this view. All the statistics were assembled: enemy killed and captured, weapons lost and found, roads secured, peasants rallied to the government, and most of all the Hamlet Evaluation Survey (HES), the computerized system which rated Vietnamese villages according to their degree of loyalty to what the National Liberation Front called "the Saigon administration." The evidence was plausible, as Westmoreland told the journalists at the Pentagon on the twenty-second of November.

Question: General, you mentioned earlier that 45 per cent of the North Vietnamese-VC main force units are combat-ineffective . . .

Westmoreland: That is according to the assessment by my military intelligence officers.

Question: Could you give us some examples of how this shows up in the battlefield, sir, because we don't see that in news reports? The news reports don't indicate this shows up—how ineffectiveness shows up on the battlefield. We don't see it in the news reports we get back here.

Westmoreland: Well, you haven't heard of any victories that they've won, have you?

Question: No. But they seem to do quite well on defense.

Westmoreland: And you don't—they don't run away?

Question: They don't seem to.

Westmoreland: Well, sometimes we try to make is possible so that they cannot run away; that's one of the objects of the exercise. [Laughter.] So that we can use our firepower against them. Well, how do we get this information? We get it from interrogation of prisoners, from defectors, from captured documents. The order-of-battle people keep detailed information on every one of these main force units. Now this can change very rapidly, I mean a unit could be ineffective because it only has half of its authorized men, but it could get in a packet of replacements from the North and after those replacements had been assimilated it could be effective again. So this is a fluctuating matter.

Question: That also includes the units that are licking their wounds and rebuilding again.

Westmoreland: Yes, that's right . . .

Question: You said that on this trip that it's conceivable to you that within two years or less we could begin to phase down the war. Those of us who have to cover other aspects of Washington wonder whether its conceivable to you that within a year, say, by next November, we could . . .

[Laughter.]

Question: . . . phase out . . .

[Laughter.]

Westmoreland: I'm not inclined to change my language.

[Laughter.]

Question: Let me clear up one point. You don't think that the battle of Dak To is the beginning of the end of anything particularly for the enemy . . .

Westmoreland: I think it's the beginning of a great defeat for the enemy.

Question: Thank you, general.

Two points: The general was accurate when he predicted that the war, or at least the American part of it, would begin to "phase down" within two years. But sixty-nine days after the press conference at which he said that enemy main force units were forty-five per cent ineffective, the Viet Cong struck at Tet. The enemy hit every provincial capital in South Vietnam, more than half the district capitals, seized the American embassy for twelve hours, and held the city of Hué for twenty-two days. The American public never recovered, and from that point on the Vietnam war was an endgame.

EIGHT

The Colonel

Southgate, California, lies to the south and west of Los Angeles Internationl Airport, out Century Boulevard past Watts. That's where the colonel was now, in Southgate on a thirty-day leave from Vietnam. The kids were underfoot all day long in the bungalow which sat on a cul-de-sac off one of the main roads; the street itself was quiet, but two blocks away there were gas stations and drive-ins and small neighborhood taverns. It was a place where people bought houses for two or three years, and then moved on. In America for seven days, the colonel was unable to adjust.

He was fighting the war every day in his memory, not talking about it very much with his wife, who has a job now and three children to raise when she is not at work, at the hospital, nursing. The colonel's parents died when he was three, and he joined the merchant marine when he was fourteen; three years later he joined the Army, so in one form or another the military has been his home, what the Spanish call a *querencia*, for all his adolescent and adult life. That is what he thinks about at home now in the evenings: the Army. Drinking a Scotch, kneading his fist into his palm, he thinks about the service, and the silence is broken only by the big jets flying low in the smog, approaching LAX. He eases back in the Barca-Lounger, legs atilt, and looks at the design over the fireplace. It is only a week before Christmas, and above the mantle is hung an odd arrow-shaped apparatus with the word HARDCORE set in relief in the middle. Now that was funny. The men of the battalion had tried to figure out ways of telling the enemy who they were, which unit was tormenting them. When they killed a gook, they wanted the gook's comrades to know who had done it. At first they stuffed division patches into the mouths of the dead. Then one of the sergeants, what a stud *that* one was, got the idea of branding the bastards; brand them on their chests. So a cumshaw artist in the battalion got together some solder and made HARDCORE, which was the battalion motto; the sergeant had showed it to the colonel and the colonel had laughed and said, No babe, it's too goddam big to lug around just to brand some gook, and where are you going to get the fire to heat it up? So the man went back to division patches in the mouths of the dead. Now the colonel was sitting in the chair and grinning, because atop the branding iron his wife had placed a white porcelain angel of mercy.

The boy was five and the girls eight and ten, wonderful looking kids, especially the boy, very bright-eyed and at odds with all the women in the family, the ones who dominate his life while his dad is away at the war. The colonel worries a little about the boy, about the females running his life. It's not good for a kid to grow up surrounded by women. And *his* friends, the old Army friends, are not there, because Southgate is not an Army town. It is a suburb like the other Los Angeles suburbs, classless and faceless, a thin gray line of houses retreating off the main streets. His wife took the family there while the colonel was in Vietnam. His wife grew up in Los Angeles, and her mother lives there still; so there is a sense of place, for the wife anyway, a sense of familiar things and people. Her husband, since he has been at war, is a little less familiar.

He is an expert in the art of small-unit infantry tactics, and with a seventh grade education as a base has managed to read and understand Hannibal and Clausewitz and, lately, the books of Bernard Fall. He told her a little sheepishly that it's *his thing*, using the vernacular with a smile because doing your thing reminded him of hippies, flower children, and here he was a colonel of infantry. I'm doing my thing, killing gooks.

"It's what I'm good at," he said.

"Yes," she said, because there wasn't anything else to say. But she does not understand the romance of small-unit maneuvers, squad leaders and point men and the mike force out in front and the mortars to the rear. Just now she's very involved with her job, and becoming someone herself. The colonel has as much interest in the subtleties of nursing as she has in the subtleties of commanding a battalion.

She has never been caught up in the Army the way other officers' wives have. Perhaps that it because the colonel is not a West Point man, and pointedly avoids the sort of polish that separates officers and gentlemen. With a friend late at night, the colonel falls to talking of life on an Army base—the Army brats and their Army brat wives, the ass-kissing, the relentlessness of the system. They have always been mavericks, these two. He told her very early on, Don't bother to politic for me; I'll make it on my own or not at all. He didn't need a woman to do it for him, and truth to tell when women meddled they did more harm than good anyway. *When we make major*, that captain's wife at Campbell had said.

His wife smiled a little at that, and moved to go into the kitchen to fetch the ice. She enjoyed the conversation, reminiscing about life as a captain at Fort Campbell, Kentucky, and as a major at other bases in other states.

"Don't talk about that now. Talk about something else while I'm gone. Talk about the Army," she said and walked into the kitchen.

She means, talk about the war; talk about assaulting a hill in South Vietnam or about HARDCORE or about the body count or the ARVN officer corps. She does not understand the war and is bored by it, and appalled by the killing. He has been away two of the past three years, three of the past five, now with one unit, now with another, at staff and at corps, but never in Saigon. He had successfully avoided Saigon because he had friends, and a truly outstanding record; his superiors permitted him to get away with it. An exasperated Creighton Abrams took the colonel's battalion command away from him after his fourth wound in Vietnam; Abrams didn't want him dead, and so moved him to corps, where he wouldn't get shot at. That was where the colonel would return, at the end of the thirty-day leave. He was thinking now about extending again. What the hell, the only war we've got; and laughing at the old, the very old joke, saying it in parody of the number of times he had heard it before.

The colonel's wife succeeded in her instructions, and when she returned with the ice the two men were back talking about Vietnam, about the son-of-a-bitch brigade commander who didn't give a damn about lives, only his own reputation, and some of the stupidities and fuckups of the war. That reminiscence led to another, and as his wife sat and listened, the colonel and his friend plunged back into the detritus of memory. It centered on battles. War stories.

"We killed a hundred and eight in that one"—he named the day and the name of the captain who commanded the company—"and two thousand five hundred and forty-eight in four months."

"Well, there must have been a hell of a lot of enemy there for you to kill two thousand men," the friend said, not really believing the statistics. "Christ, that is supposed to be a place where the pacification . . ."

"Twenty-five hundred," the colonel said, correcting the figure.

"Oh, right."

"Not two thousand. Two thousand, five hundred and forty-eight."

His memory is phenomenal, total recall of events in Korea twenty years ago, or six months ago in the Delta of South Vietnam. He can remember the date and the time of day, the name of the operation, and where it took place. He can recall the disposition of his men, and who had the point.

"Okay," he said. "Aguda. The story of Aguda. March thirty-one, nineteen fifty-one. It was a rocky goddammed hill, and we had to stack up stones and dig into the face of the hill for protection. The enemy was at the top and hell it wasn't like Vietnam where you can call in all that good air and artillery to blast the bastards off of it. 'Okay babe, you've got your six rounds of artillery,' was all they told me at battalion. *Six rounds.* The company was no damned good to us, a platoon had to do it all. To get to the top of the hill, and get those people off of it. Well, we did it. We got a small foothold, a fingerhold really, on one, just one, ridge. It was real bad.

"Now, about Aguda. It's this premonition thing. Aguda had been wounded and got back the day before wearing regular boots, not the shoe packs that we had for the cold. God, you don't know what cold is until you have been in Korea in February and March. I told him to get the shoe packs, and get them on, but I was really fencing around with him, you know, to find out if that wound had affected him. You never know with guys, what it does to them. I told him that he'd have to have the shoe-packs. 'I'm not going to be around here long enough to need them,' Aguda said.

"I didn't think much about that, although in retro-spect it's pretty obvious I should have. But I didn't. Any-way, it was Aguda and I on the fingerhold of this damn hill. And Aguda (James Aguda, I think his name was; he was a Hawaiian) had a B.A.R. Wonderful weapon, B.A.R. And the son of a bitch stands up. He stands up with the B.A.R. and takes the enemy as they're coming at us."

The colonel was up out of his seat, standing in the middle of the room, legs set wide apart, hefting an imaginary Browning Automatic Rifle in his hands. The colonel is short, no more than five-nine, but husky with forearms like bowling pins. He was crouching in the middle of the room, his arms bent with the weight of the gun, his fingers jerking and clawing for the trigger, aiming the barrel, then jamming an imaginary clip into the breech.

"Christ, and while he's shooting at them I can see him getting it. *I can see it.* I'm yelling at him, for crissakes Aguda get down, and two slugs are hitting him, one in the leg and the other in the arm"—the colonel banged the flat of his hand on his thigh, and wrenched his shoulder back—"and two more in the legs, and he's shooting like hell and finally he takes one in the chest and that swings him around and he drops and he's dead. KIA." The colonel nodded sadly. "But look: he put down effective fire. Down there. *He bought some time,* and that's what it's all about."

The colonel paused. "But there's a funny-sad aspect to it, too," he said, speaking more slowly and quietly now. "We put him in for the medal of honor, you know. He should have had it, anyone can see that. But none of us could *write.* You should have seen those letters we wrote. Pathetic. 'James Aguda saved our ass. He shot a lot of gooks.' That's what those letters were like, and up at division some smart-ass captain reads them and thinks, So what. So he fired his weapon and killed some people. That's what you're supposed to do in a war. That's the name of the game." The colonel sighed, shaking his head. "We couldn't write, that was the fact. So Aguda didn't get the medal of honor. He got a bronze star."

The colonel's wife had talked a little about the Army, saying that the period in Kentucky was fine, before the war and all the separations. There was a misconception somehow that Army life was one big scramble to keep up with the Joneses, and it wasn't true. Everyone knew what everyone made. It was there on the pay envelope. A lieutenant made $577 a month, a captain $870, a major $901, a lieutenant colonel $971, and a colonel $1,001, and it could go higher than that depending on the length of service. The general's wife can drive a Ford and you can drive a Cadillac, and if you drive a Cadillac everyone on the base knows you're eating beans for dinner. Unless your parents have money. There were a few of those, *are* a few of those, on every base.

The colonel and his wife had read *The Organization Man* with amusement, and concluded that life in an American corporation and its adjunct, the suburb, was more confining than military life ever could be. But yet, it was true when they lived in Kentucky—when people came over for dinner there were none of higher or lower rank. If you were a captain, your friends were captains. Sometimes there was an awkward moment at large receptions when the wife of a captain would call a colonel by his first name, and her husband would call him by rank or, more frequently, *sir*. Well, really, that happened all the time.

Then the colonel's wife said:

"They ought to do something about the promotions, though. They are all published in the *Army Times*, and everyone reads them at once, for the first time. You have only got ten minutes to compose yourself and walk into the office and congratulate a man you probably hate for being on the five per cent list, or for a promotion ahead of time." She was talking of what a man would have to do. "The trouble is, everybody knows everything. Your life is an open book. There's really no ... I guess it's privacy. They ought to send individual messages, and give a man time to compose himself."

The colonel was nodding at that, neither agreeing nor disagreeing. Now, back in Southgate, he was worrying the war again. Whatever defects the institution had, the solutions would have to come from others, those higher up than he. The colonel is not an introspective man, but he is reflective. He knows what he has to do. He does not visit hospitals like other commanders, on the theory that it would, after a time, become impossible for him to order men into battle if he were forced to view the results. There is no anomaly: he did not declare the war, nor is he hired to stop it. He is hired to fight it, which he tries to do with maximum effect. In the Korean war the colonel, then a sergeant, killed more than 100 men and then at some point—he mentioned a figure like 138 or 143—he stopped counting. But he has been at this war a long time, longer than Korea, and what he sees now is bungling. He speaks scornfully of the Army as "the industry," sounding oddly like a movie producer when he says it, and is quick to pronounce Vietnam a misconceived adventure. No one understood it then, and very few understand it now. The problem stems from the kind of army they have made, an army of managers and technicians, data processers, not fighters. No one read Bernard Fall and General Giap. Who read *People's War, People's Army*? No one knew what a guerrilla war was all about. They did not understand small-unit tactics, did not comprehend the guerrilla apparatus as a huge tree, with the main forces the lush foliage on top, but the real strength of the Communist political structure at the roots. Chop off the foliage and it quickly grows back; the guerrilla must be denied his roots, which is to say the people. It might have been done right away, with small and mobile counter-guerrilla forces. Might have, but wasn't.

The colonel thought about quitting the Army eighteen months before, but didn't. He probably never would. He is one of those that Westmoreland calls motivated. Anyway, the chance to win the war had been lost, and a hell of a lot of good men dead . . .

"But what about the nature of the war?"

"That's what I mean," the colonel said.

"No, no. I mean the fact that the war was against American traditions. I mean it was a *bad* war."

"Yeah, we were on the wrong side. But it could have been won."

"Okay, forget that for a moment. Can you win a war, *should* you win a war, that's fundamentally . . ."

"I don't know about that," the colonel said. "We were in it, and I had to fight it."

. . . good men are dead. Any war always claims the best men an army has, the colonel said, because they are the studs, the chargers, the can-do boys, the ones with spirit and guts and the willingness to do what needs to be done. The others, the one-year tourists, they tend to get back okay. They tend to survive. Christ, and *for what*? All the dead, and for what? There are dead men because there were too many stupid general officers, who didn't take the time to find out about the enemy. "Do you remember that stupid son-of-a-bitch brigade commander who said: 'I have entered the Iron Triangle and the Iron Triangle Is No More.' What kind of phony bullshit is that?"

His feelings mixed and conflicting, the colonel tried to find the villains. It was the Army's job, and the Army botched it. The generals, and the press, which spent too much time covering the periphery and not describing the manner of the war. The manner in which the infantry fought it. Well, give him his due: Westy had a tough goddammed job, none tougher. But the war was the Army's to fight. Hell, you had to stop Communism somewhere.

I guess I just like war, he said finally. "I like the comradeship. Adversity brings out the best in men. I believe that. I really believe it."

He knows and his wife knows that he is more at home

at Dak To than in Southgate. He can laugh at the HARD-
CORE branding iron the way other men laugh at a remembered joke at the circus, when they were kids. The
bugle in the morning, the starched fatigues, with just the
nametag and U.S. Army and the three patches, C.I.B.,
paratroopers, and ranger. Nothing more than that. And
a battalion command. You could do so goddammed
much with a battalion of men; at division there were
too many troops, and too much administration, and you
had to be some kind of manager. But a battalion, six
hundred guys; if you maneuvered six hundred men, you
could do goddammed near anything with them. And if
they were really good, volunteers, *airborne;* Christ . . .
*What I wanted to do was take that battalion and mold
it just like I would a piece of clay, take those kids and
make them into the best fighting force that I could. The
best in the country. And by God I made it go. It ended
up the best battalion in the country. No question. Well,
now I'm going to study Latin-American affairs. That's
where it's going next, because the bastards think they
can win it all now. Yessir, Latin America. COMUSMACL.*

There was time for just one more war story, "a cute
tragic story," this one about the Korean war and an
infantryman named DeBore. DeBore was the worst
trooper in the platoon, a slacker and an expert on sick
call. "He was not one of us," the colonel said. "He was a
coward. He admitted it, and we hated him for it. We all
hated him and he was an outcast. He had a sixth sense,
that DeBore did. He was never in a major firefight because he always managed to anticipate them and go on
sick call. We had a joke about him. 'Out of the dark,
dreary jungle came the call of the DeBore bird: *Sick call,
sick call, sick call.*' Anyway, this was February fifth, nineteen fifty-one, in the vicinity of Operation Killer, that
thing that Ridgway ginned up; it was a dark and over-
cast day, and DeBore had got it right again, showed up

on sick call and, hell, I had to let him go. We were going
to pull out on an operation, but the day was so bad that
we didn't move. It was too dark for the tac air, so we
stayed where we were. Next day, DeBore returned, thinking we had left, and so he was forced to go with us. We
ended up getting into a terrible fight; I took eight dead
and about twenty wounded, and we'd regrouped around
some armor and I looked out onto the ice of a pond we
were near, and there was a trooper and I knew it was
DeBore. Have you ever heard slugs ricochet off ice?

"Well, these slugs were going everywhere but I got out
next to the son of a bitch and he'd bought the farm real
bad. A gut wound, blood all over—but he was conscious,
so I gave him the old business, Come on, let's go, you're
gonna be all right. Well DeBore, this son of a bitch,
looked up at me just as cool as you want. He had this
real nice smile on his face, and said, 'Hey, Sarge, don't
bother. Get your ass out of here. You're gonna get
greased yourself. I just shit my pants. Man, I'm going.'
And he died. Just like that. So nice."

The colonel paused for a second and said, "When I told
the guys about it . . ." He stopped again, and put his head
down. "It's kinda sad. It got to me." He pushed his lips
together and didn't say anything for a full minute.

"Well, after that he was treated with dignity. He . . .
DeBore was one of the . . . heroes. You talked about the
giants, the great men of the platoon, and DeBore was one
of them."

The colonel was up now and standing, the tears
streaming down his cheeks. He shook his head and murmured something. He said, "It happens to you sometimes." He turned to one side to look out the window.
Then he brightened and poured another drink. In thirty
minutes DeBore was forgotten, and in three weeks the
colonel was back in Vietnam.

A NOTE

This book was written in Washington, D.C., and revised and edited in Pawlet, Vermont. It probably should have been the other way around: Pawlet has a serenity and distance useful for this kind of work.

A number of people cooperated in the project, although they are in no way responsible for the results. The public information office of the Department of the Army arranged interviews, and generally smoothed the way for my visits to Army bases in the United States. These are services normally accorded any accredited journalist. Officials at West Point, Fort Lewis, and Fort Bragg were especially helpful and generous with their time. My friend George Thayer kindly gave me a number of his personal files, particularly those relating to Army weaponry. The project, a risky one from the beginning, was conceived and financed by Robert Manning, the wise and thoughtful editor of *The Atlantic*.

There is a bibliography following. Huntington, Janowitz and Vagts were especially helpful. The Goerlitz book is unputdownable once you get into it. J. Glenn Gray's *The Warriors* is a classic, as is, for other reasons, the House of Representatives' *Review of Army Tank Program*. Where I have pirated quotations I have tried to indicate them.

Military Men centers on the Army because it is the

service with which I am most familiar. I have tried to abbreviate military terminology wherever possible. This will give offense to some soldiers, but I think will result in clarity for the civilian reader. All ranks and assignments of Army officers mentioned in the book are roughly as of spring, 1970.

W.J.
Pawlet, Vermont.
September, 1970

BIBLIOGRAPHY

Armed Services Investigating Subcommittee, House of Representatives: *Review of Army Tank Program.* Washington, D.C.: U.S. Government Printing Office; 1969.

Aurelius, Marcus: *Meditations,* translated by Maxwell Staniforth. Middlesex, England: Penguin Books, Ltd.; 1964.

Barnet, Richard J.: *The Economy of Death.* New York: Atheneum; 1969.

Bradley, Omar: *A Soldier's Story.* New York: Henry Holt & Co.; 1951.

Clausewitz, Carl von: *A Short Guide to Clausewitz on War,* edited by Roger Ashley Leonard. New York: G. P. Putnam's Sons; 1967.

Dean, William R. (as told to William L. Worden): *General Dean's Story.* New York: Viking Press; 1954.

Eisenhower, Dwight D.: *At Ease.* New York: Doubleday & Co. (Avon edition); 1967.

Foch, Ferdinand: *The Memoirs of Marshal Foch,* translated by Colonel T. Bentley Mott. Garden City, New York: Doubleday, Doran & Co.; 1931.

Goerlitz, Walter: *History of the German General Staff,* translated by Brian Battershaw. New York: Frederick A. Praeger; 1953.

Gray, J. Glenn: *The Warriors.* New York: Harper & Row (Harper Torchbook edition); 1959.

Hemingway, Ernest: *Across the River and into the Trees.* New York: Charles Scribner's Sons; 1950.

Huntington, Samuel P.: *The Soldier and the State.* New York: Vintage Books; 1957.

Janowitz, Morris: *The Professional Soldier.* New York: The Free Press; 1960.

Just, Ward: *To What End.* Boston: Houghton Mifflin Co; 1968.

Leckie, Robert: *Warfare.* New York: Harper & Row; 1970.

Liddell Hart, B. H.: *Strategy.* New York: Frederick A. Praeger; 1967.

Mailer, Norman: *The Naked and the Dead.* New York: New American Library (Signet edition); 1948.

Myrer, Anton: *Once an Eagle.* New York: Holt, Rinehart & Winston; 1968.

Schlesinger, Arthur M., Jr.: *A Thousand Days.* New York: Harper & Row; 1965.

Shea, Nancy: *The Army Wife.* New York: Harper & Brothers; 1941.

Taylor, Maxwell D.: *The Uncertain Trumpet.* Washington, D.C.: Harper & Brothers; 1959.

United States Government: *The Budget of the United States Government.* Washington, D.C.: U.S. Government Printing Office; 1970.

Vagts, Alfred: *A History of Militarism.* New York: The Free Press; 1959.

Weigley, Russell F.: *History of the United States Army.* New York: The Macmillan Company; 1967.

West Point Alumni Foundation, The: *Register of Graduates and Former Cadets.* New York: R. R. Donnelley & Sons Company; 1969.

Wheeler-Bennett, John: *The Nemesis Of Power.* New York: Viking Press (Compass Books edition); 1967.

A NOTE ABOUT THE AUTHOR

Ward Just was born in Michigan City, Indiana, in 1935 and grew up in Waukegan, Illinois. He attended Trinity College in Hartford, Connecticut, and then worked for *Newsweek* in Chicago, Washington, and London. In 1965 he joined the Washington *Post*, serving as a correspondent in Vietnam for eighteen months. His widely acclaimed book on the Vietnamese war, *To What End*, was published in 1968, followed by a novel, *A Soldier of the Revolution*, in 1970. Mr. Just lives in Washington, D.C., with his wife and children.

A NOTE ON THE TYPE

The text of this book was set on the Linotype in Aster, a typeface designed by Francesco Simoncini (born 1912 in Bologna, Italy) for Ludwig and Mayer, the German type foundry. Starting out with the basic old-face letterforms that can be traced back to Francesco Griffo in 1495, Simoncini emphasized the diagonal stress by the simple device of extending diagonals to the full height of the letterforms and squaring off. By modifying the weights of the individual letters to combat this stress, he has produced a type of rare balance and vigor. Introduced in 1958, Aster has steadily grown in popularity wherever type is used.

This book was composed by Cherry Hill Composition, Pennsauken, New Jersey, and printed and bound by The Haddon Craftsmen, Inc., Scranton, Pennsylvania. Typography and binding design by Bonnie Spiegel.